THE
CULTURE & ARTS
OF
KOREA

THE CULTURE & ARTS OF KOREA

CONTENTS

ROMANIZATION
The romanization of Korean words in the main text follows the McCune–Reischauer system. Korean names are written with the family name first.
In the interest of reader convenience, we have, however, used a modified romanization system in the directory, eliminating the breve that many computer systems are incapable of reproducing.

THE CULTURE & ARTS OF KOREA

Copyright © 1993 Ministry of Culture and Sports of the Republic of Korea

First published 1993.

ISBN 89—7820—003—6

Published by
Cultural Exchange Division,
Cultural Policy Bureau,
Ministry of Culture and Sports
Seoul, Korea

Project Directors:
Kim Yong- mun
Jun Young-jea
Shim Jang- sup
Whang Hye-jin

Art Director:
Park Seung-u
Art Space Publications

Edited and Designed in Korea by
Art Space Publications

Printed in the Republic of Korea

First printing: December 1993
Second Printing : December 1994

Not for sale

INTRODUCTION

Produced in the belief that the Korean culture is an important part of the world's culture and in response to the new era of internationalization and liberalization, *The Culture and arts of Korea* introduces the rich heritage of the unique Korean culture to promote a greater understanding of Korean culture and advance mutual cultural exchanges with our neighbors near and far.

Traditionally endowed with optimistic, artless and unpretentious aesthetic sensibilities born of the graceful beauty of the Korean peninsula, the Korean people were able to develop Korea's traditional culture and arts which are distinctly different from those of China or Japan. In the eyes of most non-Koreans who lack a clear understanding of the unique characteristics of the cultures of Korea, Japan and China, however, the art and culture of the nations of Northeast Asia seem quite similar.

In the interest of laying such misconceptions to rest, we have, in the first section of this volume, tried to provide a comprehensive introduction to Korea's arts and culture, and in the later section, have included as much of the important resource materials on Korean culture and arts as possible. We plan to continue to revise this volume in the future, reworking and supplementing it in order to provide readers with an even more valuable source of information.

We sincerely hope that this book will provide those interested in Korean culture and arts as well as anyone involved in the promotion of international cultural exchange with a better understanding of the Korean people and their culture.

THE ORIGINS OF KOREAN CULTURE

Korea's rich culture is often said to be unique. While it does, of course, have distinctive intrinsic characteristics, that description may be overworked or applied somewhat loosely. An understanding of the culture of Northeast Asia is essential to any study of the origins of Korean culture. The early influence of other Asian countries on the Korean peninsula can be seen in the comb-pattern pottery of the Neolithic age, and in the lute-shaped daggers, twin-knobbed mirrors and geometric patterns of the Bronze Age.

The early growth and development of the Korean people was not uniform, but generally was characterized by active contact, and sometimes struggle, involving the Chinese people. Korean culture gradually became identified with that of China when

A Silla period stoneware figure of a man playing a musical instrument

Korean society began to develop into an agricultural society centered around rice cultivation. Korea produced iron tools and weapons, and developed politically, economically, philosophically and culturally under strong Chinese influence.

An understanding of cultural exchanges alone cannot fully explain Korean culture, however. A proper understanding of the characteristics of the Korean people is also essential, and these characteristics must be explained in the context of the nation's historical development. Consider, for example, how Buddhism and Confucianism were introduced to Korea. Although the introduction of Confucianism slightly predates that of Buddhism, Koreans embraced Buddhism first because it was more conducive to the building of an aristocratic, centralized state bent on expansion.

Some attribute the Five Secular Commandments, to which the youth of Silla (57 B.C.-A.D.935) subscribed, to Buddhism while others attribute them to Confucianism. Wongwang, the man responsible for teaching the commandments in the early 600s, was a Buddhist monk who was also well versed in the teachings of Confucius. Thus the commandments may be explained either way.

The other side of the picture should also be considered, however. As society was in need of moral codes for the development of royal authority and a patriarchal family system, the promotion of the youth corps, known as *Hwarang*, and the protection of property, such as domestic animals, would have been held in high esteem even if Buddhism and Confucianism had not been introduced at that time.

The same may be said of the *Sŏn* (Zen) sect of Buddhism. *Sŏn* was introduced to Korea long before Silla absorbed the kingdoms of Paekche (18B.C.-A.D.660) and Koguryŏ (37 B.C.-A.D.668) but it did not become popular until late in the Unified Silla (668-935) period when powerful local landlords rose against the centralized ruling system. In other words, *Sŏn* Buddhism gained acceptance and importance as a religion of the local landlords.

Neo-Confucianism began to attract attention during the latter part of the Koryŏ (918-1392) period and eventually became the prevailing ideology of the Chosŏn Period (1392-1910). It is believed to have been introduced into Korea during cultural exchanges with Yüan China. However, acceptance of Neo-Confucianism is better explained in relation to the rise of the middle class, a group of medium and small landlords with the status of local gentry who entered officialdom not through hereditary rights but through the state examination system. These

Confucian ceremony

were men of probity, critical of the pro-Yüan ruling families who had come to possess large-scale holdings through illegal means. This new middle class welcomed Neo-Confucianism moral principles as a spiritual support.

These people, who subsequently became the leaders of a new kingdom, were not, as is commonly believed, worshipers of a powerful China. On the contrary, they tried to discover the historical tradition of their country, traced the beginnings back to the Tan'gun era, and supported the development of King Sejong's (r.1418-50) new Korean alphabet, *hangŭl.*

A new interest in improving Korean technology and the economy prevailed among Chosŏn scholars of the 17th and 18th centuries. Agricultural reforms were promoted, and a nationwide commercial network was organized, with Seoul and Kaesŏng as its two centers. Merchants promoted foreign trade at Ŭiju, and independent handicrafts flourished. It

was in this social milieu that *Sirhak,* the "Practical Learning" school of Confucianism, developed. "Practical Learning," aimed at reforming society through the promotion of an awareness of native historical traditions, reaped unprecedented benefits in terms of the influence of Western culture and the Xing Chinese historiographic methodology.

The development of Korean art paralleled the general development of Korean culture. The mural paintings of Koguryŏ reflect the temperament of the Koguryŏ people, a product of contemporary historical and environmental conditions.

The stone grotto shrine, *Sŏkkuram,* of the Silla Kingdom, with its magnificent Buddha in the center, represented a unified universe. The grotto seems to idealize the harmonized world. The two stone pagodas, *Sŏkkatap* and *Tabot'ap,* in Pulguk

The Buddha at Sŏkkuram
stone grotto shrine

Temple, are perhaps the best stone works of the Unified Silla period, products of an aristocratic temperament which, under the ruling system of absolute monarchy, took harmony as its ideal. As memorials to *Sŏn* monks, they are examples of *Sŏn* Buddhist art which began to appear toward the end of the Unified Silla period.

The beauty of Koryŏ celadon reflects the tastes of Koryŏ's ruling aristocracy. Although Koryŏ celadon was influenced by Song Chinese celadon, it is clearly unique to the Koryŏ aristocracy. In contrast, the simple and staid beauty of Chosŏn white porcelain exemplifies the lifestyle and attitudes of the Chosŏn military and civilian upper class, who emphasized practical use over luxury.

Although Chosŏn painting has generally been regarded as a mere imitation or a regional school of Chinese painting, its composition, brushwork and colors reflect uniquely Korean tastes. By the 17th and 18th centuries, some painters executed realistic paintings of the Korean landscape with bold brush strokes. Genre painting also flourished during this period. These paintings exude a rich Korean flavor, depicting scenes of elegant young *yangban*(aristocrats) flirting with *kisaeng*(trained entertainment girls), farmers and artisans practicing their trades, and other aspects of everyday life.

While foreign influences on Korean art cannot be ignored, it is almost impossible to appreciate the real value of Korean art without properly understanding the underlying context of Korean history and culture.

Although every work of art has its own independent and intrinsic value, once it is freed from the hand of the artist, the historic background that generated the work must not be forgotten. In this sense, works of art are historic products that transcend individual taste. ◆

LITERATURE

In old Korea, skill in poetic composition was one of the most important criteria for judging a man's ability to serve his country as a public servant, and, at the same time, was also the yardstick of a man's personal cultivation.

Poetry tended to be "I" centered, confessional. In the hands of anything less than consummate artists, this subjective tradition is severely limited, but in the hands of great masters, the reader discovers his own experience, and consequently that of all men, in the experience of the poet, moving in the process from the particular to the universal.

Poetry was also characterized by a pervading movement toward transcendence, reflecting the Buddhist tradition of freedom and liberation, and also reflecting the Confucian tradition which, while aspiring toward order and control, still seeks the ultimate in wisdom. Buddhism was dominant during the Koryŏ Kingdom when *hansi* (poems in Chinese characters) developed to maturity. Confucianism was dominant throughout the Chosŏn Kingdom when the *sijo* and the *kasa*, the two literary genres deemed to best express the Korean sensibility, reached their fullest development. Personal cultivation is integral in both systems, and traditional composition tended to be spontaneous: a visit to a temple, meeting a friend, celebrating the arrival of spring, a gift of wine.

In traditional poetry, nature was seen conceptually. An appreciation of nature led to contemplation, which in turn led to rapture, not over the physically beautiful but over the morally

beautiful. The poet did not see a mountain; rather he saw the universal essence of mountain. This approach was primarily symbolic, with the emphasis always on the inner landscape of the heart, and remains the core of the Korean tradition to this day.

The earliest Korean poetry consisted of songs of ritual worship and songs designed to accompany work. These songs were invariably linked with music and dance. Unfortunately, there was no writing system in Korea until Chinese characters were introduced, presumably in the second century, though dating remains inexact. Chinese characters quickly became popular with the elite in Korea, leading to the development of a tradition of *hansi* poetry, that is, poems in Chinese, following the rules of Chinese prosody, but written by Korean poets.

During the Silla period, a system of recording Korean sounds in Chinese characters, called *idu*, was developed, thus making it possible to record the vernacular *hyangga* which flourished during Unified Silla and the early part of Koryŏ. Twenty-five *hyangga* are extant.

The *changga* (literally "long songs") replaced the *hyangga* during the Koryŏ Kingdom. There were two divisions of *changga*: *kyŏnggichega* which were recorded in Chinese and reflected Confucian thought, and *sogyo*, exquisite little popular lyrics, which were recorded orally.

The tradition of *hansi* flourished from Silla through Koryŏ and Chosŏn. *Hansi* poems are quite different from *sijo*, a three-line poem (song), 14 to 16 syllables in each line, distributed through four distinct breath groups, the total number of syllables not exceeding 45, in the feeling they engender. This difference may derive from the fact that *hansi* were written in Chinese, the language of literature and official business, whereas *sijo* were written in *hangŭl*, the language of the home and of the common people. At any rate, *sijo* are even more private and more personal than *hansi*. An image is introduced and developed, and the poet presents a statement of his own experience, all within the narrow confines of three lines and 45 syllables.

Scholars still debate the origin of the *sijo* form. Theories abound: a development of Silla *hyangga* or of Buddhist songs imported from Ming China; a form that developed naturally in the course of translating Chinese poems into Korean; a development of the Koryŏ *tan'ga*; or a form that goes back to the Shamanistic chants of antiquity. The difficulty in unraveling the history of the *sijo* is compounded by the fact that *hangŭl* was not invented until 1446. Any *sijo* written prior to this date were either recorded originally in Chinese and only later translated or retranslated into Korean, or recorded orally from the beginning. The problem is further compounded by the fact that the first of the great anthologies, *Ch'ŏngguyŏngŏn*, was not published until 1728, and texts of individual poets are contained in posthumous collections of their writings, many of them produced long after the death of the poet.

Chinese remained the language of government and literature until the 19th century. In 1884 the Western powers and Japan forced the opening

of the ports, an event which marked the end of the Hermit Kingdom and beginning of a flood of Western influence. Following a annexation in 1910, an increasing number of young Korean intellectuals began to go to Japan for university education where they came into contact with current trends in Japanese literary circles. Within Korea the period was marked by a surge of nationalist sentiment which culminated in the March 1st Independence Movement of 1919.

The rise in nationalist sentiment was accompanied by a rejection of literature in Chinese and the Chinese tradition in favor of *hangŭl* and the Western tradition.

Korean poets were influenced by Japanese interpretations of Western literature and criticism. The result was a varied product, characterized by a *fin-de-siecle* atmosphere of world weariness, decadence and pessimism.

Kim So-wol (1902-1934) was the first of these young poets to move away from imitation and create something new on the basis of assimilated influences. Perhaps his most significant achievement was the flexibility and versatility he achieved in the use of the Korean language. "Azaleas" may be So-wol's most anthologized piece:

If you grow so sick of me
that you would wish to go,
I'll let you go gently,
    without a word.
On Yaksan, Yŏngbyŏn
I'll pluck an armful of azaleas
and strew them in your path.
Tread gently
on these flowers

that deck your parting steps.
If you grow so sick of me
that you would wish to go,
though I die, I'll shed no tears.

Chŏng Chi-yong (1902-?) and Kim Ki-rim (1908-?) ushered in the second stage of modern poetry. Both steeped in the imagist mode, they present a literary world coming to grips with modernism. Chŏng Chi-yong generates a special excitement. "Sea" reveals his mastery of imagist effects:

The channel flaps like a tent
now that the whale has crossed.
White water bundling up;
  paduk stones
tumbling, tumbling down.
The sea skylark soars: silver
  drops its flight;
vigilant half the day
to claw, to scavenge red flesh.
A shell, azalea hued, takes the sun
in a seaweed smelling rock crevice,
while a sea swallow on wing slide
glides in a plate-glass sky.
Sea—see right, right down.
Sea
green as bamboo leaves.
Spring.
What does it look like?
Little hills, lines of flower bud
  lanterns lit?
What does it look like?
Thick thickets of pine and
  bamboo?
What does it look like?
A crouching tiger
draped in a blanket.
spotted yellow and black?
And you, my friend, take
  some such scene,
a white
smoke like
sea,
and voyage far, far away.

The forced dissolution of the Korean Artists Proletarian Federation (KAPF) in the mid-1930s introduced a period of intense Japanese repression. However, following the tradition of

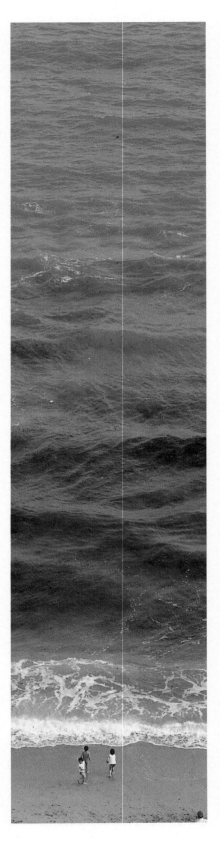

Han Yong-un (1879-1944), monk, poet, and patriot, a towering light in the 1920s, the defiant note continued to ring out in the work of Yi Yuk-sa (1904-1944) and Yun Tong-ju (1917-1945), who remain symbols of undying resistance to foreign domination. The Blue Deer Group, Pak Tu-jin (1916-), Pak Mok-wol (1919-1978) and Cho Chi-hun (1920-1968), sought to sublimate the harsh reality of Japanese oppression in nature poetry. All three are recognized as masters of lyrical language.

The Korean War made the idiom of the pre-war period seem dated and unrelated to contemporary problems. The post-war era was characterized by a poetry that was experimental in form and highly critical of the contemporary scene in content.

Beginning in the 1960s, the process of industrialization bred a profound sense of alienation, isolation, and dehumanization which was increasingly reflected in poetry. A new radical political-social consciousness was awakened, and the more radical of the committed poets, the celebrated Kim Chi-ha (1941-), for example, or the man who assumed his mantle in the 1980s, Kim Nam-ju, paid for their dissent by spending long periods in jail. The political situation in the early 1980s led younger intellectuals to lash out in anger against the poetry establishment, represented for the most part by the older generation of poets, for its failure to find a poetic voice which could prevent or even deal with such tragedy. The young intellectuals reacted forcefully, both in form and content, asserting the failure of the humanist stance to find adequate solutions.

It is of more than passing interest that four pillars of the older poetry community, Cho Byŏng-hwa (1916-), Sŏ Chŏng-ju (1915-), Pak Tu-jin (1916-) and Kim Chun-su (1922-) all produced new collections in the spring of 1990.

The 1980s were also characterized

by the reemergence with renewed vigor of workers' poetry, a genre which traces its roots back to the KAPF literature of the 1920s and early 1930s, and possibly as far back as Chŏng Ta-san (1762-1836).

Despite some seesawing in terms of popular image, Sŏ Chŏng-ju was generally recognized as the best Korean poet of this century until Chŏng Chi-yong's recent rehabilitation swung the pendulum away from him. The appeal of Sŏ Chŏng-ju's work rests first in his use of language, so distinctively of his native Chŏlla province; second, in the sensuality apparent particularly in his earlier work which has evoked comparisons with Baudelaire and Yeats, and third, in his return to the spirit of Silla, mainly Buddhist, to find the values that should inform the new Korea which is to replace the tragic Korea of the recent past. "Untitled" is typical of Sŏ's work.

So hushed
the sky
an orchid
wondering
why
opened
its petals
wide

There is obviously a profusion of poetic talent in Korea, but how the moderns will measure up to the great poets of the past in the acid test of time remains problematical.

THE NARRATIVE TRADITION

Korea's narrative tradition can be traced to a rich storehouse of myths, legends, and folk tales, the oldest surviving examples of which are recorded in the *Samguk-sagi* (*The History of the Three Kingdoms*) (1145) and *Samguk-yusa* (*Memorabilia of the Three Kingdoms*)(1285?). *New Stories of the Golden Turtle*, written in Chinese by Kim Si-sŭp (1435-1493), is usually regarded as the first work of fiction in Korea.

Korean fiction in the vernacular begins with Hŏ Kyun's (1569-1618) celebrated *The Story of Hong Kil-tong*. The novel advocates the abolition of the class system, the eradication of corruption, and the elimination of the abuse of power by greedy bureaucrats.

The Nine Cloud Dream (1689) by Kim Man-jung (1637-1692) marked the coming of age of the Korean novel. The story concerns a Buddhist monk who dreams that he is reincarnated as a successful Confucian bureaucrat. *The Nine Cloud Dream* employs sophisticated symbolism to explore the tensions between the Buddhist and the Confucian approaches to life.

During the 17th century, *Sirhak* (Practical Learning), emphasizing empirical knowledge and practical living, came into prominence. With it came a movement away from poetry toward prose as the mode of literary expression. As a result, a new more realistic kind of fiction satirizing the social prejudices of the day made its appearance.

The Story of Ch'unhyang is by far the most popular of the Chosŏn era novels. Originally a popular tale, it was developed by travelling entertainers into *p'ansori* (a folk opera genre). The novel represents a satirical treatment of corrupt officials, a sensitive delineation of social problems, a finely modulated humor centered in the minor characters, an extraordinary depiction of the ideal of faithfulness, and a lovely, playful picture of young love.

The historical novel is a distinct type of Chosŏn era fiction. *Imjin-nok*, the author of which is unknown, records the exploits of famous generals who fought against the Japanese warlord Hideyoshi. *Kyech'uk Diary*, by an anonymous court lady, records the sufferings endured by Queen Mother Inmok (1584-1632) under the tyrant Kwanghaegun (1556-1622). *Hanjung-nok*, by Princess Hyegyŏng (1735-1815), is an elegant account of court life in diary form. *The Tale of Queen Inhyŏn* recounts court intrigue during the reign of Sukjong.

The 19th century was marked by a decline in the classical novel. Toward the end of the century Korea entered a period of profound political and social change. The opening of the ports in 1884 and the treaties with the great powers which followed marked the end of the Hermit Kingdom and the beginning of a veritable flood of Western influence.

At this time a new national consciousness began to emerge, its first dawning being signaled by the *Tonghak* (Eastern Learning) Movement, an unprecedented popular revolt against corruption and injustice which occurred toward the end of the century. In the years immediately before and after annexation by Japan in 1910, the new national consciousness began to be expressed through the medium of *hangǔl* literature, called *sinmunhak* or "New Literature."

"New Literature" was a reaction against Chinese characters and the Chinese literary tradition in favor of a European-style literature in *hangǔl*. The modern novel was a new concept in Korea, and the work that appeared under its title was something in between the old Chinese romances and the modern Western novel. *Tears of Blood* (1906) by Yi In-jik (1862-1916) was the first new novel. It is a romance based on the old "reward good and punish evil" formula, while at the same time assigning a significant role to dreams. Although it had not fully developed an acceptable realistic idiom linguistically, *Tears of Blood* was the first of its kind and expressed many of the rallying cries of the age–ideas such as the freedom to select one's own spouse, the need for education, the call to enlightenment, and the urgency of modernization.

In 1908 Ch'oe Nam-sŏn (1890-1957) produced *Sonyŏn* (*Youth*), the first quasiliterary magazine. This magazine and a series of others published between 1908 and 1928 provided a forum for young writers to express their ideas. Ch'oe Nam-sŏn worked closely with another fervent young nationalist, Yi Kwang-su (1892-?), who used the novel as vehicle to promote his ideas. Yi Kwang-su's *The Heartless* (1917) was the first modern novel. It is a romantic story juxtaposing "love marriages" and arranged marriages, and emphasizes the value of overseas education, the need for sacrifice for one's country, and the opposition between the values of the old world and the new. The interests of both Ch'oe Nam-son and Yi Kwang-su were not primarily literary. Their concern lay in the promotion of nationalism and enlightenment.

The failure of the Independence Movement in March 1919 bred a climate of intellectual pessimism and disillusion that limited the roads open to Korean intellectuals. An intellectual could be completely escapist and ignore the situation altogether; he could adopt the nationalist platform of "strengthen the nation;" or he could take the Marxist option which reached its culmination in the organization of KAPF.

While the failure of the March 1st Independence Movement was traumatic, the movement did produce significant positive results, in particular the policy of appeasement which the Japanese government subsequently adopted. Under that policy the publication of Korean newspapers and magazines was permitted, organizations could be formed, and meetings could be held. All such activities, of course, took place under strict police surveillance.

One of the lessons learned from the March 1st movement was that independence was not going to be won by emotional appeals alone. This realization gave considerable impetus to the "strengthen the nation" approach. Yi Kwang-su threw his weight behind this program. Yi Kwang-su had been a radical idealist preaching independence through education, modernization and popular demonstrations up until 1919, but he then became a realist thinking in terms of what was feasible here and now, with independence as a long range goal. He called for a greater emphasis on morality and education and used his novels to propagate his ideas.

A reaction against this kind of doctrinaire literature was inevitable. It came in the form of Korea's first purely literary magazine, *Creation* (1919). Written by a group of young men studying in Japan, under the leadership of the brilliant if eccentric Kim Tong-in (1900-1951), *Creation* stated that the purpose of literature lay not in political propaganda but in depicting life as it is. "Art for art's sake" was the imported catchword.

From 1923 onward the New Direction Group began to herald a change in the literary hegemony, a change from pure literature to a propaganda literature dedicated to spreading socialist principles. In 1925 KAPF was formed and absorbed the New Direction Group. Pure literature was forgotten and once again literature entered a period of political propaganda. The literary world became a battlefield between Marxists and nationalists, an arena of theoretical disputes without any real literary creativity. The proletarian groups remained in the ascendancy until the mid-1930s when they were rooted out by the Japanese police.

For the rest of that decade there was no real dominating influence in literature. There was, however, a good deal of experimentation, notably the work of Yi Sang (1910-1938) who tried to plumb the depths of the subconscious mind in a series of stories set in red light districts.

During this period Ch'ae Man-sik wrote his inimitable *Peace Under Heaven* (1937). There is nothing quite like it in fiction anywhere. It seems to be almost a new genre, reminiscent of Dickens in the vividness of the hero's character, of Fielding in the intrusive narrator, and of *p'ansori* in narrative technique. It represents the marriage of realism and the classical romance.

During the 1930s another group of writers–notably Kim Tong-ni (1913-), Hwang Sun-won (1915-) and Yi Hyo-sŏk (1907-1942)–began writing a completely new type of story. These writers began to examine what was uniquely Korean, writing in lyrical prose of the real spirit of Korea which they looked for in the past.

The 1940s brought renewed oppression by the Japanese and was an unproductive decade in literature. Liberation in 1945 was followed by great social and political confusion, and 1950 found the country in the throes of war again.

The 1950s saw the emergence of another new generation of writers, younger writers who had experienced the horrors of civil war and who were now looking for meaning amidst the cruelty and corruption of postwar society. Existentialism, introduced before the war, was in vogue, exerting a marked influence on the literature of the period. Chang Yong-hak (1921-) and Son Chang-sŏp (1922-) are typical of the new generation in their search for meaning in a society where all order had broken down.

The quest for freedom was central. Post-war intellectuals were concerned with discovering, or rediscovering, the self and the value of the individual. *The Square* (1961), by Ch'oe In-hun

(1936-), is a representative expression of this quest for freedom. The story deals directly with the consequences of the war and a dilemma which must have faced many prisoner-of-war intellectuals: whether to choose south, north, or a neutral country after the armistice.

The mid-1960s and early 1970s saw another new generation of writers begin to make their mark on the literary scene, writers who had either been children during the Korean conflict or had been so young that they had no vivid memories of the horror of war. As a consequence, the war and its aftermath gradually became less dominant in terms of the subject matter of literature. Kim Sŭng-ok's (1941-) *Seoul: Winter 1964* is a brilliant satire of a society where all order has broken down and human relationships have become meaningless. Highly experimental in form, it is a horrifying tragi-comic depiction of alienation and the absurdity of human existence.

During this period a new awareness of social and political issues came to the fore, and, as a consequence, stimulated concern with corruption and the abuse of power. The characters in the work of Hwang Sŏk-yŏng (1943-) are mostly from the lowest levels of society, people who find themselves in conflict with an unjust society and who face inevitable defeat. *Chang Kil-san* (1975), which has attracted considerable critical attention, provides a panoramic picture of the 18th century while depicting the tragic life of a legendary rebel hero. *The Road to Sampo* (1975), one of Hwang Sŏk-yŏng's finest stories, is a delicate mood piece, told almost entirely through dialogue.

The Kwangju tragedy in 1980 brought the anomalies of contemporary society into even sharper focus. Suddenly there seemed to be an urgent need to solve the problems that beset society, in particular, the gaping wound of a divided country. The so-called "Literature of Division" has become an important literary genre in recent years. It traces its roots back to Ch'oe In-hun's *The Square*, but with a rather different emphasis. *The Age of the Hero* (1984), by Yi Mun-yŏl (1948-), depicts a hero who has freely chosen the Communist way of life, emphasizing personal responsibility in choices. Cho Chŏng-nae's (1942-) *Taebaeksan-maek* (1986) asserts that division was part of an inevitable evolutionary process inherent in the class struggle between landowners and tenants.

The 1980s also were marked by a wave of "novels of the masses" (*minjung*) and "novels of workers" (*nodongja*) which focus on the entire gamut of social problems associated with industrialization and see the working class as pivotal to social reform and the future development of the nation. ◆

PAINTING

Korean painting has developed steadily throughout its long history from the Three Kingdoms period to modern times, in spite of frequent political crises and invasions. Absorbing foreign influences, Chinese in particular, on a selective basis, Korean painting has developed its own independent styles and has influenced the development of Japanese painting.

What is the relationship between traditional Korean painting and Chinese painting?

First of all, ancient Koreans made a deliberate effort to absorb Chinese arts. Chinese painting did not appear in Korea of its own accord. From the Three Kingdoms period to the Chosŏn period, it was customary to dispatch a professional painter along with the government envoy to China, this artist's mission being to sketch Chinese landscapes, learn new trends in Chinese painting and purchase paintings at whatever cost.

Second, Koreans chose to accept only the elements they deemed beneficial to their painting and pleasing to domestic tastes. The Korean aesthetic sense was very much at work in the process of selective acceptance of foreign elements.

The third and most important point is that Koreans did not stop at imitating Chinese elements but, much to their credit, always assimilated and developed them further to create artistic styles of their own.

The Korean painting tradition first began to develop in the Three Kingdoms period. The three countries, Koguryŏ, Silla, and Paekche, developed distinct artistic styles while maintaining a close interrelationship.

The paintings of Koguryŏ in the northern part of the Korean peninsula were marked by vitality and rhythmic movement as shown in the murals found in the tombs near T'ong-gou in Manchuria and P'yŏngyang. Best represented in the hunting scene in the Tomb of the Dancers, this spirited style originated

A hunting scene from a mural in the 6th century Koguryŏ Tomb of the Dancers

in the early days of the kingdom and became firmly established in the later period. Judging from these murals, painting began to develop in Koguryŏ around the 4th century at the latest, firmly established its own tradition by the 6th century, and matured fully in the early 7th century.

The Koguryŏ painting style was transmitted to the Paekche Kingdom. Influenced artistically by Koguryŏ and the Southern Dynasties of China, especially the Liang (502-557), Paekche developed elegant and refined styles quite special to it. As exemplified by the Lotus Flowers and Flying Clouds painted in the Nŭngsan-ri Tomb and the ornamental tiles with landscape designs in relief, excavated from Kyuam-ri, the artistic work of Paekche is elegant and relaxed, a remarkable contrast to the dynamic Koguryŏ style.

The style of Silla is evident in a number of paintings done on crafts, including the Heavenly Horse Painting (*Ch'ŏnmado*) excavated from the Tomb of the Heavenly Horse in Kyŏngju. Obviously influenced by Koguryŏ and Paekche, these paintings, though inferior, show qualities quite distinct from the other two countries. While the paintings of Koguryŏ are dynamic and rhythmic and those of Paekche elegant and refined, the paintings of Silla are somewhat speculative and statical.

Thus each of the ancient nations of the Korean peninsula developed its own style despite strong influences from China and close cultural interchanges amongst themselves. Their painting styles and tradition were transmitted to Japan and contributed to the development of ancient Japanese art.

These diverse painting styles are believed to have integrated and blended into one after Silla's unification of Korea in 668. Ancient records, available only in fragments, indicate that portraits for the royal court's entertainment, blue-green colored landscapes, and Buddhist paintings prevailed at the time as a result of active cultural exchanges with Tang China. Buddhist painting must have shared Buddhist sculpture's periodic style in its representation of Buddhist deities, as witnessed in the only extant work from that period, the frontispiece of the Avatamsaka Sutra executed around 754-755.

Painting was also an important art in the other Korean kingdom of Parhae (699-926), which occupied a vast territory including Manchuria and northern Korea and rivaled Unified Silla. Murals in the Tomb of Princess Chŏnghyo reveal a mixture of Koguryŏ tradition and assimilation of Tang styles.

The Koryŏ Period(918-1392)

The art of painting flourished in great variety during the Koryŏ period. A new tradition developed as paintings began to be produced not only

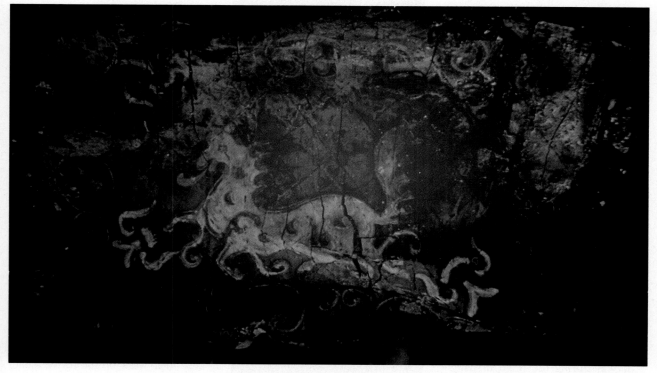

The Heavenly Horse *on a birch saddle guard which lends its name to the Silla tomb from which it was excavated*

for practical purposes but also for appreciation and spiritual cultivation by artists for whom painting was an avocation and not a profession. Unlike previous periods, members of the nobility and ordained Buddhists often enjoyed painting and so contributed to the broadening of the art.

One of the important developments in this period was the emergence of landscape paintings based on actual sketches. Though it has no direct link with the later school of Chŏng Sŏn (1676-1759) who painted landscapes based upon actual Korean scenes and subjects, the new trend nevertheless set the precedent for the depiction of actual Korean scenery.

Koryŏ Buddhist paintings, as seen from a number of works extant in Japan, are extremely elaborate and, much like the celadonware of the same period, evince a penchant for aristocratic artistry. They are all marked with the same stylistic idiosyncrasies in composition, pose of figures, and rendering of folds and patterns in drapery.

The Chosŏn Period(1392-1910)

It was during the Chosŏn period that Korean painting came into full bloom and established a firm tradition. Talented painters from the Royal Academy of Painting and prominent literati-painters contributed greatly to the development of traditional styles. Painting became more diverse and Korean elements more prominent than in the preceding period, especially in terms of composition, treatment of space, brushwork, and the depiction of trees.

Selectively absorbing the styles of Chinese masters from the Song, Yüan, Ming and Qing periods, Korean painters were able to evolve their own styles. They also played an important part in the development of *sumie* (ink painting) in Japan.

It was during the reign of King Sejong (r. 1419 - 50) that the Korean

Top, Self-Portrait by Yun Tu-sŏ, a 17th anonymous work from 14th century Koryŏ Bottom, Amitabha Triad Welcoming Souls, an century painter and scholar

tradition was firmly established, thanks to great masters like An Kyŏn, Kang Hŭi-an and Prince Anp'yŏng. These early Chosŏn painters based their work on the Koryŏ painting tradition and at the same time absorbed and assimilated highly advanced Chinese traditions to develop their own styles.

The painters of the 16th century showed a strong tendency toward conventionality and adhered to the style of the previous century, a fact which reaffirms the generally held belief that the roots of the Korean painting tradition were firmly implanted by the early Chosŏn period.

The Korean style of painting was able to maintain its unique character despite the four destructive foreign invasions that swept the country in the mid-Chosŏn period (ca. 1550-1700) mainly because the tradition was so firmly established in the earlier period.

The Korean style became even more pronounced in the paintings of the late Chosŏn period (ca. 1700- ca. 1850), which were comparable to the early Chosŏn paintings in terms of artistic standards. Whereas the early painters developed a native style by carrying on the tradition of Koryŏ and absorbing Chinese influences of Song, Yüan and Ming, the style of the later period manifested a national awareness on the part of the artists even as they embraced Ming and Qing styles.

This national awareness surged during the reigns of Yŏngjo (r. 1724-76) and Chŏngjo (r. 1776-1800) and played a vital role in society and culture in general during the late Chosŏn period. Just as many scholars of the time turned away from pedantic Neo-Confucian precepts in favor of the progressive ideals of "Practical Learning" (*Sirhak*), painters began to base their work on the native scenes and life-style of their country.

New social trends brought forth a number of new artistic trends. The new developments in technique and style may be summarized as follows: the Chinese Zhe school style, favored during the mid-Chosŏn period, was replaced by the Chinese Southern School style; Chŏng Sŏn and his followers adopted and transformed the techniques of the Chinese Southern School for use in the painting of Korean landscapes; Kim Hong-do, Kim Tŭk-sin, Sin Yun-bok and their followers produced a large number of genre paintings depicting scenes of daily life with a sense of humor and affection; and Western methods of painting were introduced to Korea via Qing China.

Another notable aspect of the paintings of this period is the introduction of Western methods from China. Western techniques of shading and perspective were brought to Qing by Jesuit missionaries and were, in turn, introduced to Korea by members of the Korean mission to Yenjing. Eighteenth century painters, including Kim Tu-ryang, Kang Se-hwang and Yi Hŭi-yŏng, were the first to employ these techniques. They also found their way into the paintings of royal ceremonies done by academy painters and folk paintings.

In the final years of Chosŏn (ca. 1850-1910), the landscape and genre painting styles found in the preceding period declined, giving way to the Chinese Southern School style (*Namchonghwa*) promoted by Kim Chŏng-hŭi and his adherents. In addition, a fresh and unusual style was initiated by a small number of markedly individualistic artists, including Kim Su-ch'ŏl, Kim Ch'ang-su and Hong Se-sŏp. Despite the pervasive influences of the late Qing styles, the painting of this period was marked by strong individuality and became the basis for modern Korean painting.

Social and political upheavals in the late 19th century caused a decline in painting, although literati painters were quite prolific with their ink brush renderings of orchids. Chang Sŭng-ŏp is regarded as the most representative and last professional academy painter of the period.

CONTEMPORARY PAINTING

The periodization of Korean contemporary art remains a problem for art historians. While this may sound strange to the general reader, we must remember that it takes considerable patience and insight to delineate when a new age has begun for the art of any country.

In Europe and America, the term "contemporary art" usually refers to the schools of art which have evolved since the end of World War II. Similarly, the term "post-war" art is applied to contemporary art in Korea. However, there is no historical justification for this. From a purist view of art history, contemporary Korean art appears to have lacked sufficient motivation, unlike that of Europe. What is now called "contemporary art" is believed to have developed as a reaction to or out of a social need brought about by the political and psychological situation the Korean people found themselves in following the Korean War.

Artists in the 1950s were obviously influenced by the harsh postwar environment. Perhaps this was why the young artists of the so-called "Korean War generation" were attracted to expressionism which had developed in post-war Europe under similarly unfortunate circumstances.

Expressionist paintings were produced in great quantities by avantgarde artists toward the end of the 1950s, especially between 1958 and

A painting by Pak Su-kŭn

Top, A painting by Yoo Young-Kuk Bottom, A painting by Kim Whan-Ki

1959. In view of Korea's geographical location and its cultural and social environments, it was only natural that it took some time before any new art movement in Europe or America was embraced by Korean art circles. The works displayed at the Modern Art Exhibition in the late 1950s showed that Korea's artists were exploring new directions rather than simply reworking what they had done earlier. Their efforts appear to have born fruit. The paintings displayed in the exhibitions in the early 1960s reveal many new values and artistic conceptions.

The founding of the Contemporary Korean Art Exhibition for Invited Artists by the major daily newspaper *Chosun Ilbo* in 1957 was an important milestone in the development of Korea's contemporary art. As the first independent exhibition in Korea, it played a major role in encouraging artists' creative activities, in contrast to the government-sponsored National Exhibition of Fine Art which was extremely academic and conservative.

Abstract art denounced the traditional order and values in pursuit of direct expressions of man's free spirit. But the new methods of expression the artists of the abstract school achieved could not bear repetition. The zeal Korean artists showed for abstract expressionism began to diminish in the latter half of the 1960s, as they were faced with the dilemma of repetition and lack of inspiration. The artists of the abstract school thus had to struggle to find a means to revitalize their art.

A new generation of artists, whom some call the "April 19 generation," because they were mainly educated after 1960 when an authoritarian government was overthrown in the wake of a fierce student demonstration, began to appear around 1968.

These young artists were inclined to geometric abstraction in reaction to the anti-formal art which had been most popular in the nation's art circles until that point. Another common tendency found in these young artists' work was that their keen interest in found objects, or "objets trouve," and the possibilities they offered.

In the early 1970s, Korean painters began to explore geometric compositions with a view to reestablishing the original value of forms. Taking control of this movement was the Origin Group, which was formed in 1966.

At the same time, some young artists in other parts of the art community were extending the concept of fine art to an appreciation of various objects in nature, in which they seemed to have discovered new aesthetic qualities. Their interest was not only in achieving artistic imagery but, more basically in a sense, in seeking a significant encounter between the human consciousness and objects as well as a union of humanity and the world. They endeavored to bring about a change in, or an expansion of, the general concepts of fine art. Leading this movement were the artists belonging to two prominent groups, the A.G. Group (or the Korean Avant-Garde Art Association) and the S.T. (Space and Time) Group, both of which were organized in 1969.

It should be pointed out that such an extended concept of fine art was not totally foreign to the majority of Korean artists. Indeed, they recognized that the idea had its roots in a traditional perspective of nature and was a universe characteristic of all Asian cultures, including Korea's. Traditionally, Koreans have seldom viewed humanity and nature from two separate perspectives. Instead, they have tried to identify with nature, and further with the whole universe. It was through this age-old tradition that the young experimentalists discovered a valuable source of artistic inspiration.

A similar pan-naturalist philosophy can be detected in the monochromat-

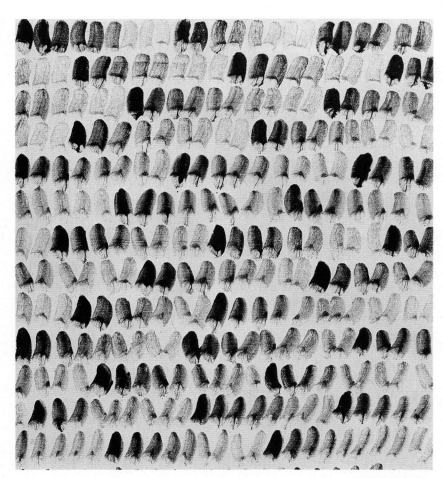

A painting by Lee U-Fan

ic pictures of the minimalist tendency, an important painting trend in the late 1970s. These paintings of a simple color scheme, which are often described as representing the "reductionist" concept in its crystallized form, attempted to avoid all illusions possibly attainable from images and composition.

Korean painting since the 1960s has been guided for the most part by abstraction, which can be further classified into abstract expressionism, post-painterly geometric abstract painting and abstract monochromatic painting.

The 1980s witnessed a powerful movement toward social messages. The birth of the "Reality and Uttrance Group" early in the 1980s signaled the initiation of this movement which has technically divorced itself from all trends of modernist painting including abstraction.

The artists of this group, who apparently banded together with the primary goal of critizing social issues, have chosen painting to give a visual voice to their politics. This tendency among young artists to seek social participation can be understood as a Korean adaptation of the worldwide trend in "New Painting." But in the context of Korea's political and social circumstances in recent years, this movement, so-called "Min Joong Art" takes on a particular historical significance, although its universal value as art is questionable.

23

Korean painting has generally been grouped into two major categories—pure painting and "functional" painting. While there is no such thing as a truly pure, academic form of painting any more than an exclusively "functional" painting, this classification still dominates the thinking of many artists, art historians, connoisseurs and art dealers. The traditional Confucian scholar's scorn of popular paintings which were colorful and contained folk motifs was at the basis of the idea that unsigned "functional" paintings were a low form of art.

"Functional" in this context can mean many things. Some "functional" paintings, for example, were used for decorations at special seasonal festivals, such as New Year's Day, and the *Tano* festival held on the fifth day of the fifth lunar month. Such paintings generally included symbols of

Tigers were a common theme of folk paintings

longevity and happiness as well as guardian images to ward off evil spirits.

The old Confucian-oriented Korean scholars classified virtually everything outside the elitist areas of calligraphy and literati or *Sŏn* painting, created for the intellectual diversion of the scholar class, as folk painting. Yet a great deal of this painting was not folk painting at all in the sense that this term is used elsewhere in the world to mean a simple form of painting executed by amateurs and with no reference to the rules of any school on art.

Korean folk painting, therefore, developed as the art of an entire nation, of all classes. The painters often did not sign their names to their works but a trained eye can usually tell what type of painter created a particular work.

The first type consisted of painters known as "passing guests," wanderers who travelled from village to village

A portion of a screen depicting the ten longevity symbols

producing paintings at individual households. Most of them were naive peasant craftsmen, but some skilled artists were found among them, usually those who had failed to become court painters.

The second group was made up of painter-monks. Talented monks who received strict training from a master usually became professional painters and were engaged in producing various Buddhist ritual paintings for temples. Those who failed to survive the strict regimen often turned to the life of itinerant painter-monks, travelling from one temple to another and earning their living by painting murals on temple walls.

The third group consisted of court painters. As far as social position is concerned, a court painter was the highest rank obtainable in Korea for an artist. It is often thought that the works of these men were only in the classical style, but they were also hired to decorate palaces and to provide ornamental designs.

Folk paintings were found in the royal court, Buddhist temples, Shaman shrines, *kisaeng* drinking houses, altars and private houses.

Korean folk painting is often classified in terms of its relationship to the concepts of Confucianism, Taoism, Buddhism or Shamanism. This classification is valid when there is a clear religious identification: paintings based on the Buddha's life are Buddhist paintings, paintings portraying the Taoist immortals are Taoist paintings, illustrations of Confucian teachings are Confucian paintings, and those of the Mountain Spirit are Shamanistic paintings. However, at times these religious motifs are interwoven with such complexity that it becomes impossible to determine to which specific religion each belongs. The end result is a general impression that in Korea there is Taoist Buddhism, Buddhist Shamanism, and Taoist Shamanism.

A folk painting depicting a group of shamans

A striking characteristic of folk painting is the extent of stylization, which leads to abstract art, expressing man's dreams, imagination, symbolism, life, humor, satire, and sense of fantasy. There is no attempt at realism, and every space is filled in, a sharp contrast to the aesthetics of open space typical of classic Oriental painting. Another unique aspect is animism, expressed in all kinds of animal, rock and tree paintings. This animism is really a reflection of Shamanistic animism. A third style, usually referred to as "the naive style," is developed by a combination of abstraction and animism which portrays a genuine, childlike world where a man's heart is more important than his name.

CALLIGRAPHY

In Korea, as in China and Japan, calligraphy has long been considered a form of art. Korean calligraphy derives from the written form of the Chinese language, in which each character is composed of a number strokes within an imaginary square and is intended to convey a specific meaning. Koreans have used Chinese characters for writing since the second or third century A.D., although their own language is of an entirely different system. Even after the invention of the Korean alphabet *hangŭl* in 1446, Chinese was used as the official script until the late 19th century. Traditional Korean calligraphers wrote in Chinese rather than in Korean.

Calligraphy was always closely connected with painting in Korea, and some believe that painting was influenced by calligraphy in terms of the vitality and rhythm of its economy of strokes. A calligraphic work would be hung on a wall like a painting and admired in the same way, each stroke praised for its attributes, the ink for its tone, and the composition for its strength, individuality, vitality and so on.

Technically speaking, the art of calligraphy depends on the skill and imagination of the writer to give interesting shape to his brush strokes and to compose beautiful structures from them. This is done without retouching or shading and, most importantly, with well-balanced spaces between strokes. Such spacing is acquired only through years of practice and training.

Dexterity of brushwork and cultivation of aesthetic sensitivity are not the only elements essential to understanding the art of calligraphy, however. In fashionable circles, the art was regarded as essential to the development of a cultured gentleman. The practical function of calligraphy as

Frontispiece to the Avatamsaka Sutra *from the Unified Silla period*

handwriting or a means of communication was often overshadowed by the philosophical implications attached to its execution.

The fundamental inspiration of calligraphy, as of all other arts in traditional Korea, is nature. Each stroke in a character, even a single dot, suggests a natural object. Like the ancient Chinese masters, Korean calligraphers recognized that, just as every twig of a living tree is alive, every tiny stroke must be made to live. This is the very property of calligraphy that distinguishes its strokes from those in a printed word.

Like the tools of a traditional ink-and-brush painter, the tools of a calligrapher are few—good ink, an ink stone, a good brush and good paper (some prefer silk). These items were affectionately called the "scholar's four friends." Great care was taken in selecting and maintaining them because they often served as a measure of the owner's aesthetic taste.

Korea boasts a long tradition in calligraphy, dating to the early years of the Three Kingdoms period when Chinese literature was taught for the first time at royal academies and state-run institutions of higher education. In spite of this long history and the efforts of numerous aristocratic noblemen and artists to promote the art over the centuries, few calligraphic works have survived the many foreign invasions and internal conflicts which have tormented the Korean peninsula. The Japanese invasions of the late 16th century, in particular, caused serious damage to historic monuments and cultural objects, not to mention a tremendous loss of human lives. Thus the number of existing fragments of calligraphy dating to the years preceding that war is less than 20.

Fortunately examples of traditional calligraphy carved in stone are more readily available. Among several inscribed stone monuments from the Three Kingdoms period is a huge stone monument erected in 414 A.D. in southern Manchuria in honor of the military achievements of King Kwanggaet'o of the Koguryŏ Kingdom.

This 6.4 meter-high stone monument carries an epitaph of some 1,800 Chinese characters engraved in an angular, epigraphic style. Most epigraphists and specialists in ancient Korean calligraphy note that the style expresses the bravery and vigor of the people of the ancient military state which ruled a considerable portion of Manchuria and the northern half of the peninsula.

More scarce are references to the standard of calligraphic art achieved in the southwestern kingdom of Paekche. In view of its high level of scholarship and refinement of art objects, it is most likely that this kingdom enjoyed a notable degree of maturity in calligraphy. The accidental discovery of the tomb of King Munyŏng and his queen in the Paekche capital of Kongju in central Korea in 1972 yielded many important archaeological finds, including a square stone tablet. Placed at the entrance to the sixth century burial chamber, it was a sort of certificate of proof that a plot of land was purchased from underground deities in order to build the tomb. The Chinese characters engraved on the stone slab are of an elegant style showing technical dexterity, which was apparently influenced by the contemporary Chinese writing of a non-cursive style.

During the Unified Silla period, devotion and adherence to the Tang culture of China gave birth to such great masters of calligraphy as Kim Saeng and Ch'oe Ch'i-won who modeled their styles after those of famous Chinese masters.

The early rulers of Koryŏ adopted a Chinese-style civil service examination to recruit officials. Handwriting was naturally included in the criteria for judgment. This system gave rise to an interest in improving handwriting among the upper classes. The court administered a separate examination for scriveners to serve in lower positions. This period, when Buddhism thrived as the state religion, produced a wealth of examples through which the standard of calligraphy can be understood. Extant examples include tombstones, woodblock prints and handwritten copies of Buddhist texts, epitaphs on memorial stupas for revered monks and temple monuments.

The calligraphy of the Chosŏn Period first followed the Tang Chinese Chao Meng-fu style of an elegant, supple touch. Prince Anp'yŏng (1418-53), the third son of King Sejong, was unrivaled for his dexterous hand in this style. By the early 16th century, however, a weakened, unimaginative style became evident, and Korean calligraphy entered a period of sterility.

The 19th century saw the emergence of individual styles related to those of the Chinese calligrapher, Wen Cheng-ming, of the 16th to the early 17th century. The new trend resulted from Korea's close cultural contacts with Xing China. Such contacts were actively pursued by a group of scholars and intellectuals eager to follow the Xing model of seeking practical approaches to better the lives of the people and to build a modern state.

The greatest master of the Chosŏn period was Kim Ch'ŏng-hŭi, a member

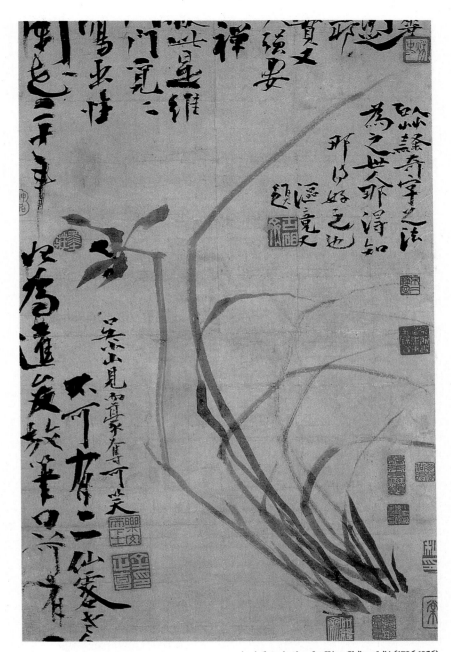

An ink painting by Kim Chŏng-hŭi (1786-1856)

of the *Sirhak* School of "Practical Learning." A distinguished calligrapher and scholar, Kim's calligraphy is derived from the Li Shu script of China, but his sense of pictorial composition, harmony within asymmetry and animation wrought by unmatched, forceful strokes led to the creation of a dynamic style of his own.

A few Chosŏn calligraphers persisted in the early decades of the present century. However, the influence of Japanese calligraphy began to be felt around 1920. Since World War II, traditional calligraphy has survived only as a minor art. A new trend since the 1960s has been calligraphy employing the Korean alphabet. ◆

SCULPTURE

The introduction of Buddhism to Korea was one of the most important factors in the formation of early Korean art. Buddhism and Buddhist art originated in India, passed through and developed in various Buddhist centers in Central Asia and China and reached Korea in the late fourth century during the Three Kingdoms period.

Sculpture in the Three Kingdoms

During this period, a large number of Buddhist monks went to China to study Buddhist doctrine. They returned with Buddhist texts, images and other religious objects. Thus the development of Korean Buddhist images is indebted to Chinese prototypes and is often traced back to Central Asian or Indian models. However, Korean artists were selective, favoring certain prototypes and developing them into distinctly Korean forms which reflect native, artistic traditions and regional differences.

The propagation of the Buddhism in Korea occurred under the patronage of the royal court and ruling aristocracy. Large temples were constructed, and many images were created for worship.

When Buddhism was first introduced to Korea, imported images must have been worshiped, but these were soon superseded by locally-produced images. The earliest extant Korean Buddhist images date from the sixth century, the oldest being a gilt-bronze Buddha discovered at Ŭiryŏng in South Kyŏngsang Province. The inscription on the back of its aureole indicates it was made in 539 A.D. during the Koguryŏ period.

Buddhist triads consisting of a central Buddha figure flanked by two attendant Bodhisattvas were among the most popular images during the second half of the 6th century. A fine example of these triads is the Rock-cut Buddha Triad found in Sŏsan, South Ch'ungch'ŏng Province, part of the ancient Paekche Kingdom. The three figures are carved in high relief

Gilt Bronze Standing Buddha with dated inscription, 539 A.D.

on a huge rock facing east.

Of the many meditating Bodhisattva images extant from the Three Kingdoms period, two large gilt bronze figures dating from around the year 600 are perhaps the most impressive. Both reflect the heights achieved in bronze casting during this period and are unsurpassed in their finely modelled facial features and harmonious interplay of form between the round body and free-flowing garment folds.

Images representing the Bodhisattva Avalokitesvara were widely worshipped during the Three Kingdoms period. This Bodhisattva can be recognized by a small seated Buddha depicted in its crown, which symbolizes that Avalokitesvara is an attendant to the Amitabha Buddha and helps beings reach the Amitabha Buddha's Western Paradise.

From the mid-seventh century, naturalistic depictions became more common in Korean Buddhist sculpture. There was a greater interest in the modelling of three-dimensional forms and in a more organic and balanced proportioning of the head and body of a figure.

The tendency toward simplicity in form, more voluminous modelling of the face and body, and a reduced number of garment folds was also a hallmark of images of Buddha during this period. One of the earliest examples of the progressive seventh century style is the standing gilt-bronze Buddha discovered in Yangp'yŏng, north of Seoul.

Buddhist Sculpture in the Unified Silla Period

When Silla unified the Three Kingdoms in 668, Buddhism enjoyed continued prosperity and was a prominent aspect of both religious life and artistic creativity of the period.

Several artistic elements contributed to the development of Buddhist art during the Unified Silla period. Silla's indigenous local tradition continued to provide an important aesthetic base, and to this foundation were added artistic traditions inherited from the deposed kingdoms of Paekche and Koguryŏ. New ideas also came from Tang China, which was then the cosmopolitan center of Buddhist culture in East Asia. By the late 7th century, many Silla monks had ventured on pilgrimages to India, either overland through Central Asia or by the sea route around Southeast Asia.

Buddhist images during the Unified Silla period were made with great refinement. Forms were full and rounded, the proportions of the body were harmonious, and an interest in realistic modelling became prominent. The gold Buddha image discovered inside a pagoda at the Kuhwang-dong temple site in Kyŏngju is a fine example of early 8th century Buddhist art.

The finest stone sculptures of 8th century Silla are undoubtedly the images in the cave temple of Sŏkkuram in Kyŏngju. At the center of the round hall is the main Buddha image seated high on a lotus throne. It is imposing in size, majestic in posture and divine in appearance. Relief images of Bodhisattvas, Brahma and Indra are in elegant postures depicted with subtle modelling of the forms. The Buddha's ten disciples are depicted with individualized facial features and expressions, and the Four

Gold Seated Buddha from Kuhwangni, Kyŏngju, 706 A.D.

29

Eleven-headed Avalokitesvara from Sŏkkuram Stone Grotto, mid-eighth century

Directional Guardians are carved on either side of the corridor leading to the main hall.

The production of seated Buddha images with the Buddha's hand in the earth-touching gesture symbolizing enlightenment, such as the Sŏkkuram Buddha, was widespread in late Unified Silla. This iconography comes from India but seems to have received special attention in late 7th century Tang China.

By the 9th century, there was an aesthetic decline in the sculptural tradition represented by the Sŏkkuram Buddha. The treatment of garment folds had become stereotyped and there was no longer any interest in modelling of the body.

In late Unified Silla, a new type of Buddha image, that of the Buddha Vairocana, began to appear. Vairocana is distinguished by his unique hand gesture in which the five fingers of the right hand hold the index finger of the left finger. This figure first appeared in Huayen Buddhism and was further developed in Esoteric Buddhism as the Supreme Buddhist Deity and the Great Illuminator whose body, speech and thought make up the life of the universe. Many images of this Buddha were made in stone and in iron during the ninth century. In Korea, these statues were especially worshiped in temples where Buddhists practiced *Sŏn* (Zen) Buddhism, which stresses meditation for the attainment of enlightenment.

The Koryŏ Period

Like the Unified Silla, the Koryŏ Kingdom also patronized Buddhism as the state religion. Many temples were constructed, Buddhist images multiplied, and complete sets of Buddhist texts were carved on wood blocks for printing. The latter was an act of supreme piety meant to insure the well-being and protection of the nation from disaster and foreign invasions.

Koryŏ sculptures vary in the quality of their workmanship. Many images were of high quality, cast in bronze, while iron and stone became a popular media for larger statues which tended to be less articulated in their modelling. Some stone statues were carved in such shallow relief that often only the contour of the image is recognizable from the surface of the stone.

In the early years of the Koryŏ Kingdom, the Unified Silla sculptural tradition lingered on, as revealed in the large iron seated Buddha found at a temple site in Ch'ungung-ni in Kyŏnggi Province. This figure generally follows the stylistic features of the central image in the Sŏkkuram cave temple in its hand gestures, draping of the folds in the figure's clothing and the cross-legged seated posture.

A fine example of early Koryŏ sculpture is the marble Bodhisattva from the Hansong temple site in Kangnŭng, Kangwŏn Province. The statue features voluminous modelling on its plump face and rounded body and in the deep carving of the necklace and scarves. These features were probably inspired by Chinese images from the late Tang or Five Dynasties periods.

Stone sculptures from the Koryŏ period tend to be almost overpoweringly large. The Unified Silla sculptural tradition persisted but changed gradually as purely Koryŏ elements developed.

Several bronze statues of fine

Top, Gilt Bronze Seated Bhaisajyaguru from Changgok Temple, 1346

Bottom, Wooden Relief Panel with Buddhist Figures from Yaksu Hermitage, Silsang Temple, 1782

workmanship survive from the late Koryŏ period. Most representative of these is the gilt bronze seated Medicine Buddha, or Bhaisajyaguru, image at Changgok Temple. Balanced in bodily proportions, with naturally flowing garment folds and a benevolent facial expression, this 14th century statue marks the high point of Koryŏ bronze casting. An examination of the interior of this statue yielded many objects including copies of sutras, colored textiles and a cloth with an ink inscription indicating that this figure was cast in the year 1346.

The Chosŏn Period

The Chosŏn Kingdom witnessed the decline of Buddhism as Confucianism was introduced as the state religion. However, private devotion to Buddhism persisted, and Buddhist images continued to be produced. Many of the images worshipped in Korean temples today date from the late Chosŏn Kingdom. They are made from a variety of materials but bronze and wood seem to have been the preferred media.

Of the many wooden sculptures from the Chosŏn period, a popular genre were the wooden relief panels carved with Buddhist images which were placed behind the Buddha like a Buddhist painting. The shape and expressions of the faces of the figures and the folds in the drapery were quite stereotyped and lacked in individuality. The somewhat heavier carving and the stylization are typical of Buddhist sculpture in the late Chosŏn period.

Faith in Buddhist teachings remains very much alive today in the minds of many Koreans. Thus Buddhist images will continue to be made, forever reflecting the unpretentious charm, human warmth, and carefree spirit of the Korean people.

Most art historians agree 1919 marks the genesis of modern Korean sculpture. In that year, Kim Pok-chin, entered the Tokyo School of Fine Art. He returned home, as the first Korean to have trained in Western sculpture. A few other students then enrolled in the same Japanese institution. Those artists, including Kim Chong-yŏng, Kim Kyŏng-sŏng and Yun Hyo-jung, soon joined Kim Pok-chin in introducing sculpture influenced by European traditions and spawning what was to become an age of modern sculpture in Korea.

At that time Japan's colonial regime wielded unchecked power over all spheres of Korean life. Japan was Korea's only window on the world, and often this window was stained with a strong Japanese bias. It is from this general perspective that the overall background and process of development of sculpture as a major aesthetic movement in the modern period should be viewed.

This early period of modern sculpture suffered from a lack of creative inspiration despite the pioneering zeal of early artists, who were largely obsessed with imitating Western sculpture. Circumstances were far from conducive to lively artistic activities as Japan was pulling its colonial reins ever more tightly in preparation for World War II. In 1945 Korea was liberated, but the overall situation did not improve and became even more hostile as ideological polarization, and eventually military confrontation, occurred between South and North Korea.

One bright spot during this unstable period was young Korean sculptors' admiration of Western sculpture. Yun Hyo-jung met Marino Marini in Venice in 1952 and was greatly influenced by the famous sculptor and his works. Another occurrence worth mentioning from those dark years was the inclusion of abstract works for the first time in the National Exhibition of Fine Art in 1954.

After the cease-fire in 1953, art circles began to gain some vitality. A few large-scale exhibitions were organized by private organizations, encouraging a remarkable diversity in

Chi-won's Face by Kwŏn Chin-gyu (1922-73)

style and technique. Among the more notable exhibitions were the annual membership show sponsored by the Korean Fine Art Association and the Contemporary Korean Art Exhibition for Invited Artists sponsored by the leading daily newspaper *Chosun Ilbo.* The latter deserves special note for providing a venue for the works of emerging artists of an avant-garde penchant.

Modern Korean sculpture had become firmly established by the end of the 1950s. The conflict between the opposing schools of realism and abstractionism was intensifying, and sculptors were employing a greater diversity of materials, including assorted metals and stone in a break with their traditional reliance on plaster and wood.

The 1960s to the 1970s saw impressive progress in Korean sculpture owing to the country's rapid economic development as well as to political

and social changes. The sculpture of this period of dramatic transitions can be divided into two major streams. The first was the so-called "anti-formal abstractionism," which had been introduced to Korea from the late 1950s to the early 1960s. The movement, inspired by the creation of the Korean Avant-Garde Art Association, breathed new life into the world of Korean sculpture throughout the 1960s. Sculptors of this vein repudiated the natural forms respected in the traditional school of academic realism and sought to give spontaneous expression to their emotions through nonrepresentational shapes. In the 1970s, this emotional abstractionism was seriously challenged by another new school, the "Sculptural Conceptualism" movement.

Sculptural conceptualism pursued "pure" abstraction, free from all emotional bonds and connotations. In terms of style, artists of this movement favored simple, daring forms in

The Echo of a Bow
by Yun Hyo-jung (1917-67)

contrast to those of the previous generation of anti-formal vanguardism who tended to be complex and intricate.

The 1980s experienced an unprecedented burgeoning in the number of active sculptors and sculptural activities, and a number of young artists become nostalgic for the past trends of a more humane nature in reaction to the cold intellectualism of the previous decade. ◆

Dream of a Spring Day *by Kim Kyŏng-sŭng (1915-)*

CRAFTS

One of the best ways to understand ancient Korean civilization is to examine the tools and crafts that have been discovered in archeological digs around the peninsula. A large number of relics from the Paleolithic, Neolithic and Bronze ages have been recovered. These artifacts provide scholars with valuable insights into life in ancient Korea, and crafts from later periods reflect everyday life and values.

METALCRAFT

Korea's metalcraft culture dates back to the Bronze Age in the 6th or 5th centuries B.C. A wide variety of bronze relics have been recovered around the country. Of note are the Liaoning-type bronze swords first made in China in the 7th or 8th centuries B.C. and introduced to Korea in the fifth or sixth century. These swords were fitted with separately molded blades and hilts. By the 4th or 3rd centuries B.C., another bronze sword modeled after the Liaoning-type was developed in Korea. The most common of the bronze age artifacts found in Korea, this "slender bronze sword" was later introduced to Japan.

In recent years, an increasing number of bronze implements have been excavated, the majority from stone cists. Among the major finds are bronze swords and sword hilts made separately to be joined together. The hilts are generally bamboo-shaped, and some have decorated pommels. Few hilts or decorated pommels have been reported from the early age of the "slender bronze swords," however.

Gold crown from fifth-sixth century Silla

On occasion, iron swords from the early iron period (ca. 300 B.C.-0) have been found together with "slender bronze sword" hilts and decorated pommels.

Bronze spearheads have been reported from the latter part of the "slender bronze sword" period, although it is difficult to trace their origin. Bronze dagger-axes consisting of a long wooden handle attached at right angles to a blade were important weapons during the Chinese Shang (ca.16th century B.C.-1027 B.C.) and Zhou (1027-221 B.C.) periods and seemed to have inspired Korean imitations at a later date.

Animal-shaped bronze buckles showing a strong influence from the bronze culture of northern Eurasia have been discovered in North Kyŏngsang Province. The buckles consisted of a round or oval ring

attached to a bar sticking out from the breast of the animal ornament.

Metalcraft reached a new level of sophistication during the Three Kingdoms period (1st century B.C.-7th century A.D.) as evidenced by the relics recovered from tombs dating to that period. Only fragmentary objects remain from most Koguryŏ and Paekche tombs because their stone or brick chambers were vulnerable to pillage, but the Silla tombs, great stone mounds, have produced a wealth of archeological evidence.

Koguryŏ metalcraft was influenced by Chinese metalcraft as well as the unique character of the Koguryŏ people accustomed to a severe climate and nomadic lifestyle.

Paekche artisans, on the other hand, produced works characterized by moderation and elegance, reflecting their kingdom's mild climate and fertile land. The Tomb of Paekche King Munyŏng (r .501-523), discovered in 1981, is a rich archaeological treasure of more than 3,000 burial objects including personal ornaments in gold and silver, weapons, a variety of vessels, and bronze mirrors. Many of these objects reflect a strong Chinese influence, and the gold ornaments used in royal head-dresses, earrings, silver bracelets, necklaces, and the like are more refined than those made in Koguryŏ or Silla.

Most of the extant metalware of any importance comes from Silla tombs. Silla artisans created many art objects of great delicacy and elegance. In Silla tombs, a wooden coffin was placed in a pit or wooden chamber and boulders were piled over it to form a mound which was then covered with earth. Since the wooden coffin and chamber decomposed as time passed and the boulders and earth mound collapsed around them, it was impossible to make additional burials or re-enter the tomb. Thus, the contents of Silla tombs were relatively well preserved.

The gold crowns discovered in Silla tombs represent the finest in Silla metalcraft. One such crown, National Treasure No. 87, dating back to the 5th or 6th century, is composed of two parts: an inner and an outer crown. A forked gold piece symbolizing the feathers of a bird stems from the inner crown and slants slightly backwards. Across the front of the outer crown are upright tree-shaped ornaments, and at the back are row antler-shaped uprights. A string of pendants hangs from each side near

Gold earrings from fifth-sixth century Silla

the front of the crown. The inner part of the crown is decorated in an open latticework of various patterns. The crown is further festooned with gold beads and comma-shaped pieces of jade, fitted with intricately carved gold caps, attached with gold wire.

Gold girdles were almost always found together with Silla gold crowns. The openwork links were fastened to a leather or cloth belt with tiny nails to form a girdle from which ornamental pendants were hung. Earrings, pendants and rings were also buried in the tombs. Most of the necklaces are of jade or gold with a few exceptions such as the crystal necklace from Kŭmnyŏng-chong Tomb. The bracelets are round and have sawtooth designs on the outside. Some are solid and others are hollow.

Gold girdle with pendants from fifth-sixth century Silla

The Kaya Kingdom, a federation of six tribal states along the lower Naktong River on the southeastern tip of the Korean peninsula (A.D. 421-562), developed its own culture that is just now being uncovered. A beautiful example of Kaya metalcraft is National Treasure No. 138, a crown cut from a thin sheet of gold. Four floral uprights stand at equal intervals around the wide headband, and the crown itself is decorated with round gold spangles. Comma-shaped pieces of jade are attached at equal intervals around the headband.

Metalcraft flourished with the introduction of Buddhism to Korea in A.D.372 as ritual implements, such a temple bells, gongs, incense burners, water sprinklers, sarira cases and the like were in great demand. The oldest extant bell is the bronze bell at Sangwon Temple cast in 725 during the reign of King Sŏngdŏk. The largest bell, measuring 3.33 meters, was also cast at that time and is named for King Sŏngdŏk. Silla and Koryŏ bells are characterized by dragon-shaped hooks and sound pipes at the top of the bells, decorated bands around the shoulder and bottom of the bells, four panels of nipple-like protuberances just below the shoulder, and relief decorations and striking points on either side of the bells.

During the Koryŏ period, many Buddhist bells were smaller than those of Silla. The diameter of the mouth of the bell was relatively large, and the designs degenerated from those of the Silla period. Chosŏn period bells are distinguished by a horizontal band around the middle of the bell and no bands at the shoulder or bottom.

Silla craftsmanship is exemplified by the ornate gold and gilt-bronze cases used to house *sarira*, the calcified remains of holy persons after cremation. These cases, or reliquaries, were enshrined in pagodas as the object of religious worship during the Silla period and were also common during the Koryŏ and Chosŏn periods. Often the *sarira* cases resembled small houses with miniature railings, ornate roof decorations, and tiny figures standing guard or playing musical instruments on the veranda.

Any discussion of traditional metalcraft would not be complete without mentioning the development of movable type in 1240, 200 years before Gutenberg's Bible. The *Pulcho chikchi simch'e yojŏl* (*The Selected Teachings of Buddhist Sages Sŏn Masters*) was printed with this type.

During the Chosŏn period, ornamental knives were a popular accessory used for decoration and occasional use. Men hung knives from their belts, and women carried them in their purses or wore them hanging from woven strings attached to their gowns. Originally these knives were intended for personal protection, especially for the protection of a woman's chastity.

The knife handles and sheaths were generally made of wood, ox-

Bronze bell dedicated to King Sŏngdŏk in 771 A.D.

bone, coral, gold or silver, and the blades were made of steel hardened by heating and pounding. A silk cord with decorative knots was generally attached to the sheath for decoration.

GLASS & CURVED JADE

Silla tombs have produced a number of beautiful examples of glass and curved jade pieces. Glass, jade, agate, crystal, and pure gold were made into curved ornaments to be hung on gold crowns, pendants and necklaces. Several glass vessels have been excavated from the major Silla tombs. In the past, all glasswares were believed to be imported, but research may prove that these glass pieces were made in Korea as glass workshop sites and other evidence indicates that there were some domestic glass-producing operations.

WOODCRAFT

Korean furniture is unique for its simple, sensitive designs, compact forms, and practicality, all emanating from the Korean custom of sitting and sleeping on the floor.

Chosŏn woodcraftsmen were famous for their attention to detail

and the blending of practicality and beauty. The use of glue and nails was avoided whenever possible by fitting carefully cut parts together.

The natural grain and texture of the wood was considered an important decorative element. Wood was polished with oils to maximize the natural grain of the wood. Paint was not used.

Metal hinges and ornaments were used on chests and other wooden furniture as a means of structural reinforcement and decoration. White bronze, bronze, copper, and iron were most frequently used for hinges, padlocks and decorations. Iron ornaments blackened with perilla oil and soot were favored for their simplicity and practicality.

LACQUERWARE

Lacquerware inlaid with mother-

of-pearl dates back to the Silla period, and Chinese accounts refer to a highly developed lacquerware culture during the Koryŏ period. During the Koryŏ Kingdom, a special lacquerware studio was established in 1272 to produce mother-of-pearl inlaid cases to hold the woodblock-printed manuscripts of the *Tripitaka Koreana*, the collection of Buddhist texts

Koryŏ lacquerware was generally decorated with dainty mother-of-pearl chrysanthemums and other floral patterns. Tin or bronze wire was used to depict the vines, and sometimes pieces of thinly sliced turtle shell, tinted yellow or red, were used for variety.

Toward the end of the Koryŏ period, lacquerware designs became bolder, larger and less dainty. A variety of larger patterns depicting peonies, grapes, phoenix and bamboo took the place of the delicate floral patterns of the earlier period.

Portable dining table from 19th century Chosŏn

The term *hwagak* refers to a uniquely Korean woodcraft in which ox horn is applied to chests, boxes and small accessories. The origins of this craft are uncertain but it has been traced back to the development of mother-of-pearl in the Koryŏ period and has long been popular, especially for decorating women's quarters.

In *hwagak*, ox horns are boiled to remove their inner cartilage, thinly sliced and ironed flat. The slices of horn are then polished until translucent. Bright pigments mixed with glue made from ox hide are applied to the slices of horn which are then glued onto the wooden surface, painted side down.

POTTERY AND PORCELAIN

Early Earthenware

The Korean people began using earthenware kneaded from clay and fired at low temperatures during the Neolithic period. These vessels were generally used to store food, a necessity that arose when mankind advanced from gathering and hunting to tilling the soil and raising domestic animals. Comb-pattern earthenware has been excavated in almost every part of the Korean peninsula, principally from sites along the coasts and the banks of major rivers.

In the Three Kingdoms Period, this earthenware was fired at high temperatures. Of the Three Kingdoms, Silla and Kaya produced the highest quality earthenware fired at temperatures exceeding 1,200 C. The surface of this earthenware was gray and very hard. A variety of shapes and designs were created, indicating that the vessels may have been used for ritual or ceremonial purposes.

The Unified Silla Period was marked by a transition from earthenware to porcelain. Earthenware was no longer used for burial accessories and was made solely for daily use. Shapes became softer and more curved, and there was a shift toward floral designs.

Silla Celadon and Koryŏ Porcelain

Koreans learned of porcelain from celadons imported from China during the Six Dynasties period. Porcelain

Stoneware jar from fifth-sixth century Silla

(from celadon and white porcelain) from the late Tang had been introduced to Korea since the 9th century together with the techniques for producing early celadon and coarse green celadon. In the first part of the ninth century, celadon was produced at coastal sites that had established ties with the Yuezhou kilns of Zhejiang in China. This technique spread to nearby areas, and coarse green celadon was fired in kilns scattered along the eastern and southern coasts of Korea from the latter half of the 10th to 11th century.

Kilns producing celadon of the earlier green type were located in Kangjin County in South Chŏlla Province. The production of true celadon in the Kangjin area beginning in the mid-ninth century was instigated by the maritime activities of Chang Po-go, the leading maritime trader of Northeast Asia.

These kilns developed under government control and direction. Koryŏ ceramics were perfected during the 10th and 11th centuries, a transitional period during which Chinese influence on shapes and designs gradually diminished and Korean ceramicists developed their own style.

This refinement advanced still further by the middle of the 12th century as glazes became semi-transparent and lighter, and the designs incised or carved in relief began to show more ordered development. Koryŏ potters also developed a new technique, known as *sanggam*, for delineating designs through inlaying.

Koryŏ's celadon culture blossomed during the reigns of King Injong (r.1122-1146) and his successor King Ŭijong (r.1146-1170) and continued to develop in spite of political upheaval and confusion in the aristocratic society. Early in the 13th century, however, the Mongol invasion dealt a serious blow to the Koryŏ Period. From the reign of King Ch'ungyŏl (r.1274-1308) onward, there were gradual changes in the shapes and designs of celadon and in the methods of firing, as elements of West Asian culture were introduced from the Yüan empire.

Koryŏ celadon and porcelain began to decline from the early 13th century. Inlaid celadon and plain celadon were the only ceramics to be produced continuously throughout this period. The dëgeneration that took place in the second half of the 14th century affected both the shapes and designs of this celadon and the methods used to fire them. This late Koryŏ celadon was replaced by *punch'ŏng* during the Chosŏn Period.

A second flowering in Koryŏ celadon was manifest in the unique inlaying techniques. Restrained and yet clear and bright in its subtle jade color, Koryŏ celadon was unified in its well-articulated forms and the first in the world to create bright red through the use of copper oxide underglaze on the surface of a vessel.

Chosŏn Era Ceramics

Inferior inlaid celadon was produced at small kilns scattered throughout the country during the late Koryŏ and early Chosŏn Period. These celadon vessels gradually developed into *punch'ŏng* ware, stoneware glazed a transparent light greenish-white.

From the early part of the Chosŏn Period through the 15th century, some celadon and white porcelain in the Koryŏ tradition was produced, although in smaller quantities than *punch'ŏng*

Punch'ŏng and new white porcelain formed the mainstream of Chosŏn ceramics until the 16th century. The newly centralized government undertook a nationwide survey of existing kilns, and an Office of Ceramics was established to administer these kilns. The state operated a central kiln as well as branch kilns near the capital and oversaw the work at provincial kilns scattered

White porcelain jar with iron underglaze design from late 17th century Chosŏn

39

around the country.

According to *Kyŏngguk Taejŏn (Grand Code of State Adminstration)*, the Chosŏn court employed 380 potters at the state-run *Saengwon* (Office of Ceramics) and 99 artisans to supervise provincial kilns under the centralized system. The most important task of the provincial kilns was to supply ceramics to the royal household in Seoul and to satisfy the demands of local government offices.

White porcelain from the early period was made in a variety of shapes and is imbued with a soft nobility. Pure white porcelain, without any decorations, was most highly valued during the Chosŏn Period.

With the introduction of Mohammedan blue during the reign of King Sejong (r.1418-1450), blue and white porcelains (*ch'ŏnghwa paekja*) were produced in limited numbers.

Chosŏn ceramics suffered greatly as a result of the Japanese invasions stretching from 1592 to 1598. Many competent potters were taken to Japan where they made a decisive contribution to the production of porcelain and to the general development of Japanese ceramics. The Japanese aggression also marked the turning point in Chosŏn era ceramics. *Punch'ŏng* disappeared along with the last vestiges of Koryŏ celadon culture.

In mid-17th century, white porcelain ware was first used in the ancestral rites in the homes of commoners. Its general use had been prohibited from 1466 by a court order which restricted manufacturing to pieces especially ordered by the royal household.

The final period of Chosŏn ceramics covers the span between King Yŏngjo's reign in the mid-18th century to the end of the 19th century. This period was characterized by remarkable developments in shape and design, interrupted only by the Janapese invasion.

A cessation of state support and the employment of Japanese craftsmen as well as the introduction of alien methods caused a rapid deterioration of time-honored traditions in porcelain manufacture. The import of cheap Japanese pottery, mass-produced in factories in the Kyushu area, further accelerated the decline of the Korean ceramics industry.

In the final years of Chosŏn ceramics, generally speaking, function began to take precedence over beauty.These traditional crafts have played an important role in Korea's culture, reflecting the Korean people's sense of form, aesthetics and workmanship. With Korea's opening to the West in the late 19th century, however, there have been radical changes in lifestyle and values, and as a result, the demand for traditional crafts has declined dramatically.

In response to the decline in traditional crafts, the National Assembly passed the Law for the Production of Cultural Properties in 1962. Under this law, many traditional handicrafts, as well as music, folk art and dances, were designated Intangible Cultural Assets. At the same time, an effort to locate and recognize artisans skilled in traditional crafts was launched. These "Living National Treasures" have since been provided with direct and indirect government support so as to sustain the artisans themselves and train young people to perpetuate these unique traditions for future generations.

White porcelain jar with iron underglaze design from late 17th century Chosŏn

Handicrafts and their makers have been appreciated in the western world, but Korean artisans, responsible for a wealth of excellent handicraft items, have traditionally been dismissed as humble in origin and trade. Even today, as Korean eyes have been open to the beauty of traditional handicrafts, some of which have been designated national treasures, the names of the craftsmen remain unknown. Occupational and class discrimination was so severe in the past that craftsmen, though they made pieces of unsurpassed skill, function and beauty, were never remembered.

The development of modern Korean craft arts, since the modernization of the country can be divided into two phases: the modern crafts from 1910-45, and contemporary crafts from 1945 to the present. The modern period coincides with the Japanese colonization of Korea. It was a relatively dark age for traditional arts and only a very few pieces of notable value were produced as Koreans were endeavoring to maintain a national identity under brutal foreign domination.

It was also a time of change brought about by the emergence of a new generation educated in the ways and thoughts of the West. With the introduction of Western arts, people began to look at crafts in a different way. It was with this new outlook that Kim Pong-yong opened a studio for mother-of-pearl inlaid lacquerware in 1925, where he was to train numerous artisans over the next 20 years. The year 1928 was marked by Korea's first one-man design show by Yi Sun-sŏk. Craftsmen responded eagerly to the inclusion of handicrafts in the annual Chosŏn Arts Exhibition in 1932, which was the most prestigious public art exhibition in Korea. From

Contemporary crafts have made a distinct departure from the traditional handicrafts of earlier periods.

Echo *by Won Tae-jŏng*

then until its final show in May 1944, a year before Korea's liberation from Japan, the exhibition provided opportunities for many craftsmen to show their works. Chang Ki-myŏng, Kim Chin-gap, Kang Ch'ang-won, Kim Pong-yong, Kim Sŏng-kyu and Kim Chae-sŏk are some of the artists who became known through the exhibition. However, it should be noted that Kim Pong-yong and Kim Sŏng-kyu had already won a silver prize and a copper prize, respectively, for the mother-of-pearl inlaid lacquerware work they submitted to the Paris World's Fair in 1925.

Despite the appearance of a new breed of craftsmen educated abroad in modern craft arts, many dedicated themselves to preserving and passing on the traditional arts of ceramics, mother-of-pearl lacquerware and cabinetmaking. It is through the efforts and dedication of these craftsmen that traditional Korean handicrafts survived.

With national liberation in 1945 came an age of confusion and turmoil. Political unrest caused by factional strife between the right and the left was detrimental to artistic activities. Nevertheless, the Chosŏn Industrial Association was organized in 1945, and the Association of Chosŏn Craft Artists was formed in 1946. Many universities and colleges set up courses in fine arts and crafts, and art exhibitions were held more frequently.

Artistic activities suffered another setback with the outbreak of the Korean War in 1950. The country was ravaged by war for three years and many artists were either killed or taken to North Korea.

The National Art Exhibition was reopened in 1953 after the government moved back to Seoul from Pusan, where it had sought refuge during the war. As it more or less marked the official resumption of artistic activities, contemporary craft arts should perhaps be said to have started in that year. As the exhibition was held over the years, the opportunities for craft artists to reassert themselves increased and led to the development of a new image of Korean craft arts. The number of craftsmen increased as more universities and colleges opened courses in craft arts. The Korean Industrial Artists Association, which had replaced the Chosŏn Industrial Artists Association, continued to grow and hold annual exhibitions.

From the end of the 1960s through the early 1970s, there emerged a number of craft artist groups which, through innovative techniques, experimentalism and camaraderie, exerted a strong influence on the world of craft arts. Thanks to their efforts, galleries, art magazines and other publications specializing in craft arts were launched and in turn motivated more creative activities.

Contemporary crafts, including the industrial arts that are constantly exposed to new ideas and trends, made a distinct departure from the traditional handicrafts of the folk art character.

The Korea Industrial Design Exhibition, established in 1968 to coordinate education in crafts with industrial needs and to upgrade the designs of craft products, has produced many artists and designers through its exhibitions comprised of three departments - commercial design, crafts and industrial arts. The Medium and Small Industry Promotion Corporation has also backed a nationwide folk arts and craft contest for a number of years and staged three exhibitions for Olympic souvenirs to encourage creative participation by craft artists in the Olympic Games held in Seoul in 1988.

Many artists work and exhibit actively through the organizations they are associated with such as the Korean Designers Association, the Korea Craft Artists Association, the Tojŏn Exhibition, the Korean Metalcraft Association, the Korean Ceramic Artists Association, the Colorist Group, and the National Craft Artists Association.

Meanwhile, the Traditional Handicraft Exhibition has introduced highly skilled craftsmen in metal crafts, ceramics, jade carving, woodcraft, bambooware and lacquerware, rush products, textiles, paper making and other areas. It has also been instrumental in promoting public appreciation of the craftsmen known as human cultural properties and their works.

Besides these exhibitions, opportunities abound for craftsmen to introduce their works to the public as numerous exhibitions are held in Seoul and other major cities year round. Many are backed by influential newspapers and broadcasting systems. Many universities and colleges and junior colleges also offer craft courses that range from design to production.

International exchange shows and overseas training programs for craft artists are also becoming much more numerous. ◆

Mountain and River *by Yi Sun-sŏk*

ARCHITECTURE

Prehistoric Architecture

The earliest dwellings in Korea were natural caves. The Chinese history *Sanguoji* and other historical records indicate that there were three types of prehistoric dwellings on the Korean peninsula: pit houses, log houses, and elevated houses. However, only the remains of pit houses have been identified. In Pusan, post-holes have been found together with small stones which were used as foundations inside the holes. These pit dwellings were made by excavating a hole one or two meters deep and leveling the earth inside it. In some cases, fireplaces were found at the center of the dwelling, but in the northern part of Korea, stone slabs were used for a kind of under-floor heating system, which later developed into the *ondol* heating system used in Korean homes even today. The early *ondol* system of heating floors constituted of under-floor flues through which hot smoke from a heating fire was channeled. Today, hot water is pumped through pipes embedded in a cement floor.

Neolithic pit dwellings reconstructed on the site of the Amsa-dong archeological dig

The Koguryǒ Kingdom

There are no remains of wooden architecture from this period; however, examples of stone architecture, such as tombs and city walls, have been discovered. Sites of palaces and temples which had once been built of wood have also been excavated, and paintings in tombs, as well as written records, provide evidence of wooden structures during the Koguryǒ period.

Stone tomb chambers were built so as to imitate wooden architecture. The roof construction and bracket system of the Tomb of the Heavenly King and Earth Spirits are similar to those of a wooden structure, and the entrance to the Tomb of the Double Columns is flanked by two octagonal columns.

The Paekche Kingdom

No wooden structures from the Paekche Kingdom survive today, but there are several temple buildings in Japan which were built by artisans from Paekche, providing modern scholars of Paekche architecture with some valuable clues. A small gilt bronze pagoda from the Paekche period now housed at the Puyǒ National Museum also provides many hints about wooden architecture during this period.

Archaeological excavations temple sites in the Puyǒ area reveal the high level of technical skill and refinement achieved by Paekche craftsmen as well as the splendor of the buildings they created.

Among the many finds have been stone lanterns and the foundation stones for the columns and terraces on which the temple structure stood.

Private houses were simple structures with wooden floors. One record indicates that these houses were reached by ladders. Archaeologists excavating the Mirŭk and Imgang temple sites have exhumed

Top, The five storey stone pagoda found at Wanggungni was built during the Paekche period.
Bottom, the Mirŭk Temple site in North Chǒlla Province

tall foundation stones on which wooden floors would have rested. The raised floor and heating system later became a characteristic structure of the Korean house.

The Silla Kingdom

Architectural remains from the Silla Kingdom include the Ch'ŏmsŏng-dae observatory in Kyŏngju. This structure consists of a round tower built on a square base with four large stone beams placed transversely over the top of the tower. Another stone structure is the pagoda at Punhwang Temple, erected in 634.

Wooden pagodas were also built, but only the foundations remain today. Judging from these foundations, octagonal pagodas were common throughout the Koguryŏ, Silla and Koryŏ periods, although it is unclear whether Paekche had such pagodas.

Archaeological evidence of Silla palace architecture includes the Wolsŏng site, of which the gate has been most recently excavated. Stone mountain fortifications can be found around the country.

Unified Silla Kingdom

The largest architectural work of the Unified Silla Kingdom, the construction of Anapchi Pond and Imhaejŏn, the palace buildings that surrounded it, was undertaken during the reign of King Munmu (r. 661–681) immediately after unification of the Three Kingdoms. The site of these structures has been excavated, and two of the pavilions have been reconstructed.

Buddhism flourished during the Unified Silla so it is no wonder that Buddhist temples constitute some of the greatest architectural masterpieces of the period. Temple architecture was chiefly made of wood, including many of the pagodas. More than ten

Top, Anapchi *Pond in Kyŏngju*
Bottom, Ch'ŏmsŏngdae *Observatory, constructed in 633 in Kyŏngju*

Nirvana Hall at Pongjŏng Temple, North Kyŏngsang Province

of these temples are still in operation today, although their wooden structures are all of more recent construction. The most famous of these temples is Pulguk Temple in Kyŏngju, built in 752 by Kim Tae-sŏng. The temple sits on terraces of natural and dressed stones. These terraces are surrounded by stone railings. The temple is approached by four stone staircases which lead to a pair of pagodas and the two main halls.

Kyŏngju is also home to *Sŏkkuram,* a man-made grotto which consists of a rectangular antechamber connected to a large rotunda by a small passageway.

The Koryŏ Kingdom

The use of brackets with curved bracket arms in temple and palace architecture was a key feature of Koryŏ architecture, revealing the influence of Silla culture as well as

the growing influence of architectural trends from Song China. These brackets (*chusimp'o*) rested on top of the columns only. As a result, the framework of the building was quite simple and the interior ceiling was left bare without covering panels or canopies. Most roofs were gabled. The Nirvana Hall (*Kungnakjŏn*) at Pongjŏng Temple and the Amitabha Hall (*Muryangsujŏn*) at Pusŏk Temple are two examples of the column-head bracket system.

From the mid-Koryŏ period onward, a multi-cluster bracket system (*tap'o*) introduced from Yüan China began to emerge. This style was much heavier in that it had clusters of brackets not only on top of the columns but on the horizontal beams between columns as well.

Stone pagodas were built in the Koguryŏ and Paekche styles in the former territories of those kingdoms. They generally had three, five, seven,

or nine storeys, but toward the end of the Koryŏ period there were also examples of 13 storey pagodas.

Private houses followed the pattern of the Silla period. The *Samguk sagi* (*The History of the Three Kingdoms* written by Koryŏ scholar Kim Pu-sik in 1145) indicates that there were regulations on the size of private houses, depending on the rank of the inhabitants.

The Chosŏn Kingdom

Compared to earlier periods, a relatively large number of structures from the Chosŏn Period are extant today, although the majority of these were built after the Japanese invasions at the end of the 16th century. The only example of original court architecture constructed prior to the 16th century is Namdaemun, one of the four original city gates built into the wall that surrounded the capital of Seoul.

Of the existing palaces, Kyŏngbok, Ch'angdŏk, Ch'anggyŏng, and Tŏksu Palaces are all in Seoul. Kyŏngbok Palace was built by the founder of the Chosŏn Period, King T'aejo, as an audience hall, but was burnt down during the Japanese invasions.

There were also various official buildings for administration, education, transport and military purposes. Chongmyo was the ancestral shrine for sacrifices to heaven, and Munmyo was devoted to Confucian rites.

The construction of Confucian shrines and private and public Confucian academies flourished under the Chosŏn court which established Confucianism as the state ideology, but construction of Buddhist temples declined drastically because of official suppression of Buddhism. A few temple buildings retained the Paekche type of bracket system, perhaps a carryover from Koryŏ building techniques. In the early Chosŏn period, both the *chusimp'o* and *tap'o* bracket systems were in evidence, but after the disruptions at the end of the 16th century, a mixed type, known as *ikkong*, was introduced. The structure supporting the eaves became increasingly complicated as the number of individual brackets increased. The eaves themselves became correspondingly wider, with long rafters, and there were also instances of double eaves.

Official buildings and temples were decorated with *tanch'ŏng*, multi-colored patterns that were first used during the Koguryŏ period.

City walls and stone bridges were the principal stone structures of the Chosŏn Period, and pagodas and stupas were no longer commonly built. However, even wooden structures were set on stone foundations or platforms. Private houses were also influenced by this practice. A *taettol*, or stone step set below the wooden-floored veranda surrounding a house, was a common feature of residential structures during this period.

Private houses were standardized in appearance after the 16th century. In earlier times, the kitchen had been a separate building, but as the population shrank and the economy worsened, the kitchen was more frequently attached to the hearth, which heated the main dwelling through the *ondol* under-floor heating system.

Upper-class houses were built on a sturdy foundation and featured many decorative elements, although the use of the colorful *tanch'ŏng* patterns was restricted to temples and palaces. The houses of the lower class were generally made of logs and had little decorative woodwork. They were usually thatched. No ordinary house, be it of the upper- or lower-class, could exceed 99 *kan* (a term referring to the square space inside four pillars).

With the collapse of the Chosŏn Kingdom in 1910, the number of wooden structures decreased. After 1945 traditional methods of wooden construction were almost forgotten, and the importation of modern architecture radically changed the face of Korea.

Kŭnjŏngjŏn, *the main hall at Kyŏngbok Palace*

MODERN ARCHITECTURE

Seoul's ever-changing skyline testifies to the speed with which Korea has developed in recent decades as well as its struggle to accomplish modernization amidst the flow of Western culture and civilization. The city offers a kaleidoscopic view of the works of innumerable architects and engineers from both ancient and modern periods. Modern high-rises stand cheek to cheek with ancient royal palaces, private houses, temples, shrines, and gates.

The impact of Western architecture was first felt during the last decades of the 19th century when Korea began to enter into treaties with foreign governments. In 1900, a British architect, at the request of the ruling family of the Chosŏn Kingdom, designed a royal residence in a Renaissance-revival style on the grounds of Tŏksu Palace in downtown Seoul. The two-story stone edifice, completed in 1909 and later used

as the National Museum, was one of many Western-style buildings erected by foreigners in Seoul and major provincial cities around the turn of the century. Buildings from that time include the Gothic-style Myŏng-dong Cathedral (1898), the Renaissance-style Bank of Korea Main Building (1912) and Seoul Railroad Station (1925), the Romanesque Seoul Anglican Church (1916) and the Seoul City Hall (1925).

Western-style buildings continued to pop up around Seoul, until the 1930s. Western architects and engineers built many of them, especially churches and offices for foreign legations, but the Japanese gradually took over construction as their political power increased. The Japanese constructed a number of new buildings for public offices, banks, schools and businesses, most in classical Western styles modified to suit their particular tastes. The most important of the remaining structures from this colonial period is the building that housed the offices of Japan's government-general,

though Korean interest in it as an architectural monument was overshadowed by the political implications of its design and location directly in front of Kyŏngbok Palace. The four-story, Renaissance-style granite structure, designed by a German architect, was completed in 1926 after 10 years of construction, and was used for the central government offices of the Korean government after liberation in 1945 until 1983. It was renovated extensively from 1983 to August 1986 when it became the home of the National Museum of Korea. The structure is now scheduled for relocation in order to restore the Kyŏngbok Palace grounds to their original state.

The two decades from the late 1930s to the 1950s were a dark period in the history of modern architecture in Korea. Japan was engaged in a prolonged war overseas and Koreans suffered from extreme economic deprivation and harsh political suppression at home.

In the early years of modern architectural development, Koreans

Modern buildings on Yŏŭi Island in the center of Seoul

49

acquired new ideas and skills from Western architects and engineers while they worked on important construction projects. Some young engineers were employed by the Japanese government, and a few were successful enough to open their own firms later. Among these early pioneers were Pak Kil-yong, who designed the Hwashin Department Store building, and Pak Tong-jin, who designed the main building of Korea University. These architects, active in the early 1930s, are two of the most significant figures in the history of Korean architecture as they were the first Korean designers of important structures about whom there is any recorded history. Traditionally, Korean archi-

tecture relied on apprenticeship, and carpenters and masons were trained under master technicians. Formal education in Western architectural concepts and engineering was not introduced in Korea until 1916.

Korean architecture entered a new phase of development during the post-Korean War reconstruction boom with the return of two ambitious and talented young architects from their studies overseas—Kim Chung-ŏp from France and Kim Su-gŭn from Japan. The office-residence of the French Embassy in Seoul designed by Kim Chung-ŏp and the Liberty Center designed by Kim Su-gŭn, both constructed in the early 1960s, were refreshing additions to

Seoul's architectural environment. Both architects were influenced by Le Corbusier's Brutalism, but their distinct approaches have contributed greatly to the development of Korean architecture and have been a subject of constant academic debate.

Some structures of special note in Seoul include Kim Chung-ŏp's Samillo Building, significant for its introduction of new technologies in the 1970s; Ŏm Tŏk-mun's Sejong Cultural Center; Pak Chun-myŏng's 63-story Daehan Life Insurance Building, and Kim Su-gŭn's Kyŏngdong Methodist Church and the Olympic Stadium, which shows the influence of Chosŏn ceramics. ◆

The main Olympic stadium designed by Kim Su-gŭn

*The following
institutions are related to
the preceding articles*

The National Museum

1, Sejongno, Chongno-gu, Seoul, 110-050,
Republic of Korea
Tel: 02-738-3800, Fax: 02-734-7255

Aims: The National Museum of
Korea was established to collect, conserve and exhibit relics; to excavate,
research and study of relics; and thus
to diffuse and enhance the understanding of traditional culture.

Divisional Responsibilities

• Establishment, examination and
analysis of principal business programs
• Maintenance and operation of buildings, machines, electric installations
and other equipment
• Management of national properties
exhibitions
• Excavation and investigation
• Regular scientific investigation: excavation of historic relics through

The National Museum

investigation of ancient history
- Urgent relief excavation: urgent investigation of historic relics which are in danger of destruction
- Scientific research and study
- Archaeology: study of ancient life through historic relics, efforts to make archaeology more scientific
- Artistic history: study through the revival and restoration of traditional art and crafts
- Publication of scientific materials
- Materials for art, report on excavation of historic relics, journal of archaeology, pictorial record of collections, pictorial record of special exhibitions
- Management of collections and in the custody of the nation relics

Principal Establishments
● **National Museum (Seoul)**
● **Regional Museums:**

Kyŏngju National Museum
76, Inwang-dong, Kyongju,
N. Kyongsang Prov. (0561-2-5192)

Kwangju National Museum
San 83-3, Maegok- dong, Puk-gu, Kwangju
(062-571-1419)

Chŏnju National Museum
893-1, Hyoja-dong, Wansan-gu, Chonju N.
Cholla Prov. (0652-223-5650)

Ch'ŏngju National Museum
San 81, Myongam-dong, Ch'ongju
N. Ch'ungch'ong Prov. (0431-55-1631)

Puyŏ National Museum
San 16-1, Tongnam-ri, Puyo-eup, Puyo-gun,
S. Ch'ungch'ong Prov. (0463-33-8561)

Chinju National Museum
171-1, Namseong- dong, Chinju,
S. Kyongsang Prov. (0591-42-5950)

Kongju National Museum
284-1, Chung-dong Kongju, S. Ch'ungch'ong
Prov. (0416-54-2205)

The National Folk Museum

1, Sejongno, Chongno-gu, Seoul, 110-050
Republic of Korea
Tel:02-734-1346, Fax: 02-723-2272

Aims: The collection, research, conservation and exhibition of artifacts and materials of traditional Korean life and customs and social education

Principal Activities
- Regular and special exhibitions
- Research on traditional life
- Comparative study of Korean and foreign folk customs

The National Folk Museum

The National Museum of Contemporary Art

San 58-1, Makgye-dong, Kwach'on, Kyonggi
Prov. , 427-080, Republic of Korea
Tel: 02-503-7744/5, Fax: 02-503-9167

Aims: The National Museum of Contemporary Art was established to contribute to the development of Korean art by giving recognition to current domestic and foreign artistic trends, by popularizing and extending an artistic awareness among the public through a general education in the arts, thereby raising cultural consciousness.

Principal Activities

Exhibitions:
The Permanent Collection, with its representative examples of both domestic and foreign art, provides a comprehensive survey of contemporary art. The museum also regularly presents special exhibitions of art with important implications for art history and actively pursues international exchanges of exhibitions and information.

Collection and Conservation:
The curators stay abreast of trends in contemporary art, systematically collecting artworks and related reference materials to promote a genuine understanding of art today. These are preserved using the latest techniques and housed in scientifically controlled environment.

Educational Services:
The museum plans various programs in conjunction with special exhibitions to help attract the general public to the museum and to encourage the

public's appreciation for art. These include lectures on art history, as well as seminars and symposiums on a variety of subjects. Studio workshops also help promote creative activities. And the audio-visual room, center for data and research, and the library continuously add to their materials and equipment to provide resources for the study and enjoyment of art.

Investigation and Research:
Research activities focus on major historical trends in contemporary art, both foreign and domestic. The museum art historians actively promote international exchanges of information in order to improve the museum's educational services. Likewise, the curators constantly seek new technical expertise in such areas as display, collection, and preservation of artworks.

International Exchanges:
The museum actively encourages international exchanges of artists and art specialists. In so doing, it hopes to introduce Korean art to other countries and to broaden appreciation for international art in Korea.

Other Programs:
Varied programs are planned to help attract the public to the museum and promote a broad appreciation of the fine arts. Included are concerts, dances, plays, films and live performances. These combine visual art with other cultural fields to diversify the appeal and function of the museum.

Principal Facilities
- Exhibition Galleries
- Open-Air Sculptural Garden
- Main Auditorium
- Small Auditorium
- Rehearsal Room
- Library

National Museum of Contemporary Art

MUSIC

A-ak, the music of the ruling class and literati of the Chosŏn period

TRADITIONAL MUSIC

Korea's traditional music can be classified into two major categories: *A-ak*, "proper or upright" music; and folk music. As its name implies, *A-ak* refers to the music of the ruling class and literati of the Chosŏn period. *A-ak* is characterized by subdued melodies and a very slow, formal tempo as befits the Confucian mindset. The genre is largely comprised of ceremonial music for court banquets and military music, ritual music, including Confucian music and royal shrine music, and non-court music for

the listening enjoyment of the literati. Vocal music includes *kagok*, long lyric songs, *kasa*, narrative songs, and *sijo*, short lyric songs.

Traditional ritual music is still performed in its original form at the royal ancestral shrine or during the biennial memorial services honoring Confucius held at the Munmyo shrine on the campus of Sŏnggyun'gwan University. Banquet music was, of course, mainly performed at courtly banquets, the most famous composition being the *Sujech'ŏn*, a court piece played on wind instruments.

The music of the ruling class and

literati consists of *p'ungnyu*, a kind of ensemble music, *kagok*, the most sophisticated lyric genre, and sijo. *P'ungnyu* is an archaic term that originally referred to music in general but later came to denote a state of mental and physical leisure in which man removes himself from everyday life through the appreciation of poetry, music and female companionship. When referring to classical music, however, the term connotes upper-class ensemble music.

The lyrical *kagok* consists of a rhythmic pattern of either a 16-beat *changdan* (literally "long-short") or a

variation based on a 10-beat *chang-dan*. The song is accompanied by an instrumental ensemble consisting of a *kŏmun-go*, a six-string zither, *kaya-gŭm*, a 12-string zither, *yanggŭm*, a Korean-style dulcimer, *haegŭm*, a two-string fiddle without a fingerboard, *p'iri*, a cylindrical oboe, and *changgo*, an hourglass drum.

Unlike *chŏng'ak*, folk music is fast tempoed, dynamic and exuberant. There are many different types of folk music in Korea's traditional culture. Instrumental music includes: solo music, or *sanjo*; ensemble works, or *sinawi*; farmers band music known as *nong'ak*; and *samulnori*, a four-piece percussion ensemble. There is a broad range of vocal folk music including: the operatic *p'ansori*; *minyo*, or folk songs; and *chapka*, secular songs performed by itinerant entertainers.

Nong'ak, or farmers music, is generally performed by a six member team of musician-dancers led by the gong-playing *sangsoe*. The *changgo* (hourglass drum) player usually follows the *sangsoe*. The *changgo* is slung over the player's shoulders and played with a light bamboo stick in one hand, giving a sharp tone, and a wooden-tipped mallet in the other, producing a deeper tone.

The remaining members of the *nong'ak* band play the *ching*, a large gong, the *taep'yŏngso*, a conical oboe, and a round drum.

Religious music comprises songs derived from and performed in Shamanistic ceremonies, and Buddhist music, including *pŏmp'ae*, a song in praise of the Buddha and performed today by only a few monks.

The origin of *p'ansori*, a narrative-dramatic vocal form of folk music sung by a single performer accompanied by a drummer, is uncertain. Some believe the genre grew out of songs sung by shamans in the southern part of the Korean peninsula, while others believe that it originated

Top, Haegŭm *performers in a Confucian ceremony*
Bottom left, Taegŭm *Right*, *farmers' band music*

in the chanted recitation of classical literature. The theory that *p'ansori* grew out of shamanistic songs seems most credible, however, since the minstrels who traditionally performed *p'ansori* are believed to have originally been the musicians who provided the musical accompaniment during shamanistic rituals.

It is not clear when *p'ansori* became an independent genre but the mention of *p'ansori* performers in historical records from the late 17th century indicates the genre existed at that time. *P'ansori* was largely a form of oral literature handed down from performer to performer until the latter part of the mid-Chosŏn period. A total of 12 *p'ansori* works were handed down through history but all that remain are the five *p'ansori* works we know today, reorganized and codified in written form for the first time in the mid-19th century and become a

P'ansori *virtuoso Pak Tong-jin*

stage art by *p'ansori* patron Sin Jae-hyo (1812-1884).

The varied form of *p'ansori* which is known today as *Ch'anggŭk* is a

kind of Korean traditional folk opera. Ch'ang means the singing part of *p'ansori* and dialogue part, recitative, is called aniri. Because *p'ansori* was performed by a single vocalist, it was unsuited for large theaters. In the latter years of the Chosŏn period as society modernized and foreign influences increased, a new musical genre was needed. Chinese troupes staged traditional Chinese opera in Seoul, and soon after, Korean *p'ansori* performers began to follow the Chinese example, dividing up the different roles found in traditional *p'ansori* pieces among several vocalists and thus creating a new musical genre known as *ch'anggŭk*. In the early 19th century, *ch'anggŭk* was performed in a theater without any stage decorations. The roles of the original *p'ansori* piece were allocated to both male and female singers.

Ch'anggŭk, Shim ch'ong-ga, *Korean traditional folk opera*

Of several theories as to when Western music was introduced to Korea, the most commonly accepted is that it was through the hymns taught by foreign missionaries. In line with that view, 1885, the year American missionaries Horace G. Underwood and Henry G. Appenzeller arrived in Chemulp'o Port (today's Inch'ŏn), can be regarded as the beginning of Western music in Korea.

From that time, music from the West began to permeate Korea's musical cultures. It flourished so that around the turn of the century, conflicts between pro-Western and pro-Korean musical viewpoints began to arise. Many asked why Koreans should indulge in Western music.

There was not much qualitative development during the Japanese colonial rule, but some pioneer musicians did sow the seeds for future growth.

While traditional Korean folk songs formed the musical mainstream from the 1920's to the 1945 liberation, Western-style songs like "Pongsŏn-hwa," composed by Hong Nan-p'a in 1919, enjoyed increasing popularity. Some of the most popular composers during that time were Ch'ae Tong-sŏn, Hyŏn Che-myŏng, Yi Hŭng-yol, Kim Se-hyŏng, Kim Tong-jin, Cho Tu-nam, and Kim Sŏng-t'ae. Many of their songs have remained popular.

In 1948 Chŏng Hoe-gap presented a composition of his own entitled String Quartet No. 1 at a concert commemorating the graduation of the first class of the Music College of Seoul National University. Two years later an opera composed by Hyŏn Che-myŏng called *Ch'unhyangjŏn*, which was based on a traditional love story by the same name, opened and was enthusiastically received. These two events gave rise to expectations for active composition; however, the Korean War (1950-1953) brought a brutal halt to such movement.

Korea's music world was introduced to modern compositional techniques in 1955 when the country began to recover from the devastation wrought by the war. Around that time, composer Na Un-yŏng began to present to the public works based on a 12-note system and soon other musicians began to join the mainstream of world music. In 1958 the members of the Composition Department of the Music College of Seoul National University formed a composers club

that played an important role.

Composers like Yun Yi-sang residing in West Germany, and late Ahn Ik-tae, composer of the Korean national anthem, won world-wide fame for their distinctive musical talents in composition.

More and more composers turned to chamber music during the 1970's, increasingly employing the techniques of their Western contemporaries. Leading musicians at this time included Chŏng Hoe-gap, Yi Sŏng-jae, Kang Sŏk-hŭi, Paek Pyŏng-dong, Kim Yong-jin, Pak Chae-yŏl, Na In-yong and Yi Yŏng-ja. A group of young composers centered around Kang Sŏk-hŭi won prizes in competitions sponsored by the World Association of Modern Music, showing the level to which composition in Korea had risen.

Korea's first symphony orchestra was established in September 1945 under the name Korea Philharmonic Orchestra Society. The Seoul Philharmonic Orchestra was inaugurated in 1957 and the KBS (Korean Broadcasting System) Symphony Orchestra was formed in 1956. There has been a rapid growth of orchestras in the provincial cities as well in recent years. The symphony orchestras of Pusan, Taegu, Inch'ŏn, Kwangju and Suwon hold regular concerts. The Korean Symphony, a privately operated orchestra, held its inaugural concert in 1985.

The quality of music performed in concerts, however, has been weak in light of the number of orchestras, ensembles and other groups. This is due in part to the interrupted growth of instrumental musicians caused by the Korean War. Another reason is that it has only been since the mid-1960's that there have been quality performances by musicians who have returned home from studying abroad.

The first opera performed here was Verdi's *La Traviata* in January 1948. Many opera groups have emerged and disappeared in the past 40 years. The National Opera Group, the Kim Cha-kyŏng Opera Group and the Seoul Opera Group led by Kim Pong-im are the most active. The National Opera Group, opened in 1965 with a performance of Puccini's *La Boheme*. The Kim Cha-kyŏng Opera Group opened in 1968 with *La Traviata*.

Church choirs have been leading chorus activities for a long time in Korea. The first professional chorus came into being in 1973 with the formation of the National Chorus. Nan Yong-su, one of the nation's foremost chorus conductors, has contributed to the raising of chorus music into art. The Seoul City Chorus was established in 1978. The Daewoo Chorus, a privately operated chorus, came into being in 1983.

An increasing number of Korean musicians are performing in concerts and other fields abroad. Many have won highest acclaim from foreign critics and audiences. A number have taken top awards in international competitions, and some have assumed prestigious posts as conductors or in other musical roles.

Among them are Chŏng Kyŏng-hwa, one of the world's most acclaimed violinists; violinist Kang Tong-sŏk, a prize winner at the Elizabeth Concours; and violinist Kim Yŏng-uk, who is based in New York. Pianists performing abroad include Han Tong-il, who resides in the United States, Paek Kŏn-u, who resides in Paris, and Sŏ Hye-gyŏng and Sŏ Chu-hŭi. Baritone Ch'oe Hyŏn-su won top honors in the voice section of the Ninth International Tchaikovsky Musical Competition in July 1990 in Moscow. He also received the Tchaikovsky Award, a prize for the best interpreter of Tchaikovsky's music. Conductors working abroad include Chŏng Myŏng-hun who was appointed music director and principal conductor of the French National Bastille Opera.

Yewon and the Seoul Arts High School are two well-established schools that provide training in the arts for talented young people. Numerous graduates from these schools have gone on to study at music conservatories of international fame, including the highly regarded Juilliard School of Music. In addition, the Korean National University of Arts was established in 1993 to train professional musicians and artists. The students of these schools are expected to contribute much to the development of music in Korea. ◆

DANCE

Korean dance is more than simply a form of entertainment. It is an expression of a metaphysical philosophy. Koreans have traditionally believed that the human body is a universe unto itself and that man's ideal existence lies in harmony with heaven and earth.

The earliest evidence of Korean dance is found in historical records from China and Korea and in the murals found in *Muryongch'ong*, the Tomb of the Dancers, dating back to Koguryŏ. Among the extant written records is the *Akhak Kwoebŏm*

(*Canon of Musical Science*), a comprehensive study of Korean music and dance compiled during the reign of Chosŏn King Sŏngjong (r. 1469-1494). This record provides explicit descriptions of dances, costumes, props, procedures and instruments and has helped modern artists recreate many traditional dances.

Korean traditional dance is generally divided into two categories: court dance and folk dance. Court dance dates back to the Silla period and was actively promoted during the Koryŏ Period, a period known for its love of festivals. Court dance took its present form during the strictly Confucian Chosŏn period. In the Chosŏn period,

court dance was divided into *chŏngjaemu*, which was performed at court festivals, and *ilmu*, which was a ritual dance.

Both *chŏngjaemu* and *ilmu* are characterized by extreme formality, an economy of movement, and solemn music. Each physical motion is deliberate and executed with the piety of a religious ceremony. The individuality and spontaneity found in folk dance are repressed in Chosŏn era court dance.

The *chŏngjaemu* dancers are dressed in magnificent costumes combining the five cardinal colors—yellow, blue, white, red, and black—with flower-like gold crowns on their

Sŏnyurak, *the Boating Dance*

heads. The costumes often have long rainbow-striped sleeves which cover the dancers' hands and trail along the ground.

One of the most popular *chŏngjae-mu* is *ch'ŏyongmu*, the Dance of Ch'ŏyong, which depicts the ninth century Silla legend of Ch'ŏyong, a man who danced to expel evil spirits. Originally a solo, and later performed as a duet or quintet, *ch'ŏyongmu* was performed to exorcise evil from the royal court prior to the New Year. The dancers, all male, wear brown masks adorned with peonies and earrings and costumes in the five cardinal colors.

The *Hangmu* (Crane Dance) is performed by two dancers dressed as enormous cranes. The giant birds peck at two lotus buds on a rear stage, and two small children emerge from the petals. These lotus flowers are important symbols derived from Buddhist thought.

The other court dance genre, *ilmu*, is a Confucian ritual dance featured the ancestral ceremonies held at the national shrine Chongmyo and during the memorial services held to honor Confucius and his disciples twice a year at the Confucian shrine. This dance is performed by 36 dancers aligned in six rows of six or 64 dancers in eight rows of eight. The dancers are dressed in formal court robes and tall hats. The slow-moving dance is more of a bowing ritual than a dance and embodies the people's reverence for the spirits of their ancestors and revered sages. The dance is accompanied by slow music played on stone gongs, bronze bells and other traditional instruments.

Folk dance is filled with vigor and rhythm, a far cry from staid court dance. Buddhism, Shamanism and Confucianism all contributed to the development of folk dance. Therefore, a brief discussion of the influence of these philosophies is in order. Buddhism brought a variety of

Sŭngmu, or Monk's Dance

musical and dance genres to Korea when it was first introduced in the late fourth century. Among the many ceremonial dances introduced were *nabich'um*, the Butterfly Dance, and *parach'um*, the Cymbal Dance, in which two or four monks swing large brass cymbals as they dance. These dances were part of traditional Buddhist rituals and laden with rich Buddhist imagery. For example, humanity is epitomized by the meta-

morphosis of the butterfly.

Another Buddhist dance, *pŏpko-ch'um*, the Buddhist Drum Dance, is a thrilling solo piece in which a dancer plays a large temple drum to invoke a spirit. In modern times, the dance has lost much of its traditional religious connotations and now involves highly developed acrobatics.

Shamanism made a great contribution to traditional dance through the *kut*, the shamanistic exorcism ceremony. In fact, some people believe the *kut* is the source of all Korean folk dance. The Fan Dance is a popularization of the Shaman's solo dance. *Salp'uri*, one of Korea's oldest dances, is also derived from shamanistic ceremonies. *Salp'uri* refers to the rapid pace of the dance as well as the shamanistic rite to exorcise evil and welcome good. The dancer flourishes a length of white silk as she flexes and relaxes her body at intervals. *Salp'uri* embodies the Oriental philosophy of "universal energy."

T'alch'um, or mask dance, is a unique development emerging from the ancient tradition of integrating dance, music and drama into rituals that relate man to a power larger than himself. During the Chosŏn period a number of mask dances satirizing the hypocritical ruling class, corrupt religious leaders and other social contradictions were popular. These dances

Salp'uri, *the Exorcist Dance*

were performed by male dancers who flung their limbs about vigorously in exaggerated movements. *T'alch'um* remains popular today because of its humorous commentary

and audience participation. The performance usually ends with the audience joining in the dance to the music of a shrill horn.

Nong'ak, mentioned in the discussion of traditional music, also remains popular today. Many of the costumes worn by *nong'ak* performers reveal Buddhist influence (e.g. the paper flowers and lotus blossom shapes) but the dance itself is more Shamanistic in nature as it is traditionally performed on special occasions when the performers dance through the village to ward off evil spirits, much like a kut.

Kanggangsulle, a circle dance performed by a large group of young women, is performed on the full moon of the first and eighth lunar months. The dance starts very slowly and gradually builds to a whirling climax.

Kanggangsulle

MODERN DANCE

Until the 1920's, the Korean dance community had few opportunities to become familiar with the dance traditions of the West. In 1921, however, an event occurred that was to be of great importance for dancers in Korea who wanted to learn of the modern school. A group of Korean students residing in Vladivostok visited their homeland to give performances of European classical music and dance in Seoul and Wonsan, a port city along the east coast of what is now North Korea. The Korean Students Music Company, which consisted of 11 college and high school students, provided Korean audiences with their first glimpse of Western dance. The program consisted of Cossack, Hungarian and Spanish folk dances and classical music and ballet numbers.

An event of even greater importance took place the next year. Baku Ishii, a pioneer of modern dance in Japan who had once studied under Isadora Duncan, visited Seoul to present his *Dance Poem*. His performance created a stir among the

Korean modern dance

Korean audience, especially the young students who had longed for a change to appreciate the new dance of the time. The impact of Ishii's Seoul performance was so great that some young dance students left immediately for Tokyo to study under the famous Japanese master. Among them were Cho T'aek-won and Ch'oe Sŭng-hŭi, who would later make distinguished contributions to the development of modern dance in Korea.

Another memorable artist from this early period was Pae Ku-ja. Pae organized her own dance company, experimented in creating ballet pieces using Korean folk themes and stage settings, and opened a dance studio in Seoul in 1929. It was not until 1939, however, when Russian ballerina Eliana Pavlova visited Seoul to give a performance that Korean dance lovers were provided the opportunity to enjoy classical ballet of international standards.

An increasing number of people were becoming interested in Western dance about this time as part of the fascination with the Western arts and humanities of various disciplines including literature, philosophy, music and the fine arts. They were discovering that Western dance could appeal as much to Korean aesthetic sensibilities as their own dance legacy in spite of historical and methodological differences. Proof of this growing fascination was the ever increasing number of students going to Japan to study. Many trained under Ishii, so his influence on Korean dance was naturally strong for a considerable period of time until World War II.

Of all the dancers who studied in Japan around this time, none was more instrumental in the development of new dance forms than Cho T'aek-won and Ch'oe Sŭng-hŭi. Both were devoted to creating their own dance expressions by incorporating the modern Western dance tech-niques they had learned in Japan and the spiritual motifs they drew from Korea's traditional dances. A number of outstanding dance pieces were composed by the two artists. They successfully combined the subtle lyri-cism inherent in Korean emotion and the indigenous atmosphere of Korean folklore with fresh stage idioms bor-rowed from contemporary Western dance.

From 1945, when Korea was liber-ated from Japanese colonial rule, artists of all fields enjoyed increased freedom in their creative activities. However, dance circles were not given sufficient impetus to recover from the stagnation they had suffered during the last years of the colonial period. Political turmoil and econom-ic hardship in the ensuing years destroyed many artists' hope of pro-moting a flourishing of the arts in their newly liberated country.

The Seoul Ballet Company, led by Han Tong-in, was among the groups which carried out relatively impres-sive activities during the period between liberation and the outbreak of the Korean War in 1950. Despite various difficulties, the company struggled to continue to perform. Its repertoire included such classical favorites as *Les Sylphides* and its own creations inspired by ancient Korean folk tales.

Im Sŏng-nam, a leading male dancer, returned home in 1956 after studying ballet in Japan. He estab-lished a studio in Seoul soon after-ward and organized a performing group of his own. He distinguished himself as a leading choreographer, teacher, and principal dancer in the Korean ballet world which was suf-fering from a chronic shortage of male dancers. He was named director of the National Ballet Company upon its inauguration in 1973. Under his leadership the National Ballet grew steadily and expanded its repertoire so that it now includes *Swan Lake*, *The Nutcracker*, *Coppelia*, *Scheherazade* and a number of original pieces employing themes from popular Korean legends and tales like the *Pae Pijang Story*. And when Kim Hye-sik was named new director in 1993, the National Ballet Company had a oppor-tunity to broaden it's performing area.

Another mainstream of modern Korean dance has been led by a group of artists of a more innovative vein. Yuk Wan-sun introduced the techniques of Martha Graham. She achieved remarkable success with the modern dance drama, *Jesus Christ Superstar*. She was chief choreogra-pher and lead performer in this dance piece which was performed in vari-ous cities across Korea for many years.

Korea's history and cultural her-itage have been explored as a valu-able source of inspiration by many other dancers. Numerous small dance groups have been organized, not only in Seoul but also in major provincial cities. Many have sought to rediscov-er the value of Korea's indigenous dance culture and translate it into modern dance expressions to achieve an effective communication with audiences in Korea as well as with those of the world.

Another movement in Korean dance in the modern period has been masterminded by those artists who have maintained the original style of traditional Korean dance. They often rearrange the formats of the perfor-mance, however, to suit the modern stage. This has been necessary in view of the nature of traditional Korean dances which have been handed down either as a kind of salon art for the entertainment of aris-tocrats or as the communal rituals of village people. Kim Paek-pong and Kang Sŏn-yŏng SongPŏm, Kim Mun-suk, Kim Jin-gŏl rank among the senior dancers who have excelled in this field. ♦

DRAMA

EARLY DRAMA

Korean drama originated in the religious rites of prehistoric days. Simple Silla (57 B.C.-A.D. 935) dance movements performed to a musical accompaniment appear to have been developed into a kind of drama called *Ch'ŏyong*. *Ch'ŏyong* was actually a series of dramatic dances rather than actual drama. In addition to *Ch'ŏyong*, several other shows were performed for royal and popular entertainment during the Silla period, but again their primary emphasis on dance movements with music accompaniment disqualifies them as true drama.

Dancing with musical accompaniment has always been important in Korean classic performances of all kinds regardless of their official designation as dance or drama. The *sandae* drama of the Koryŏ period (918-1392) contained more definite dramatic elements than *Ch'ŏyong*. It was performed on stage by masked actors following a script with a story and occasional spoken lines. Dances and songs dominated the play. The *sandae* drama was further developed during the Chosŏn Kingdom (1392-1910) when it became one of the official functions of the court. Eventually, it lost its royal patronage and was performed for the entertainment for the common people. This most representative of Korean classic dramas found wide popular acceptance whereby the subjugated masses of agrarian Korean society found solace in a humorous, satirical masque which ridiculed the privileged classes — Buddhist monks and *yangban* aristocrats.

Puppetry

No description of Korean drama would be complete without a word about puppet shows. Several references in Chinese classical books indicate puppet shows were performed from the outset of the Three Kingdoms era. Apparently the repertoire was quite extensive, but only three plays survive today.

Of the three, two are nothing more than the simple manipulation of dolls with musical accompaniment and are without script or story. The third, the *Kkoktukaksi*, is a drama in every sense of the word. It has a clear scenario and a definite cast of characters. The *Kkoktukaksi* has declined with changes in modern tastes but is still played occasionally in village marketplaces. It is a typical example of the ridicule to which the leading classes of traditional Korea society were subjected by itinerant performers. These itinerant performers travelled in troupes of six or seven members, three of them usually musicians.

The stage was set up in any village square capable of holding a crowd. Four poles were erected to cover about 2 square meters of ground. Curtains were draped around the poles to hide the puppeteers from public view.

The puppets were carved of wood and clad in appropriate costumes, some with long beards as the characters demanded. The dolls were of varied heights, from 49 to 90 centimeters. The show was presented in the evening, and the stage was illuminated by torches made of cloth soaked in oil tied to the ends of sticks.

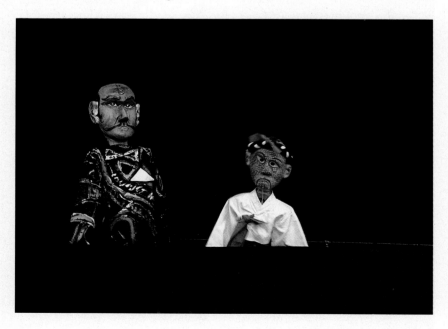

Kkoktukaksi *Puppet Play*

Masked Performance

The earliest authentic reference to the masque play appears in the *Samguksagi* (*The History of the Three Kingdoms*) which mentions three types performed during the ninth century of the Unified Silla period. The masque continued to be performed during the Koryŏ period as indicated by the *Koryŏsa* (*History of Koryŏ*) which refers to it as one of the plays offered in the 31st year of the reign of King Kojong (1244). During the Chosŏn Kingdom, an official post was created for the express purpose of handling masque shows, which accordingly prospered as an official function of the court. In 1634, however, this post was abolished, and the masque was relegated to the common people.

Masked performances fall into four distinctive categories, three named for the localities where they were played.

Top, The Hahoe *Masque*
Bottom, Yangjupyŏlsandae *Masque*

The *Sandae* Masque

Of the four masque, *sandae*, named after the royal nomenclature for the office responsible for handling masque shows, is the best known. It consists of 10 acts and 13 scenes named for the main character in each act or scene. It satirized the Chosŏn Kingdom nobility and taunted apostate monks.

The *sandae* had an all-male cast which performed and danced to the accompaniment of traditional Korean drums, strings, and winds blaring tunes based on folk songs, Buddhist invocations, Shamanist invocations and the like. It was performed on a makeshift open-air stage in the village square on holiday occasions, such as the *Tano* festival on the fifth day of the fifth month of the lunar calendar, or shaman prayer-days for rain. Starting after sunset, the show continued deep into the night.

This unique Korean drama has lost

much popular support and is kept alive today by a single troupe in a village in Yangju County, Kyŏnggi Province. A group was organized in Seoul around 90 years ago to preserve the *sandae* in latter-day Korea, but it disbanded after 50 years. Today the drama has been revived with government support and has been designated an intangible cultural asset.

The *Haesŏ* Masque

The Haesŏ masque, from the Haeju area of Hwanghae Province, northern Korea, was also performed during the Tano festival. Its origin cannot be traced, but the seven-act play is believed to have been created at about the same time as the *sandae*. The roles varied slightly according to the locality in which it was performed, but the overall cast of characters was similar to the *Kkoktukaksi* and the *sandae*.

The *Hahoe* Masque

The Hahoe masque, from the Hahoe district of North Kyŏngsang Province, was performed on the occasion of the village festival held on the second day of the first lunar month. According to the old men of the village, this masque dates back more than 500 years.

The purpose of the Hahoe masque was to appease the spirits of two departed women who were believed to possess potent spiritual powers over the village. The masque was part of a ritual observed to exorcise the village of evil spirits.

The *Ogwangdae* Masque

The fourth type of mask performance, appearing in South Kyŏngsang Province, was an acrobatic affair known as the *Ogwangdae*, or "Play of Five Clowns." The clowns apparently were the "Generals of the Five Directions," that is the generals who guarded the cosmic directions, the north, south, east, west, and center. It

was performed on the 15th day of the first lunar month by amateur performers under the direction of village elders versed in the tradition of the masque.

Western drama was first staged in Korea in 1908 at the newly opened Wongaksa Theater in Seoul. The advent of "New Drama," as it was known, as opposed to the traditional dramas of the masque and puppetry, was perhaps inevitable at a time when the influence of Western culture and civilization was so powerful.

The "New Drama" movement was pioneered by Yi In-jik, who had studied drama in Japan. It was Yi who made the Wongaksa a success. He not only wrote the plays for Korea's first theater proper, but managed, supervised and directed them as well. He was followed in 1911 by Im Sŏng-gu whose works were greeted with standing ovations from the outset. Im, however, turned to less-serious drama later, catering to popular romantic sentiments in what became known as "New-School Plays." In 1912, another modernist, Yi Ki-se, appeared with two more troupes. The world of Korean theater was suddenly crowded. By then, a considerable number of professional actors, actresses, stage directors and playwrights were available to put the "New Drama" on a solid footing.

A more serious group, calling itself the Drama Arts Society, was organized in 1921, mostly by students who had returned from Japan. A significant contribution to this Western-inspired movement was the 1923 formation of the *T'owŏlhoe* (Earth-Moon Society) by a group of students then studying in Japan. Figures such as Pak Sŭng-hŭi and Kim P'al-bong, who later became an eminent writer, returned home during school vacations to play major roles in "realistic" plays.

An entry in the Korea Drama Festival

Though its members were amateurs, the *T'owŏlhoe* surpassed any other professional group with its high artistic standards and introduction of "realistic" themes. The society's repertoire consisted mostly of original works written by its own members, but also included translations and adaptations of imported masterpieces. In fact, the troupe was so popular it presented a total of 180 performances in its ten year existence—a record-breaking feat for that time. Its influence has been felt in Korean dramatic circles ever since.

The most significant landmark in the next decade was the formation of the Society for the Study of Dramatic Arts in 1931. Organized by members of Korea's theatrical and literary elite, this society staged numerous imported masterpieces as well as original works by its members. Unfortunately, the Japanese Governor-General forced the Society to disband soon after its establishment because of its nationalistic tendencies. Nevertheless, the individual members carried on by organizing another body, the Drama Study Troupe. Under this name, the company lasted until the end of the decade when the Japanese again forced its dissolution. The 1930s saw the rise of socialistic thought which was reflected in the theatrical world by the Modern Theater, the New Construction troupe, and several other groups, all sympathetic to the leftist cause. Koreans were increasingly mobilized to support the Japanese war efforts during the early 1940s, and as a result, further theatrical development was stifled by intensified Japanese pressure.

The tragic post-liberation division of the Korean peninsula and the ensuing political cleavage brought chaos to Korean dramatic circles. Numerous groups, each with its unique political color, sprouted up one after another, only to fold as quickly. With the establishment of the Republic of Korea government in 1948 and the resulting establishment of a definite ideological line in the south, confusion ended, and a National Theater was formed in 1950.

Following the Korean War, the New Drama Society, an organ of the National Theater, revived interest chiefly in Shakespeare and Yu Ch'i-jin, one of Korea's foremost dramatists. The boom of motion pictures and television deprived the stage of both talent and audience, however, and a decline in theater soon set in.

Nevertheless, several courageous groups carried on, creating what is known as the "Small Theater" movement. They emphasized artistic presentations as opposed to the professional endeavors that sought large box office and better financial returns for the producer. The more serious-minded organized the Korean National Center of International Theater Institutes in 1958 and engaged in international cultural exchanges. ◆

An entry in the Korea Drama Festival

*The following
institutions are related to
the preceding articles*

The Korean
National University of Arts

700, Seoch'o-dong, Seoch'o-gu, Seoul, 137-070
Republic of Korea
Tel: 02-520-8114, Fax: 02-520-8000

Aims: The provision of a systematic education for artistically talented young people in order to cultivate a new generation of professional artists

Principal Activities
• Specialized education and training in the arts

The Korean National University of Arts

The National Theater

The National Theater

San 14-67, Changch'ung-dong 2-ga, Chung-gu,
Seoul, 100-392, Republic of Korea
Tel: 02-274-1151/8, Fax: 02-267-7186

Aims: The National Theater of Korea
was opened in April 1950 for the purpose of developing indigenous culture and advancing the theatrical arts.

Principal Activities

• Development of indigenous culture
  and advancement of theatrical arts
• Promotion of theatrical arts
• Search for creative art and support
  for activity

Principal Facilities

• Main Hall
• Small Hall
• Open-air Stage (*Nori-Madang*)

The National Theater

Six Resident Companies:
- The National Drama Company
- The National *Changgŭk* Company
- The National Dance Company
- The National Ballet Company
- The National Chorus Company
- The National Opera Company

The Korean Traditional Performing Arts Centre

(National Classical Music Institute)
700, Seoch'o-dong, Seoch'o-gu, Seoul,
137-071, Republic of Korea
Tel: 02-580-3333, Fax: 02-580-3025, 3065

Aims: The Korean Traditional Performing Arts Center (National Classical Music Institute) was founded by presidential decree for the preservation and development of Korean traditional music and dance.

Principal Activities
Performances
- Regular Saturday concerts
- Invitational concerts in Seoul and other cities
- Ritual music ceremonies at the Royal Ancestral Shrine and the Confucian Shrine
- Concert tours to culturally disadvantaged areas
- Regular concerts in Seoul (eighty times a year)
- Overseas performances

Korean Traditional Performing Arts Center

Research and Publication
- Research on the renovation and improvement of musical instruments
- Modern staff editions transcribed from original notations
- Collections, scores and copies of intangible cultural properties within Korean music
- Distribution of informational books and pamphlets
- Publication of musical scores, records and research papers

Education
- Regular monthly six week courses for beginners
- Advanced one year courses for various instruments
- Special basic course for music teachers of all junior and senior high schools twice a year
- Extra courses for intermediate, high school and college students .
- Regular or request broadcasts
- Lecture tours to the provinces

Archives
- Preservation of traditional records, books and music scores
- Conservation of ancient documents

Promotional Activities
• National music contest once a year
• Exhibitions of Korean musical instruments
• Supporting performances for events in the provinces
• Public contests to foster new musical compositions

Principal Facilities
Large Hall
This building, to be completed by 1995, will consist of six stories with a seating capacity of 1000.

Small Hall
The main auditorium with two floors seats 324. In addition, tiered wings on both sides can be opened to increase the seating capacity to 606. The stage can be slightly enlarged or reduced according to the number of perform-

ers. The first floor seats can be lowered to form a "village square" type of stage. In the first and second floor foyers are showrooms which display Korean traditional musical instruments. The basement has a large room suitable for receptions after performances. This area in turn has access to the underground parking lot.

Administration Block
This building has three floors and a basement. The first and second floors consist mainly of individual, small and large practice rooms for musicians and dancers. The third floor contains the General Affairs, Performance, Promotion and Arts Research Divisions, a research library and a conference room.

Education and Research Block
This block, when completed, will consist of lecture and practice rooms, individual and group research rooms, a reference room and a room for the sale of materials.

Seoul Arts Center

700, Seoch'o-dong, Seoch'o-gu, Seoul,
137-070, Republic of Korea
Tel: 02-580-1114, Fax: 02-587-5841

Aims: The Seoul Arts Center was
built to provide a space for culture
and arts so as to contribute best to the
creation and development of national
culture, to promote cultural well-
being, and to form the basis for a
greater audience for culture and the
arts.

Principal Activities

Performance
- Orchestra Festival
- Chamber Music Festival
- "Pan" Music Festival
- Concert for Korean creative music
- Program for animation of musical creation
- Concert of Young Musicians
- International Choral Festival

Exhibitions and Educational Programs
- Retrospective exhibitions of calligraphers
- Permanent Calligraphy Exhibition
- Exhibition of Young Korean Calligraphers
- Calligraphic education and exhibition for appreciation of students
- Various exhibitions for visual arts
- Summer school for visual arts

Principal Facilities

• Seoul Concert Hall
• Seoul Calligraphy Hall
• Hangaram Art Gallery
• Seoul Arts Library
• Seoul Opera House (Opera House, Towol Theater, Chayu Theater)
• Cultural Theme Park

Seoul Performing Arts Company

700, Seoch'o-dong, Seoch'o-gu, Seoul, 137-070
Republic of Korea
Tel: 02-523-0981/7, Fax: 02-523-0855

Aims: The Seoul Performing Arts Company was established to contribute to the development of the performing arts and the progress of culture and the arts.

Principal Activities
• Regular performances
• Performances in the provinces
• Visiting performances
• Overseas performances

MOVIES

The first motion picture was shown in Korea in 1903. The first Korean-made film, entitled *Righteous Revenge*, was shown to the general public in 1919. That "kinodrama," directed by Kim To-san, was designed to be shown together with a stage performance. The first feature film, *Oath Under the Moon*, appeared four years later. In 1926, the classic *Arirang*, a protest against Japanese colonial oppression, was produced by actor-director Na Un-gyu.

With the great success of *Arirang*, the number of Korean films produced annually increased to about 10 per year until the film industry was stifled by the Japanese colonial government in 1930. Production dropped to only two or three films a year after that. The first sound film, *The Tale of Ch'unhyang*, based on the old love story of the same title, was produced in that period by director Lee Myŏng-u.

The Japanese dominated the Korean cinema until Korea's liberation in 1945. More than 140 films, mostly of a propagandistic nature, were produced from 1919 to 1945. With liberation, the film industry was reborn, and the first color film, *The Diary of a Woman*, directed by Hong Sŭng-gi, was made in 1949. The Korean War (1950-1953) dealt a severe blow to the fledgling film industry, and only a few war documentaries were produced during that period.

In 1955, the government exempted domestic film-makers from taxation in an effort to promote further development of the movie industry. This led to a rapid increase in the number of film-makers and heralded a golden age of cinema. In the late 1950s, approximately 100 films were produced annually, and by the 1960s, the number had risen to approximately 200.

Scence from To the Starry Island

Korea's movie industry has been in a slump since 1970, however, largely because of the rapid development of television and the decline in the number of moviegoers.

In 1971, the government, in a fresh effort to help the movie industry, launched a financial assistance program aimed at promoting film production and script writing, and established the Motion Picture Promotion Corporation to strengthen the local cinema community with financing and technological support. The government also provided outstanding producers with permits to import foreign films subject to an annual quota. But this promotion policy ended when the new cinema law came into effect in January 1987.

A trial-and-error method has been

used for the application of the Korean Motion Picture Act to date. Now the Ministry of Culture and Sports is preparing to revise the Act. A new Motion Picture Act is expected to be announced in 1994.

Mabu (*Horse Driver*) won a special award at the 1961 Berlin International Festival, but it wasn't until the 1980s that Korean film began to make a name for itself on the international scene. Kang Soo-yeon won the best actress award at the 1987 Venice Film Festival for her performance in *Surrogate Mother*, and the following year Shin Hye-soo won the best actress award at the Montreal International Film Festival for her role as a deaf-mute girl in *Adada*.

Korean filmmakers' dream of winning first place at a major film festival came true at the 42nd Locarno International Film Festival when direc-

Scene from **White Badge**

tor Bae Yong-kyun's *Why Bodhi-Dharma Has Gone to the East?* took the grand prize. This film depicts the Zen Buddhist search for enlightenment through meditation. *White Badge*, directed by Chung Ji-young, won the Grand Prix and best director award at the 1992 Tokyo International Film Festival. In 1993, Lee Dukhwa won the best actor award at the Moscow International Film Festival for his lead performance in *I Will Survive*. *Sŏp'yŏnje*, Im Kwon-taek's *p'ansori* film, reaped a best actress award for newcomer O Chŏng-hae and best director award for Im Kwon-t'aek at the Shanghai International Film Festival.

Hwaumkyong, a story about a boy's travelling to reach Buddha's nirvana, directed by Chang Sun-woo won the Alfred Bauer Award at the 1994 Berlin International Film Festival.

Foreign films rarely run at a loss when screened in Korea. Until the mid-1980s they served as an effective fund raising procedure for Korean film-makers. In 1985, a law designed to separate film-making from film-importing was enacted. It required companies wishing to engage in either activi-ty to register with the government. In the past only licensed film-makers who produced at least four motion pictures a year were permitted to import foreign films.

The promulgation of a new cinema law in January 1987 allows foreigners to engage in the film production business in Korea and to distribute foreign films here.

As a result, the Korean movie industry must survive through technological and artistic improvements and the accumulation of capital.

It is yet to be seen whether the opening of the domestic film market will stifle the Korean film industry or stimulate it to improve the quality of locally produced films and compete with foreign films on the Korean market. ◆

Scene from Sŏp'yŏnje

*The following
institutions are related to
the preceding articles*

Korean Motion Picture Promotion Corporation

34-5, Namsan-dong 3-ga, Chung-gu, Seoul, 100-043, Republic of Korea
Tel: 02-755-9291/5, Fax: 02-774-0531
Telex: K28385 KOMOPRO

Aims: The Korean Motion Picture Promotion Corporation (KMPPC) was established on April 3, 1973, to promote, foster, and support the Korean motion picture industry. Its establishment is based on Article 14 of Chapter 4 of the Motion Picture Law.

Principal Responsibilities

• Formulation and implementation of plans to promote domestic motion pictures and to foster and assist the motion picture industry
• Importation of movies of high artistic merit, providing that they would not compete with local motion picture importers
• Promotion and encouragement of Korean movies; introduction to foreign markets and international film exchanges
• Financing of motion picture productions
• Study and research in the area of producing, promoting, and developing motion picture production facilities, technology and film know-how
• Installation and operation of the latest in motion picture producing facilities, technology and film know-how
• Promotion and Protection of the welfare of motion picture artists
• Provide motion picture distribution services, if this is recognized as necessary and is approved by

Design for the KMPPC studio complex

the Minister of Culture and Sports
• Other activities associated with the promotion of films

Principal Activities

Operation of the Advisory Committee

To collect diverse opinions from throughout the Korean film industry and to create in cooperation with film experts, KMPPC operates an advisory committee consisting of 24 members, including film artists, film critics, film professors, film reporters, producers, etc.

Supporting Quality Films

Excellence in technical and artistic film quality is always a goal at KMPPC. To induce film makers to produce quality films and to attract filmgoers to view these films, each year KMPPC provides monetary awards to the producers of 18 films selected for their high quality.

Financing

To promote the production of high quality films, KMPPC provides film makers with a partial production budget during the pre-production stage when a producer's scenario, along with a production schedule, are selected by the Selection Committee. The producer is not obliged to pay back this preliminary support nor is he or she subject to any interest liability. KMPPC also finances producers' production costs without charging interest. KMPPC assists producers in obtaining bank loans.

Sets at the KMPPC studio complex

Screenplay Bank

In order to discover new screen writing talent, KMPPC sponsors screenwriting contests which provide monetary prizes for the best synopses and screenplays. KMPPC distributes the winning synopses and screenplays to producers free of charge, and also operates a screenplay fund to encourage existing screen writers.

Training

KMPPC conducts lecture programs, inviting film professionals locally and from abroad, and sends film makers abroad for on-the-job training to refresh their skills. KMPPC estab-lished the Korean Academy of Film Arts (KAFA) in 1984 to train new film students. KAFA carefully selects prospective film makers, trains them intensively during a one-year course and assists them in joining the film industry after completion of the program.

Korean Films Abroad

KMPPC supports Korean films' partici pation in international film festivals and provides attractive incentive programs for winners, as well as assisting in the sales of Korean films in international film markets. KMPPC also publishes various publicity materials in foreign languages and distributes them to foreign film buyers.

Research and Publication

KMPPC continuously analyzes Korean films looking for ways to improve them. Thus, KMPPC collects all necessary information related to film at home and abroad and furnishes that information to the Korean film community, and publishes various books and magazines related to film.

Modernization of Film Production Facilities

KMPPC has endeavored to enhance the quality of Korean films by accumulating the latest technology through modernization of our print-

A scene from Sŏp'yŏnje

ing lab, sound recording studio, synchronized sound recording system, etc. By renting out equipment and facilities at cost, KMPPC is able to keep film production rates to a minimum.

Plan for New Studio Complex
KMPPC has started to build a large-scale studio complex with the latest, most sophisticated equipment to enhance the quality and international competitiveness of Korean films.
In addition, the plans include the construction of a large-scale indoor location set, a film museum, film information center, and recreation area includ-

ing outdoor location sets.

Principal Facilities
- Screening Room
- Library for film-related publications
- Exhibition Hall
- Film Lab
- Sound Recording Studio
- Special Photography Studio
- Editing Room
- Film Subtitling Facilities
- Film Studio Complex
  (Under Construction)

Korean Film Archive

B1, Arts Library of Seoul Arts Center, 700, Seoch'o-dong, Seoch'o-gu, Seoul, 137-070, Republic of Korea
Tel: 02-521-3147/9, Telex: ARTCNTR K29150
Fax: 02-582-6213

Aims: The Korean Film Archive (KFA) was established in January 1974 to contribute to the prosperity and culture of mankind through the collection, preservation, exhibition and mutual exchange of films and books/documents related to films, as well as through research and study of film arts, emphasizing the importance of artistic, historical and educational value in film.

Principal Activities
- Collection of films and materials related to film
- Preservation and restoration
- Film screening, exhibition and education
- Cataloguing, documentation, and research

MAGAZINES & BOOKS

Korea boasts a long history of modern printing methods, and as a result, the publication of books, magazines and periodicals, along with newspapers, has played an influential role.

The use of movable metal type is believed to have started in the mid-12th century in Korea, about 200 years before such printing was developed in Europe by Johann Gutenberg.

It was in November 1896, however, that the country's first modern magazine, the *Bulletin of the Independence Society*, was published with the purpose of enlightening the masses through the dissemination of information, education and opinion.

There were already two English-language magazines being published prior to the *Bulletin*, however: *Morning Calm* (July 1890-October 1936) and *Korean Repository* (1892; 1895-1898), both monthly publications put out by the local missionary community.

In 1900, the Hansŏng Club published the *Hansŏng Monthly Bulletin* in both Korean and Japanese editions with the purpose of fostering Korean-Japan friendship, for which the club had been set up. As the annexation of Korea by Japan became more imminent, a number of other such magazines came into being.

After annexation, no magazines except for a few innocuous publications were allowed to be published until 1920. That year, the Japanese colonialists introduced the Newspaper Law. In 1922, for the first time in a decade, a Korean periodical, *Kaebyŏk* (*The Beginning of the Universe*) was

permitted to print literary works and commentaries under strict Japanese censorship.

Kaebyŏk was followed by other magazines such as *Shinch'ŏnji* (*New World*), *Chosŏn jikwang* (*Light of Korea*), *Shinsaenghwal* (*New Life*) and *Tongmyŏng* (*Eastern Light*). All these managed to incite anti-Japanese sentiments so that the Japanese government resorted to stricter censorship and suppressive measures once again.

Kaebyŏk enjoyed the longest existence of that period (72 months), but it was forced to shut down in August 1926. After that, censorship and other restrictions as well as penetration by Japanese journals combined with the attempted suppression of the vernacular language to crush interest in magazine journalism.

There can be no doubt, however, that magazines played an important role in enlightening the general public in a period when every straw of information about the outside world was badly needed. Korean magazines also contributed greatly to the forma-

tion of a systematic Korean syntax and wide dissemination of the Korean alphabet, paving the way for literary and journalistic development in later days. The nation's liberation in 1945 unleashed a torrent of publishing businesses that have persisted, though with extreme ups and downs. Press freedom, which was restored with liberation, was one of the most important impetuses to this active trend.

As of the end of 1992, a total of 5,941 periodicals were registered with the Ministry of Information. There has recently been a notable proliferation of specialized magazines, focussing on a range of special interests ranging from house-keeping, sports and leisure activities to science and technology, health care, literature and art. In addition, more and more businesses are publishing in-house magazines.

With the exception of student textbooks, 20,858 titles, totaling 48.2 million copies, were published in 1992. Topping the list was literature with 4,654 titles, followed by books of juvenile interest with 3,925.

During 1992, Korea imported 11.1 million copies of 1,748 foreign periodicals and 204,299 titles of foreign books, with total sales of just over 3.59 million copies. The imported periodicals and books were valued at US$ 54.6 million.

In order to promote the local publishing industry, the government designated 1993 "The Year of Books" sponsoring together with private groups, numerous exhibitions, seminars and other programs. ◆

*The following
institutions are related to
the preceding articles*

The National Central Library

San 60-1, Panp'o-dong, Seoch'o-gu, Seoul,
137-042, Republic of Korea
Tel: 02-535-4142, Fax: 02-599-6942, 02-535-4167

Aims: The National Central Library was establishes to collect and preserve national collections of library materials, including a comprehensive collection relating to Korea and Koreans.

The Library provides services to other libraries to improve their own services as well as to the public to gain access to materials and information sources. It is also responsible for integrating the national library system by providing guidance, coordination, support investigation and research activities for other libraries.

Principal Activities

- Management of the legal deposit system of publications in Korea
- International book exchange
- ISBN, ISSN national centre
- Affiliation of International organizations: IFLA, FID, ICA, etc
- KOLIS-NET(Korean Library Information System Network) centre
- Standardization of scientific schemes of classification and cataloguing
- Cooperation with other institutions in the national interest

Publications

- Korean National Bibliography, Bibliographic Index of Korea, The Union Catalog of Foreign Books In Korea, The Classified Catalogue (annually)
- Library Journal (quarterly)
- Literary Information, Newsletter of Libraries (monthly)

Principal Facilities

- 11 General reading rooms, 1 Electronic Materials Room, 1 Branch

The National Central Library

GLIMPSES OF KOREA'S CULTURAL LEGACY

Historic sites and relics are located all over Korea. More than 22,000 have already been confirmed, and archaeologists and other scholars say there are probably many more. The sites and relics date from the early Paleolithic Age to modern times, evidence that the Korean peninsula has been inhabited for hundreds of thousands of years.

Many of the sites have been carefully excavated and researched, and a number of them have been restored. Some have undergone emergency excavation because they were discovered during the construction of roads, dams, buildings and the like. Some of the more important sites and relics are introduced here.

Prehistoric Sites

Paleolithic Sites

Twenty paleolithic sites, including Kulp'o-ri in Unggi, Sŏkchang-ri in Kongju, Turubong in Ch'ŏngwon, Chŏmmal cave in Chewon, Chŏn-gok-ri in Yŏnch'ŏn and Pillemot cave on Cheju Island, have been identified and excavated in Korea.

Chŏn-gok-ri is one of the most important sites. Located on red clay deposits developed over a basalt substrata near the Hant'an River basin in Chŏn-gok-myŏn, Yŏnch'ŏn County, Kyŏnggi Province, it was excavated over a five-year period from 1979 to 1983 by a team of paleolithic experts and scholars. The results of the excavation have contributed much to the understanding of Korea's paleolithic culture which is characterized by bifacial handaxes and cleavers. Some scholars assume that potassium-argon dating may show that the site dates back to 270,000 years ago.

Neolithic Sites

More than 150 neolithic sites have been identified all over the Korean peninsula. Fifty have been excavated. The sites have been grouped into four geographical regions: the Taedong River group; the Lower Naktong River group; the Lower Tuman River group; and the Han River group. Two of the most important sites are at Osan-ri, Yangyang County, Kangwon Province and Amsa-dong in Seoul's Kangdong-gu area.

Located on a sand dune along the east coast, Osan-ri has been excavated since 1981 by an archaeological team from the Seoul National University Museum. Ten round and oval dwelling sites with one or two hearths each have been uncovered. Artifacts excavated from these settlements include flat-bottomed pottery, some with appliqued pieces, a clay mask, saws, compound fishhooks, knives and an obsidian tool. This site shows that Korea's Neolithic Age goes back at least to 6,000 B.C. Carbonized acorns uncovered from the site suggest the subsistence pattern of the people who inhabited this site.

Located on sand deposits near the Han River, Amsa-dong was excavated from 1972 through 1975. The excavation revealed several pit dwellings dating to around 4,000-3,000 B.C.. Artifacts discovered from these settlements include comb pattern pottery, handmills for grinding grain and other stone implements now displayed in the National Museum. Five of the excavated dwelling sites have been reconstructed in situs.

Bronze Age Sites

The beginnings of Korea's Bronze Age can be traced back to approximately 700-800 B.C. It ended around 300 B.C. with the beginning of the Early Iron Age. Bronze Age people lived in subterranean dwelling pits, used plain coarse pottery and bronze implements, and buried their dead in jar-coffins and stone cists. A dwelling site in Hŭnam-ri, Yŏju, Kyŏnggi Province and a burial site in Koejŏng-dong, Taejŏn, South Ch'ungch'ŏng Province are two of the most important sites discovered in South Korea.

Located on a hillside near the Han River, the Hŭnam-ri site was excavated by a Seoul National University archaeological team. The excavation of the subterranean dwelling site produced many important artifacts including plain coarse pottery and stone implements as well as some carbonized rice and barley grains, all valuable to the study of prehistoric life.

The Koejŏng-dong burial site was discovered accidentally in 1967. Artifacts unearthed during its excavation included a bronze dagger, a mirror, a bronze object in the shape of a shield, comma-shaped pieces of jade, polished stone arrowheads, plain coarse pottery and black burnished pottery.

Saddle pommels from Bronze Age, 3rd-2nd century B.C.

Sites of the Koguryŏ & Early Paekche Kingdoms

Koguryŏ Kingdom

The Koguryŏ Kingdom dominated the northern part of the Korean peninsula from 37 B.C. until it was defeated by Silla, a kingdom that ruled the southern part of the peninsula, and its ally Tang China in 668 A.D. A granite monument located in Ipsŏk-ri, Kagŭm-myŏn, Chungwon County, North Ch'ungch'ŏng Province is the most important Koguryŏ relic in the southern part of the Korean peninsula. It is 1.35m high and 0.55m wide and is inscribed with with a 400 character inscription. It is valuable to the study of fifth century Koguryŏ.

Early Paekche Sites in Seoul

Little was known about the Songp'a-gu, Wall Fortress in I-dong, Kangdong-gu, Seoul until a partial excavation was conducted by the Seoul National University Museum in 1983.

The wall was built with earth sometime in the early days of Paekche along the natural contour of the land by the Han River. Along its northern end were traces of palisades, obviously used to enhance the defensibility of the wall. Base rocks were hewn almost vertically to prevent an approach from the outside. Its overall function seems to have been defense against attacks from the north.

Sites of three gates, Paekche earthenware, weights for fish nets, and jar coffins were found during the excavation.

Sŏkch'on-dong Tombs

Some stone mounds at Sŏkch'on-dong, Songp'a-gu, Seoul, have been determined to be tombs from the early Paekche period. Evidence for this was found through excavations conducted in 1974 and 1983 by the Seoul National University Museum.

They are of a style that prevailed in the neighboring kingdom of Koguryŏ from before the time of Christ. To construct them, the land was first leveled, large, long stones were then laid to make a frame, and finally natural stones were laid in several terraces.

Tomb No. 3 has three terraces and

An archeological dig

measures 49.6m from east to west, 43.7m from north to south, and 4m high. It is assumed to be a king's tomb constructed in the fourth or fifth century. The style supports the theory that the Paekche Kingdom was founded by a branch of the royal family of Koguryŏ who moved south and settled here to found the Paekche Kingdom. It was reconstructed in situs.

Pang-i-dong Tombs

There are six tombs of early Paekche origin located in Pang-i-dong, Songp'a-gu, Seoul. Four of them were excavated in 1974-76.

Tomb No. 1 has a 2.2m-high circular mound with a diameter of 12m. A 2.3 x 1.06m passageway with a 1.10m-high ceiling leads into the chamber which is 3 x 2.46m with a 2.15m-high ceiling. A 2.4m-long, 2.1m-wide, 0.3m-thick stone table on which a corpse would be placed stands in the chamber.

Tombs No.2 and 3 are similar in construction, the circular mounds being supported by a stone base. One is 2.7m high with a diameter of 13.4m and the other is 2.9m high with a diameter of 13.12m.

Tomb No. 6 also has a circular mound which is 10.6m round and 2.1m high. Unlike the others, however, the chamber is divided into two room: a west one for the corpse and an east one for funerary objects.

The other two tombs are located 150m to the east of these mounds.

Puyŏ & Kongju

As Kongju was the capital of the Paekche Kingdom from 475 to 538 and Puyŏ was its capital from 538 to 660, these two towns have an abundance of cultural relics and sites. The Songsan-ri tombs, including the tomb of King Munyŏng, the Kongsansŏng Wall Fortress and a recently excavated pond are among the most important sites in Kongju.

The Pusosansŏng Fortress, a military grain storage, Nakhwaam where 3,000 court ladies jumped into the Paekma River when Paekche was defeated, and the site of Chŏngnim Temple are among the most important sites in Puyŏ. An 8.5m-high, five-story stone pagoda marks the site of the temple.

Also of great note is the site of Mirŭk Temple in Iksan, North Chŏlla Province. The temple is believed to have been Paekche's largest.

King Munyŏng's Tomb

The tomb of King Munyŏng (r.501-523), the 25th ruler of Paekche, and his queen was discovered accidentally in 1971. Miraculously, it was intact and yielded many valuable relics including two plaques inscribed with information about the tomb and its occupants, gold floral ornaments, porcelain lamps, and weapons. A total of 2,560 relics were uncovered.

The tomb comprises a main chamber and a passageway, both of which are tunnel-shaped and lined with hard grey bricks decorated with lotus designs in relief. It was reconstructed in situs in 1984.

Mirŭk Temple Site

An extensive excavation of the site of Mirŭk Temple, built during the reign of King Mu (r.600-641), the 30th ruler of Paekche, has been underway since 1980. Conducted by the Cultural Properties Research Institute, it has revealed that the temple was about 80,000㎡ and divided into three sections by covered corridors. It has also revealed that each section has a large hall with a pagoda in front of it.

The site has long been famous for the remains of a large stone pagoda that is believed to have been nine stories high. It and the Chŏngnim Temple pagoda are considered the prototypes for Paekche pagodas.

Chŏngnim Temple site

Silla & Kaya Sites

Silla Kingdom

Kyŏngju, the capital of the Silla Kingdom from 57 B.C. until around 935 when the kingdom was replaced by Koryŏ, is a museum without walls. Within and around it are numerous vestiges of both the power and glory that was Silla and the golden age Buddhism enjoyed from the time it was made the state religion in 527. These include the crumbling remains of palaces and fortress sites as well as centuries-old temples, pagodas, monuments, sculptures and pavilions.

Palace Sites

Wolsŏng, or Pan-wolsŏng as the castle is popularly known, is one of the oldest palace sites in Kyŏngju. The half-moon-shaped structure was constructed in 101 A.D. to enclose the Silla palace. It was partially excavated in 1981. The excavation revealed that the castle was encircled by a moat.

Anapchi and Inhaejŏn

Built in 674, Anapchi Pond was the focal point of a palace garden that was planted with trees and plants and dotted with a number of pavilions. It was excavated and restored in 1970s at which time the Imhaejŏn Pavilion, which is recorded to have had a seating capacity of more than 1,000, was restored to one-fourth its original size. The excavation yielded thousands of relics including a gilt-bronze Buddhist image and a wooden boat.

Pulguk Temple and *Sŏkkuram*

Pulguk Temple and its grotto-shrine annex *Sŏkkuram* represent Silla's Buddhist architecture at its best. Constructed in 751-774, the temple was one of Silla's largest with more than 80 buildings. It was burnt down during a Japanese invasion in 1593. Though the main hall and a few other buildings were rebuilt, it was not until 1969-73 that it was completely restored.

Built in 752, *Sŏkkuram* is one of Korea's most magnificent works of art. It consists of a domed hall connected to a small antechamber by a short passageway. There are a total of 37 Buddhist images including 3.5m-high main Buddha that sits on a pedestal in the rotunda.

Mt. Namsan

Often called "Sacred Namsan," Kyŏngju's Mt. Namsan is literally dotted with Buddhist images in the round, engraved, and high and low relief, pagodas, stupas and other stone objects. Among the most interesting are the relief carvings at Ch'ilburam, the "Seven Buddhas Hermitage," a large carving of a Buddha on a high cliff in Samnŭng Valley, the Sambulsa triad, the Sŏch'ulji pagodas, and Porisa Temple. The adventuresome hiker can find a treasure trove of Buddhist carvings in the mountain's Yongjang and Samnŭng valleys.

Buddhist sculptures on Mt. Namsan

Hwangnyong Temple

Hwangnyong Temple, which was built over a 92-year period from 554 and burnt down during a Mongol invasion in the 13th century, is believed to have been the largest Silla temple and the center of Buddhist prayer for national security throughout the Silla period. An eight-year excavation of the temple site from 1976-83 revealed the temple grounds to measure approximately 82,080㎡.

Over 40,000 relics were excavated from the site. They include a 1.82m-high ornamental ridge-end tile and a standing gilt-bronze statue of the Buddha.

Kamŭn Temple

Twin three-story pagodas mark the site of Kamŭn Temple that was recently excavated and partially restored. The construction of the temple was ordered by King Munmu (r.661-681), the 30th ruler of Silla who unified the peninsula under one state for the first time, in the hope of securing the aid of the Buddha to resist Japanese invaders. He died before it was completed and it was finished during the reign of his son, King Shinmun (r.681-692), in 682.

A special structure believed to be a symbolic resting place for King Munmu since he was buried in an underwater tomb in the East Sea was uncovered. A tunnel to the East Sea was also found.

Taewang-am

The world's only underwater tomb, Taewang-am is the burial place of King Munmu. As the king willed that his body be cremated in a simple ceremony and that he be reincarnated as a great dragon, his body is said to have been cremated and the remains buried under a large granite rock sub-

O-nŭng, "Five Tombs"

merged in the sea about 19.8m from the shore, not far from the site of Kamŭn Temple.

Muyŏl's Tomb

Located in a pine forest at the foot of Mt. Sŏndo is the tomb of Silla's 29th ruler, T'aejong Muyŏl (r.654-661). It is one of the few tombs that can be positively identified with a Silla ruler.

He defeated the neighboring kingdom of Paekche in 660 with an alliance with Tang China and thus paved the way for his son, King Munmu, to unify the peninsula under one state by defeating Koguryŏ.

O-nŭng

Located in a shady grove of pines are five large mounds which are thought to be the tombs of Silla's first five rulers - four kings and a queen. The tomb complex is called *O-nŭng* or "Five Tombs".

Tumuli Park

A lovely landscaped area, Tumuli Park contains 20 large earthen mounds that are actually Silla royal tombs. Some of them have been excavated and have yielded a wealth of valuable relics. The most famous is the *Ch'ŏnmach'ong*, or "Heavenly Horse Tomb," so named because of a painting of a flying horse on a birch bark saddle guard found inside it. It has been partially restored as a museum.

Tomb of Kim Yu-shin

Located on Mt. Songhwa overlooking the city of Kyŏngju is the tomb of Kim Yu-shin, the general responsible for Silla's defeat of Paekche and Koguryŏ that led to the unification of

the peninsula under Silla's rule. The tomb is decorated with relief carvings of the 12 animals of the Oriental zodiac. The carvings are considered the best preserved zodiac figures on any Silla tomb.

Other Tombs

There are many other tombs in and around the Kyŏngju area as well as in other parts of North Kyŏngsang Province. One of the most important archaeologically is Sunhŭng Tomb, which is named for its location.

Located on Mt. Pibong in Sunhŭng-myŏn, Yŏngp'ung County, North Kyŏngsang Province, Sunhŭng Tomb

Stoneware Stand from fifth century Kaya

is an early Silla tomb excavated in 1985. The walls of the passageway and the burial chamber are covered with plaster and painted with murals. The paintings include a phoenix, a flame design, clouds, trees, birds, lotus, mountains and human figures including a wrestler holding a snake.

Kaya

A triangular region on the lower reaches of the Naktong River was collectively called Kaya because the name of six tribal states that dominated the area all ended with *"kaya"*. The states were gradually absorbed by their more powerful neighbors with the last, Tae Kaya, falling to Silla around 542.

There are a number of Kaya tombs in the area that have been excavated and yielded many valuable relics. Two of the most representative are the tomb of Kim Suro, Kaya's first king, in Kimhae, South Kyŏngsang Province and the tomb of Kuhyŏng, its last king, in Sanch'ŏng, South Kyŏngsang Province.

Pokch'ŏn-dong Tombs

Located on a hillside in Pokch'ŏn-dong, Tongnae-gu, Pusan, is a cluster of Kaya tombs recently excavated by the Pusan University Museum. A number of important artifacts including a gilt-bronze crown, an iron helmet, some armor, a horse bell and a saddle fitting were uncovered. These are not only valuable to the study of Kaya culture of the fourth and fifth centuries but also to the study of cultural relations between Kaya and Japan.

The Royal Palaces of Seoul

Among the most impressive sites in Korea are the four palaces in Seoul where the Chosŏn kings lived and ruled and the royal ancestral shrine where they honored their ancestors in elaborate Confucian ceremonies. The palaces are emblazoned with rainbows of *tanch'ŏng* patterns embodying good luck and protective symbols for the buildings, their inhabitants and the nation. They were built to be auspicious centers from which the king could transmit the will of Heaven to his subjects.

The Chosŏn kings resided in Kyŏngbok Palace from 1395 to 1592 when it was destroyed by fire during the 1592-98 Japanese invasions led by Toyotomi Hideyoshi and in the detached palaces of Tŏksu Palace from 1593-1611 and Ch'angdŏk Palace from 1611-1872. With the reconstruction of Kyŏngbok Palace from 1865-68, the original palace once again became the center of power and remained so until the king moved to Tŏksu Palace in 1897. In 1907, the throne was moved to Ch'angdŏk Palace from which the king reigned until the end of the Chosŏn Kingdom in 1910 and where the last of the royal family still live in *Naksŏnjae*, a residence first constructed for widowed queens and favored concubines.

Each generation of kings and their families added their own touches to the palaces. They left a splendid legacy of ponds, gardens, stonework, and structures rich in history as well as romance and intrigue.

Kyŏngbok Palace

The "Palace of Shining Happiness," Kyŏngbok Palace was constructed in one year by order of King T'aejo beginning in 1394. It was the main palace until the 1592-98 Japanese invasions when it was burnt down. Because the site was not considered very auspicious, the palace was left in ruin for 273 years until the Taewon-gun, the father of King Kojong (r.1863-1907), had it reconstructed from 1865-68.

Most of the palace's 200 buildings were torn down after Japan annexed Korea in 1910, and a large granite building housing the offices of the Japanese government-general was constructed in front of the palace. The building now houses the National Museum of Korea. *Kŭnjŏngjŏn*, the main throne hall, *Chagyŏngjŏn*, a residential structure, and *Kyŏnghoeru* and *Hyangwonjŏng* pavilions are among the most interesting of the palace structures.

Ch'angdŏk Palace

The best preserved of all the palaces is Ch'angdŏk Palace, the "Palace of Illustrious Virtue." Built in 1405 as a detached palace, its layout is not of the classical design of Kyŏngbok Palace. It boasts Seoul's oldest gate, *Tonhwamun*, which was constructed in 1412 and survived the

Kyŏnghoeru *in Kyŏngbok Palace*

1592 fires that destroyed most of Seoul, as well as the Korean War, and a 200,000㎡ garden known as *Piwon*, or the "Secret Garden."

Including the 28 structures in *Piwon*, the palace has 41 structures. Among the most interesting are *Injŏngjŏn*, the main hall which has an elaborate throne; *Taejojŏn*, the king's residence; *Hŭijŏngdang* the queen's residence; *Naksŏnjae*, the residence of the last descendents of the royal Yi family; the fan-shaped *Kwallamjŏng* Pavilion; the hexagonal *Chodŏkjŏng* Pavilion; *Ŏsumun* Gate; and, *Yŏngyŏng-dang* Mansion.

Interior of Injŏngjŏn *(Hall of Benevolent Government), Ch'angdŏk Palace*

Frontal view of Injŏngjŏn

Ch'anggyŏng Palace

The "Palace of Glorious Blessings,"
Ch'anggyŏng Palace was built by King
Sejong in 1418 as a residence for his
father, T'aejong, who had abdicated
the throne on his behalf. It was greatly enlarged in 1484 to house a number
of widowed queens. It was burnt
down in 1592, rebuilt in 1616, burnt
down again in 1830, and reconstructed
in 1834. During the Japanese rule,
some of the palatial structures were
torn down and a zoo, a botanical garden and a museum constructed in
their place.

The zoo and the garden were
removed and many of the palatial
structures were recently restored as
part of a restoration project begun in
1983.

Myŏngjŏngjŏn, *Ch'anggyŏng Palace*

A panoramic view of Ch'anggyŏng Palace

*Top, **The main gate at Tŏksu Palace***
*Bottom, Chunghwajŏn, **the main hall at Tŏksu Palace***

Tŏksu Palace

The "Palace of Virtuous Longevity," Tŏksu Palace was first built as a villa for Prince Wolsan(1454-88), an elder brother of King Sŏngjong(r.1469-94). As the main palace was burnt down in 1592, it was used by King Sŏnjo (r.1567-1608) and then Kwanghaegun (r.1608-23), who named it Kyŏng-un Palace, until 1615 when he moved to the reconstructed Ch'ang-dŏk Palace. It was used by King Kojong (r.1863-

1907) from 1897 until his abdication in favor of his son in 1907. His son, Sunjong (r.1907-10), moved the seat of government to Ch'angdŏk Palace and made it his father's residence and renamed it Tŏksu Palace.

The palace is not representative of traditional Chosŏn architectural styles. Many of the buildings date from 1906 when they were constructed to replace the ones destroyed in a 1904 fire.

Chongmyo

The royal ancestral shrine of the Chosŏn Kings, Chongmyo dates from 1395 when King T'aejo had it built for the memorial tablets of his ancestors which he had brought to Seoul from Kaesŏng. The buildings, however, date from 1608 when they were built to replace the ones destroyed in 1592 by Japanese invaders.

Chŏngjŏn, the main hall, houses the memorial tablets of the kings who had direct heirs to the throne, their queens and other immediate family

members. The tablets of the kings who died without heirs and their family members are enshrined in a hall called *Yŏngnyŏngjŏn*. Ritual vessels and other ceremonial items are displayed in some of the other buildings.

Confucian ceremonies were held at *Chŏngjŏn* five times a year and at *Yŏngnyŏngjŏn* two times a year throughout Chosŏn. The ceremony is now held only once a year, every first sunday in May.

Top, Chongmyo, the royal ancestral shrine of the Chosŏn kings
Middle, A Confucian ceremony   Bottom, Musicians performing in a Confucian ceremony

Fortresses

Namdaemun, one of Seoul's main gates constructed in the Chosŏn period

City Wall

The Namdaemun, Tongdaemun, Ch'ang-ŭimun, Kwanghŭimun and Sukchŏngmun gates that are located throughout Seoul are reminders of the wall King T'aejo had constructed around his capital. The 18.5km-long wall made of earth and stone was built in 98 days in 1396. Nearly 200,000 people were mobilized from throughout the country to do the work.

Parts of the wall were replaced with carefully hewn stones in 1422 by order of King Sejong. It was partially destroyed during the 1592-98 Japanese invasions. It was extensively repaired during a six-year period from 1704 and has been repaired many times since.

The remains and sites of walls like this one that were constructed to defend ancient capitals, towns and strategic spots along transportation routes can be seen throughout the countryside. Some of the more interesting are introduced here.

Suwon City Wall

Built in 1794-96 by order of King Chŏngjo (r.1776-1800), the Suwon City Wall once encircled Suwon City. The wall, which was originally 5.52km long, was built as Chŏngjo planned to move the court from Seoul to Suwon to be near the tomb of his father, Prince Changhŏn. The most scientifically designed and constructed of Korea's ancient fortress walls, it was built to withstand spear and arrow as well as rifle and cannon attacks.

The wall and its facilities were damaged during the Korean War. It was restored partially during a three-year period from 1975. One of the wall's loveliest spots is the Yong-yŏn reflecting pond located below a pavilion for watching the moon called *Panghwasuryujŏng*. *P'altamun*, the wall's south gate stands in the heart of Suwon.

Namhan Mountain Fortress

Located about 30km southeast of Seoul near Sŏngnam City, Namhan Mountain Fortress is a walled fortress where Injo, the 16th king of Chosŏn, took refuge during a Manchu invasion in 1637. The 8km-long fortress, which actually dates to the Three Kingdoms period (57 B.C.-A.D.668), had been greatly renovated from 1624 in anticipation of the invasion.

The wall had numerous facilities including 12 gates, four command posts, a palace, a variety of office buildings, several shrines and seven temples. The existing facilities include four gates, a command post, two shrines, several temples, a two-story pavilion called *Suŏjangdae*, and several other pavilions and halls.

Kanghwa Fortresses

Some of the best preserved and picturesque fortresses are on Kanghwa Island about 56km northwest of Seoul. The whole spectrum of Korea's history from the nation's founding by the legendary Tan'gun to its opening to the West in the late 19th century can be observed in the island's numerous monuments and relics.

The fortresses, which dot the island's eastern shore, include *Kapkottondae*, *Kwangsŏngbo*, *Tŏkchinjin* and *Ch'ojijin*. First constructed during the reign of King Kojong (r.1213-59) of Koryŏ and rebuilt during Chosŏn, they saw much action against French, American and Japanese naval expeditions in the late 1800s.

Chinju Fortress

Chinju Fortress, lowted on a cliff overlooking the Nam River in Chinju, South Kyŏngsang Province, is the site of an important victory against Japanese invaders in 1592 and a defeat the following year. It is most well-known for the patriotic suicide of a female entertainer name Non'gae. When the Japanese were celebrating their 1593 capture of the fort, she

Namhan Mountain Fortress

Chinju Fortress

seduced the Japanese general and, cleverly led him to a nearby cliff, clung to him tightly and jumped into the river below.

The fortress may date to the Silla period but ancient records indicate it was constructed in 1354 during Koryŏ. There are several temples, shrines and pavilions within the fortress. Of particular note is the Ch'oksŏngnu Pavilion and Ŭi-am, an inscribed rock that marks the spot where Non'gae jumped into the river.

Haengju Mountain Fortress

Located atop Mt. Haengju about 25km northwest of Seoul is Haengju Mountain Fortress. The fortress, which overlooks the Han River, was the site of one of the fiercest battles of the 1592-98 Japanese invasions of February 12, 1593. The fortress was attacked nine times from three directions by a 30,000-strong Japanese army but the 10,000 defenders led by General Kwon Yul were able to repel the attacks and defeat the Japanese who lost 10,000 men in the fighting.

A monument atop Mt. Haengju is a reminder of the great victory. There is also a shrine called Ch'ungjangsa, which houses a portrait of General Kwon, a memorial hall and two pavilions in the area.

Hyangp'aduri Fortress

Located on Cheju Island, Hyangp'aduri Fortress is the site of a 1273 battle between the *Sambyŏlch'o* (Three Elite Patrols), the core military force that resisted the peace the Koryŏ court made with Mongol invaders in 1270, and a Mongol army. The fortress was constructed by the *Sambyŏlch'o* after they fled to Cheju Island in mid-1271 when their base of resistance on Chin Island was captured. All of the *Sambyŏlch'o* including their leader Kim T'ong-chŏng, were killed in the battle.

Korea's Buddhist Legacy

More than 1,000 temples, some dating from as far back as the sixth century, are scattered throughout Korea, mostly on mountains and in deep valleys. Some of the most interesting are introduced here.

Pusŏk Temple

Located north of Andong, North Kyŏngsang Province, Pusŏk Temple, or the "Temple of the Floating Stone," was established in 676 by Silla's Buddhist priest Ŭisang after he returned from ten years of study in China. It was named Pusŏk Temple because of a large stone on the temple grounds that appears to float above the rocks under it. The temple boasts the oldest wooden structure in Korea which was constructed sometime before 1,376. It also has some of Korea's oldest murals.

Haein Temple

Set in the Mt. Kaya National Park between Taegu and Pusan is the highly impressive Haein Temple that dates to the Unified Silla period. It was established by two monks in 802 and once comprised 93 buildings.

It is most famous as the repository for the more than 80,000 woodblocks for printing Buddhist sutras known as the *Tripitaka Koreana. Taejanggyŏnggak*, the specially designed library housing the woodblocks, was constructed in 1488.

The temple boasts a number of treasures besides the *Tripitaka Koreana.* These include a relief carving of the Buddha, a seated stone Buddha, a three-story pagoda, and the regal garments of Kwanghaegun (r.1608-23) and his wife as well as 70 items of historic value.

T'ongdo Temple

Korea's largest temple, T'ongdo Temple was constructed during the Silla period by a high priest named Chajang in 646 to preserve some Buddhist artifacts including a robe and some bones and teeth of Buddha which he brought from Tang China. The main image of the Buddha is missing because the Buddha's bones and teeth are enshrined in the altar.

The temple comprises 65 buildings of various architectural styles that are covered wtih some of the nation's loveliest Buddhist murals. The temple also has some exceptional artworks as well as a number of cultural treasures.

Hwaŏm Temple

Located at the foot of Mt. Chiri near Kurye in South Chŏlla Province is Hwaŏm Temple, first founded in

Pusŏk Temple in North Kyŏngsang Province

544. It was expanded in 634 by the esteemed Silla monk Ŭisang who used it to propagate Avatamsaka Buddhism. It was burnt down during the 1592-98 Japanese invasions and restored in 1630.

The temple boasts several national treasures including a three-story pagoda supported by four-stone lions, a two-story hall called *Kakhwangjŏn*, and Korea's largest stone lantern.

Ssanggye Temple

Located in Hadong, South Kyŏngsang Province, Ssanggye Temple is famous for the unusual architectural style of its main hall. Located on the grounds of the temple are a stone monument dedicated to a *Sŏn* master named Chin-gam, which was erected in 887, and a stone stupa.

Ssanggye Temple was built in 723. However, most of the present buildings are believed to have been built during the late Chosŏn period.

Songgwang Temple

Along with T'ongdo Temple and Haein Temple, Songgwang Temple is one of Korea's three greatest monasteries. Tucked away in a pine forest southeast of Kwangju in South Chŏlla Province, it has been a center of *Son* (Zen) Buddhism since the 12th centurt. Many of its structures have been designated cultural treasures. Of special note is the temple's museum which is filled with Buddhist relics.

Songgwang Temple was established in 1197. It has been burnt down and repaired numerous times since then.

Pŏpchu Temple

Located in Mt. Songni National Park, Pŏpchu Temple is an expansive temple which once accommodated 30,000 monks. It was built in 553 by a revered Silla monk named Ŭishin. It was burnt down during the 1592-98 Japanese invasions and rebuilt in 1624.

Pŏpchu Temple houses three national treasures: a rare five-story structure called *P'alsangjŏn*; a carved lantern supported by twin lions that is a rare example of the magnificent sculpturing of Unified Silla; and a stone water cistern shaped like an open lotus flower. The temple also has many other cultural assets.

Tombs, Shrines and Other Memorials

Yŏngnŭng

The elaborate tomb of King Sejong and his queen, *Yŏngnŭng*, is a monument to the significant impact the great king had on Korea. It is located in Yŏju, Kyŏnggi Province. A small museum located within the tomb complex contains some sundials, rain guages and other examples of the many achievements made during Sejong's 32-year reign.

Stone statue at Yŏngnŭng, *King Sejong's tomb*

Hyŏnch'ung Shrine

One of the most impressive shrines is the beautifully landscaped 32.8-hectare *Hyŏnch'ung* Shrine in Asan, South Ch'ungch'ŏng Province that was first built in 1706 and reconstructed in 1932. It is dedicated to Admiral Yi Sun-sin who used ironclad battleships called *kŏbuksŏn*, or "turtleboats" to defeat a Japanese fleet during the 1592-98 Japanese invasions.

The shrine has a small museum in which are displayed a replica of a turtleboat and some of the admiral's personal belongings. The admiral's house has been reconstructed on the grounds.

Ch'ilbaegŭich'ong

Located in Kumsan, South Ch'ungch'ŏng Province is *Ch'ilbaegŭich'ong,* a tomb of 700 volunteer soldiers who died fighting a large army of Japanese invaders in 1592. A shrine and a monument were erected to the patriots in 1952. Memorial services for the 700 are held at the shrine annually.

Maninŭich'ong

A mass grave for nearly 10,000 soldiers, public officials and villagers, *Maninŭich'ong,* literally means "Grave of 10,000," is located in Namwon, North Chŏlla Province. Many of them were killed defending Namwon Fortress against Japanese invaders in 1597, and many were massacred after the fortress fell to the invaders.

Tosan Sŏwon

Located in Andong, North Kyŏngsang Province is a lovely Confucian shrine-academy called *Tosan Sŏwon*. It was established by Yi Hwang (T'oegye, 1501-70), one of Korea's most famous Confucian scholars.

Ojukhŏn

The birthplace of Lady Sin Saimdang (1504-51), a role model for Korean women who excelled in scholarly achievements, and her son Yi I (Yulgok, 1536-84), a renowned philosopher, scholar and statesman, is *Ojukhŏn* in Kangnŭng, Kangwon Province. It is a well landscaped complex that contains the home of Sin Saimdang, first built by a Confucian scholar named Ch'oe Ch'i-won (1390-1440), a studio called *Ojukhŏn* (Studio of Black Bamboo), a portrait hall and a small museum in which some paintings and calligraphic works by Lady Sin are displayed.

Tosan Sŏwon, *a Confucian shrine-academy in North Kyŏngsang Province*

Office of Cultural Properties

5-1, Chŏng-dong, Chung-gu, Seoul, 100-120, Republic of Korea
Tel: 02-318-4700, Fax: 02-319-1130

Aims:
• Conservation and management of cultural properties
• Research and study of cultural properties

Principal Activities
• Designation, cancellation, protection and management of cultural properties
• International exchange of cultural properties
• Diffusion and enhancement of cultural properties

• Protection and management of palaces
• Maintenance of cultural properties
• Excavation and research of cultural relics
• Scientific research for conservation of cultural relics
• Control of illegal acts in relation to cultural properties

Divisional Responsibilities
Cultural Properties Planning Officer
• Planning and adjustment of management business of cultural properties
• Compilation and operation of budget
• Decree, regulation, statistics and inspection
• Litigation for the state

General Services Division
• Safety
• Official applications and approvals
• Matters related to appointment, service, training, pensions and allowances of officials and other personnel matters
• Control, publication, conservation and management of official documents
• Other matters which are not related to other divisions

Tangible Cultural Properties Division
• Listing and delisting, protection and management of cultural properties which are classified into the following categories: folk materials, traditional buildings, edifices, fine art and

handicrafts
- Management of cultural property materials and tangible cultural properties listed by municipal or provincial authorities
- International exchange of cultural properties
- Control of illegal acts in relation to cultural properties
- Readjustment of directional signs to give information about cultural properties
- Measures for fire prevention

Intangible Culture Properties Division
- Conservation and management of intangible cultural properties
- Diffusion and enhancement of intangible cultural properties
- Direction and supervision of the Foundation for the Preservation of Cultural Properties of Korea

Monument Division
- Listing and delisting, protection and management of cultural properties which are classified into historical sites, places of natural beauty, monuments and natural monuments
- Overall control of the administration of the Cultural Properties Committee
- Direction and supervision of the National Research Institute of Cultural Property
- Exchange of cultural properties between the south and the north of Korea

Properties Management Division
- Overall management of national properties, namely, cultural properties
- Assessment and collection of revenue from management of cultural properties

- Transfer and adjustment of the assets in special accounts of cultural properties

Palaces Maintenance Division
- Protection, management and maintenance of palaces, gardens surrounding mausoleums and tombs and related national cultural properties
- Direction and supervision of palaces, royal ancestral shrines and branch offices

Cultural Properties Maintenance Division
- Maintenance of national cultural properties (excluding maintenance of palaces, gardens surrounding mausoleums and tombs)
- Drawing up and updating general plan for maintenance of civil and provincial cultural properties and cultural property materials
- Composition of reports on the maintenance of cultural properties

Cultural Properties Research Institute
- Excavation and research on indices of cultural relics
- Scientific exchange for conservation and management of cultural properties
- Scientific research and study on fine arts, handicraft, sculpture, antique buildings, performing arts and folk customs
- Management of cultural properties abroad
- Scientific control for conservation of cultural properties
- Direction and supervision of the provincial Research Institute of Cultural Property and of the Mokp'o Office of Control of the Conservation of Marine Relics

Five Palaces:
Ch'anggyŏng Palace,
Ch'angdŏk Palace,
Tŏksu Palace,
Kyŏngbok Palace,
Chongmyo Royal Ancestral Shrine
- Protection and management of cultural properties, facilities and trees of the palace grounds
- Affairs related to public inspection

Twelve Branch Offices
- Protection and management of palaces, mausolea, gardens, tombs and sites
- Affairs related to public inspection

Hyounch'ungsa Shrine Management Office

100, Baigam-ri, Youmchi-up, Asan-gun,
S. Ch'ungch'ong Prov. , 337-815,
Republic of Korea
Tel: 0418-44-2161/3, Fax: 0418-44-0478

Aims: The Hyounch'ungsa Shrine Management Office was established to take charge of business matters relating to the conservation and maintenance of the historical site and monuments connected with Admiral Yi Sun-Sin. In so doing, its objectives are to strengthen the will for the defense of the nation and to encourage patriotism.

Principal Activities
• Celebration of the anniversary Admiral Yi's birth
• Guidance of visitors to the shrine
• Maintenance of facilities

Principal Sites
• Main Shrine
• Old Main Shrine
• Museum of Relics
• Admiral Yi's Tomb
• Admiral Yi's House
• Archery Ground

Ch'ilbaeguich'ong Shrine Management Office

166-1, Euchong-ri, Keumsong-myon, Keumsan-gun, S. Ch'ungch'ong Prov., 312-910,
Republic of Korea
Tel: 0412-53-8701, Fax: 0412-53-5700

Aims: The Ch'ilbaeguich'ong Shrine Management Office was established to conserve and manage effectively the Ch'ilbaeguich'ong Shrine, and to enhance the spirit and great achievements of *Ch'ilbaeguisa* (700 martyrs).

Principal Activities
• Rite for *Ch'ilbaeguisa*
• Maintenance of facilities
• Guide of visitors to the shrine

Principal Facilities
• Main Shrine
• Museum of Relics
• Monument

King Sejong Shrine Management Office

San 83-1, Wangdae-ri, Neungso-myon, Yoju-gun, Kyonggi Prov., 469-810,
Republic of Korea
Tel: 0337-85-2606, Fax: 0337-84-0922

Aims: The King Sejong Shrine Management Office was established to effectively conserve and maintain the Yŏngnŭng Tombs and to draw public attention to the great works and achievements of King Sejong.

Principal Activities
• Commemorative ritual on birthday of King Sejong

Principal Buildings, Sites and Facilities
• Tomb Mounds
• *Suragan* (Royal Kitchen)
• *Chongjagak* (Main Shrine)
• *Pigak* (Stele Pavilion)
• *Subokbang* (Guard House)
• *Chaeshil* (Tomb keeper's House)
• Sejong Hall
• Tomb Management Office

The Independence Hall of Korea

230, Namhwa-ri, Mokch'on-myon, Ch'onan-gun, S. Ch'ungch'ong Prov. , 333-840, Republic of Korea
Tel: 0417-60-0114, Fax: 0147-62-0815

Aims: The Independence Hall of Korea collects, studies and exhibits historic artifacts and materials related to the Korean national resistance to aggression, the fight for independence, the search for a national identity and the record of development and progress. It is intended to awaken the Korean national consciousness and promote patriotism.

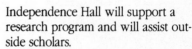

Principal Activities

- Collection, Preservation and Exhibition of Materials: Materials related to efforts to resist aggression, overcome national crises and achieve national development will be collected, preserved and exhibited in the exhibition halls.
- Study of Materials: Materials will be traced, located and studied to reveal their historic significance. The Independence Hall will support a research program and will assist outside scholars.
- Exhibition of Materials and Public Education: Public education will be conducted through exhibitions and other programs in order to promote the spirit of independence and patriotism.
- Publications: Catalogues, lists and reports of research on the historic materials in the Independence Hall collection will be published, and rare and valuable documents will be copied and distributed for research purposes.
- Maintenance and Expansion of Facilities: Facilities will be maintained and expanded in accordance with long-time plans.

Principal Facilities

- The Grand Hall of the Nation
- Exhibition Halls
- The Circle Vision Theater
- Train Ride Hall
- Underground Rest Area

Foundation for the Preservation of Cultural Properties

80-2, P'il-dong, Chung-gu, Seoul, 100-271,
Republic of Korea
Tel: 02-266-9101, Fax: 02-278-1776

Aims: The Foundation for the Preservation of Cultural Properties was established to serve the purpose of preservation of traditional culture and assets and their promotion and diffusion.

Principal Activities
• Performances of important intangible cultural assets
• Exhibition of traditional handi-crafts
• Photographic contest on traditional culture
• Writing contest for students on traditional culture
• Drawing contest for students on traditional culture
• Open-air folklore festival for college students
• Lectures on traditional culture
• Organizational support for traditional culture
• Exploration of domestic and foreign cultural monuments

Korea House
- Propagation of knowledge concerning traditional foods
- Operation of Folk Art Theater
- Introduction and diffusion of traditional handicrafts
- Traditional weddings
- Other cultural events for promotion of traditional culture

Handicraft Art Museum
- Permanent exhibition of traditional handicraft works
- Acquisition and conservation of folk materials in the domain of handicrafts
- Study and research on traditional handicrafts
- Production and distribution of scientific documents related to traditional handicrafts
- Discovery, preservation, and diffusion of traditional handicrafts skills
- Support for traditional craftsmen's creative activities and diffusion and exhibition of their work

Principal Facilities
• Korea House
• Handicrafts Art Museum
• Open-air Theater
  (Seoul Nori-madang)
• Intangible Cultural Properties Center

A traditional wedding ceremony

DIRECTORIES

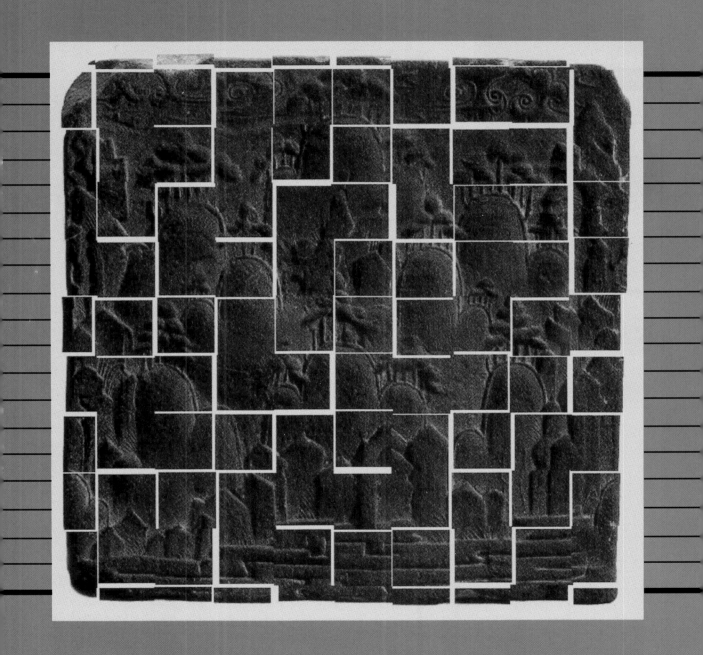

Organization

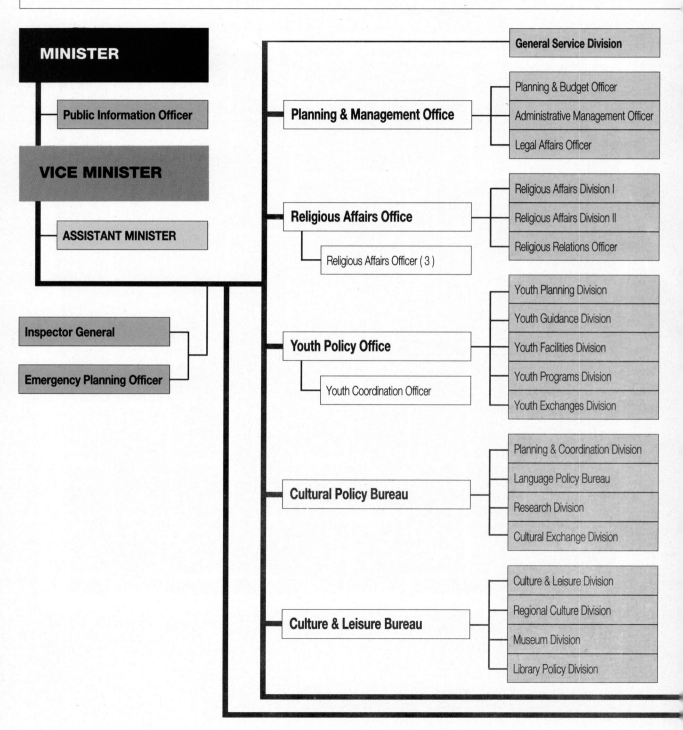

MINISTER

Public Information Officer

VICE MINISTER

ASSISTANT MINISTER

Inspector General

Emergency Planning Officer

General Service Division

Planning & Management Office
- Planning & Budget Officer
- Administrative Management Officer
- Legal Affairs Officer

Religious Affairs Office
- Religious Affairs Division I
- Religious Affairs Division II
- Religious Relations Officer
- Religious Affairs Officer (3)

Youth Policy Office
- Youth Planning Division
- Youth Guidance Division
- Youth Facilities Division
- Youth Programs Division
- Youth Exchanges Division
- Youth Coordination Officer

Cultural Policy Bureau
- Planning & Coordination Division
- Language Policy Bureau
- Research Division
- Cultural Exchange Division

Culture & Leisure Bureau
- Culture & Leisure Division
- Regional Culture Division
- Museum Division
- Library Policy Division

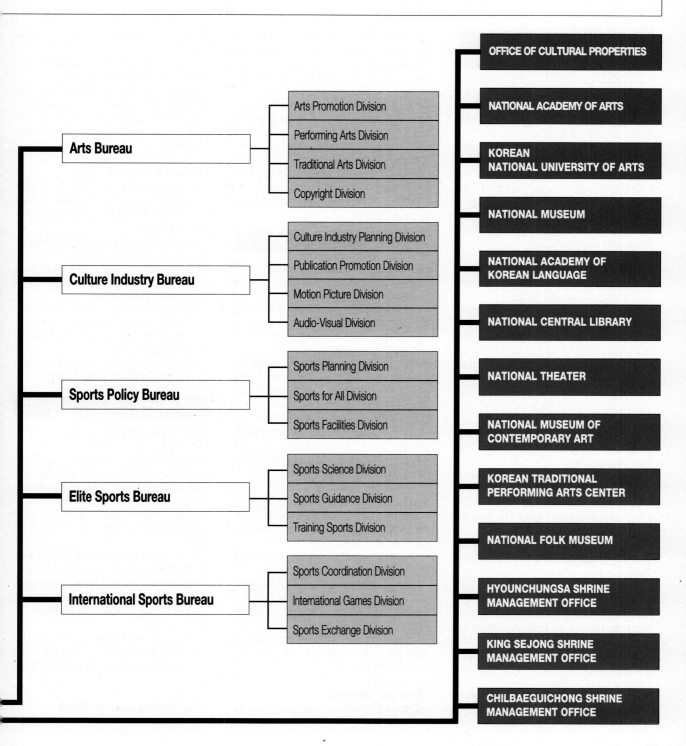

Arts Bureau
- Arts Promotion Division
- Performing Arts Division
- Traditional Arts Division
- Copyright Division

Culture Industry Bureau
- Culture Industry Planning Division
- Publication Promotion Division
- Motion Picture Division
- Audio-Visual Division

Sports Policy Bureau
- Sports Planning Division
- Sports for All Division
- Sports Facilities Division

Elite Sports Bureau
- Sports Science Division
- Sports Guidance Division
- Training Sports Division

International Sports Bureau
- Sports Coordination Division
- International Games Division
- Sports Exchange Division

OFFICE OF CULTURAL PROPERTIES

NATIONAL ACADEMY OF ARTS

KOREAN NATIONAL UNIVERSITY OF ARTS

NATIONAL MUSEUM

NATIONAL ACADEMY OF KOREAN LANGUAGE

NATIONAL CENTRAL LIBRARY

NATIONAL THEATER

NATIONAL MUSEUM OF CONTEMPORARY ART

KOREAN TRADITIONAL PERFORMING ARTS CENTER

NATIONAL FOLK MUSEUM

HYOUNCHUNGSA SHRINE MANAGEMENT OFFICE

KING SEJONG SHRINE MANAGEMENT OFFICE

CHILBAEGUICHONG SHRINE MANAGEMENT OFFICE

Divisional Responsibilities

Cultural Policy Bureau

Planning and Coordination Division
- Establishment and coordination of synthetic projects on cultural policies
- Planning and coordination of cultural and artistic exchanges between South and North Korea
- Matters related to preparation and operation of financial resources for the pormotion of culture and arts
- Direction and supervision of the Korean Culture and Arts Foundation
- Matters regarding the cooperation and support from bussiness corporations for culture and arts

Cultural Research Division
- Planning and forwarding of research and study on cultural policies
- Research and study on cultural consciousness and coultural index
- Collection and classification of the materials related to cultural policies and the operation of policy materials library
- Cooperation with domestic and foreign institutes and experts on cultural policy
- Development of the social education programs implemented by public culture organizations

Language Policy Division
- Establishment and implementation of a comprehensive plan for Korean language and Korean alphabets
- Systematization and spread of Korean language and Korean alphabets
- Distribution abroad of Korean language and literature
- Matters related to the operation of the consultative on Korean language
- Direction and supervision of the National Academy of Korean language and King Sejong Shrine Management Office

Cultural Exchange Division
- Planning and coordination of international exchanges in culture and arts
- Matters related to international cultural agreements and cultural conventions
- Cooperation with international cultural institutions and foreign government agencies
- Collection and management of international cultural information
- Support for exchanges in culture and the arts at home and abroad
- Support for introducing materials of Korean culture

Culture and Leisure Bureau

Culture and Leisure Division
- Affairs related to the culture and leisure of the populace
- Direction and promotion of the cultural activities of enterprises
- Guidance and assiting to grow of cultural organizations related to recreational and leisure life of the people
- Matters related to instruction, development and diffusion of national culture
- Direction and supervision of Hyounchungsa Shrine Management Office, Chilbaeguichong Shrine Management Office and the Independence Hall of Korea

Regional Culture Division
- Establishment of comprehensive projects on regional cultural development policy
- Development and diffusion of regional culturlal exchanges
- Setting-up regional cultural centers and supporting their activities
- Direction and support for construction of cultural facilities
- Matters on improvement, widening and growth assistance of cultural environments

Museum Division
- Establishment of comprehensive projects on the promotion of museums
- Guidance and growth assistance for public and private museums
- Matters on consultation for the establishment of national museums
- Direction and supervision of the National Museum and National Folk Museum

Library Policy Division
- Establishment and coordination of a comprehensive plan for basic policy for library development and readership promotion
- Matters on preparation and operation of the fund for library
- Establishment and implementation of the plan to promote the national book-reading campaign
- Drawing the basic plan to build networks among libraries nation wide
- Support and direction for the public and private libraries
- Providing guidelines and supervision for the National Central Library

Arts Bureau

Arts Promotion Division
- Promotion of literature
- Promotion of visual arts such as painting, sculpture, craft, architecture, photography, design and environmental art
- Support for creative activities and related bodies in the above-mentiond fields
- Promotion of welfare of persons engaged in culture and arts activities
- Matters on international exchanges of literary and plastic art works
- Growth assistance and support for art museums
- Direction and supervision of the National Academy of Arts and the National Museum of Contemporary Art

Performing Arts Division

• Promotion of performing arts such as contemporary music and dance, theatre and entertainment
• Support for creative activities and related bodies in the above-mentioned fields
• Affairs related to the registration of performers, performing places except special places for videos and movies
• Matters on international exchanges of the art categories specified in the article
• Matters on performances in Korea of foreign performing arts
• Guidance and supervision of the Korean National University of Arts, the National Theater and the Seoul Arts Center
• Matters related to the Korean Public Performance Ethics Committee

Traditional Arts Division
• Matters for the promotion of the traditional Korean music, dance and other arts
• Support for creative activities of the arts forms in the above-mentioned fields and organizations engaged in related activities
• Matters on research on modernization of traditional Korean arts and its popularization
• Matters regarding overseas popularization of traditional Korean Arts
• Guidance and supervision of the Korean Traditional Performing Arts Center
• Growth assistance and support for the National High School of Traditional Music

Copyright Division
• Establishment of comprehensive project on copyright policy
• Matters related to the granting of copyrights and registration of copyrights
• Matters related to the operation of the Copyright Deliberation and Coordination Committee

• International exchange of copyrights

Cultural Industry Bureau

Culture Industry Panning Division
• Establishment and implementation of the promotion of cultural industries
• Research on the promotion of cultural industries
• Support for formation projects for the basis of cultural industries
• Matters on development and popularization of cultural products based on Korean culture
• Matters not falling under the jurisdiction of the other divisions of the Bureau

Publication Promotion Division
• Establishment of comprehensive projects on publication printing policies
• Matters related to the registration of publishing companies and printing offices
• International publishing exchanges
• Matters related to the improvement of the distribution structure of the book publishing industry
• Support for publication of wholesome books
• Matters related to the registration of import trade in foreign books

Motion Picture Division
• Promotion of motion picture
• Support for productive activities and related bodies in the above-mentioned field
• Matters related to importation and export of motion picture
• Matters on adjusting supply and demand of motion picture
• Matters regarding the guidance and supervision of movie houses and film makers

Audio-Visual Division
• Promotion of discs and video

• Support for productive activities and related bodies in the above-mentioned fields
• Matters regarding the development and popularization of high-technology cultural programs
• Matters regarding the registration of discs and video production
• Matters on the importation, bringing in and reproduction of foreign audio-video discs
• Matters for growth assistance and distribution of whole some discs and audio-videos

Religious Affairs Office

Religious Affairs Officer
• Assisting the chief of the Religious Affairs Office in cooperation and support for religious affairs

Religious Affairs Division I
• Establishment and execution of comprehensive project on religious policy
• Management and support for affairs relating to Buddhist organizations and protection of their properties
• Management of properties of local schools annexed to Confucian shrines

Religious Affairs Division II
• Management and support for matters related to Protestant Christian bodies
• Management and support for matters related to Roman Catholic bodies

Religious Relations Officer
• Research and study on the actual state of religious activities
• Support for religious exchanges with the north of Korea and Eastern Europe
• Support for exchange of foreign religious bodies
• Support for religious activities of missionaries abroad and foreign missionaries in Korean.

MINISTRY OF CULTURE AND SPORTS
Telephone Numbers

HEAD OFFICE
82-1, Sejongno, Chongno-gu, Seoul, 110-703,
Republic of Korea
Tel: 02-736-7946/9, Fax: 02-736-8513

Title of Organizational Head:
Minister (one vice minister, one assistant minister)

Public Information Officer	02-722-0901
Inspector General	02-722-2140
Emergency Planning Officer	02-720-4282
General Services Division	02-720-3812

Planning & Management Office
Planning & Budget Officer	02-720-3810
Administrative Management Officer	
	02-720-4903
Legal Affairs Officer	02-720-4904

Religious Affairs Office
Religious Affairs Officer	02-720-4136
Religious Affairs Division I	02-720-4281
Religious Affairs Division II	02-720-3432
Religious Relations Officer	02-720-9672

Youth Policy Office
Youth Coordination Officer	02-734-5281
Youth Planning Division	02-734-0183
Youth Guidance Division	02-734-0184
Youth Facilities Division	02-734-0186
Youth Programs Division	02-722-2876
Youth Exchanges Division	02-734-0185

Cultural Policy Bureau
Planning & Coordination Division	02-720-2664
Language Policy Division	02-720-4926
Cultural Research Division	02-720-4037
Cultural Exchange Division	02-720-4038

Culture & Leisure Bureau
Culture & Leisure Division	02-720-3816

Regional Culture Division	02-737-3836
Museum Division	02-720-2665
Library Policy Division	02-722-9181

Arts Bureau
Arts Promotion Division	02-720-3820
Performing Arts Division	02-720-3822
Traditional Arts Division	02-720-3830
Copyright Division	02-720-4967

Culture Industry Bureau
Culture Industry Planning Division	02-722-1329
Publication Promotion Division	02-720-4905
Motion Picture Division	02-720-3821
Audio-Visual Division	02-720-4967

Sports Policy Bureau
Sports Planning Division	02-734-0813
Sports for All Division	02-734-0811
Sports Facilities Division	02-734-0812

Elite Sports Bureau
Sports Science Division	02-734-2189
Sports Guidance Division	02-734-0815
Training Support Division	02-734-0814

International Sports Bureau
Sports Coordination Division	02-734-0816
International Games Division	02-734-0817
Sports Exchange Division	02-734-5289

OFFICE OF CULTURAL PROPERTIES
5-1, Chông-dong, Chung-gu, Seoul, 100-120
Republic of Korea
Tel: 02-318-4700, Fax: 02-319-1130

Cultural Properties Planning Officer	
	02-318-7453
General Services Division	02-318-7455
Tangible Cultural Properties Division	02-318-7457
Intangible Cultural Properties Division	

	02-318-7458
Monument Division	02-318-7459
Properties Management Division	02-318-7460
Palaces Maintenance Division	02-318-7461
Cultural Properties Maintenance Division	
	02-318-7462
Royal Museum	02-744-6638
General Affairs Division	02-752-0735
Exhibition Division	02-753-2582

National Maritime Museum
Maintenance	0631-78-4291
Curatorial Office	0631-78-4292
Changgyonggung Office	02-762-9515
Changdokkung Office	02-762-0648
Kyongbokkung Office	02-732-1931
Chongmyo Office	02-765-0195

Cultural Properties Research Institute
General Affairs Division	02-736-6077
Archaeologic Studies Office	02-737-9436
Artifacts & Relics Office	02-737-6685
Folkloric Studies Office	02-737-8477
Conservation Science Office	02-737-8476
Kyongju Regional Office	0561-772-4136
Puyo Regional Office	0463-33-5901
Changwon Regional Office	0551-85-1314

EXECUTIVE OFFICE,
THE NATIONAL ACADEMY OF ARTS
San-94, Panp'o-dong, Seoch'o-gu, Seoul, 137-042,
Republic of Korea
Tel: 02-596-6214, Fax: 02-596-6209

General Affairs Division	02-596-6213
Operations Division	02-596-6216

THE KOREAN
NATIONAL UNIVERSITY OF ARTS
700, Seoch'o-dong, Seoch'o-gu, Seoul, 137-070,
Republic of Korea
Tel: 02-520-8011/4, Fax: 02-520-8000

Office of Academic Affairs

Academic Affairs Division 02-520-8041

Executive Bureau

General Affairs Division 02-525-4818
Planning Division 02-520-8031

THE NATIONAL MUSEUM

1, Sejongno, Chongno-gu, Seoul, 110-050,
Republic of Korea
Tel: 02-738-3800, Fax: 02-734-7255

Executive Bureau

General Affairs Division 02-732-7110
Maintenance Division 02-720-2718
Cultural Exchange & Education Division
02-720-2714
Curatorial Office 02-739-3871
Registration Department 02-739-3873
Archeology Department 02-730-8796
Fine Arts Department 02-720-2723

Kyongju National Museum 0561-2-5192
Kwangju National Museum 062-571-1419
Chonju National Museum 0652-223-5650
Puyo National Museum 0463-33-8561
Ch'ongju National Museum 0431-55-1631
Chinju National Museum 0591-42-5950
Konngju National Museum 0416-54-2205

THE NATIONAL ACADEMY OF KOREAN LANGUAGE

5-1, Chông-dong, Chung-gu, 100-120,
Republic of Korea
Tel: 02-779-4810, Fax: 02-779-4819

General Affairs Division 02-269-9211
Research Department I 02-269-9213
Research Department II 02-269-9215
Research Department III 02-269-9217

THE NATIONAL CENTRAL LIBRARY

San 60-1, Panp'o-dong, Seoch'o-gu, Seoul, 137-042,
Republic of Korea
Tel: 02-535-4142, Fax: 02-599-6942, 02-535-4167

Library Management Department

General Affairs Division 02-535-4272
Planning & Cooperations Division
02-595-6905
Cultural Research & Training Division
02-595-6904
E.D.P.S Officer 02-535-5694

Library Services Department

Public Services Division 02-535-5693
Deposits Division 02-535-4273
Acquisition & Technical Services Division
02-535-4274
Bibliographic Control Division 02-535-4275

THE NATIONAL THEATER

San 14-67, Changch'ung 2-dong, Chung-gu, Seoul,
100-392, Republic of Korea
Tel: 02-274-1151/8, Fax: 02-267-7186

Executive Bureau

General Affairs Division 02-274-1163
Performance Division 02-274-1171
Stage Management Division 02-274-1174

THE NATIONAL MUSEUM OF CONTEMPORARY ART

San 58-1, Makgye-dong, Kwach'eon, Kyounggi
Prov., 427-080, Republic of Korea
Tel: 02-503-7744/5, Fax: 02-503-9167

Executive Bureau

General Affairs Division 02-503-9673
Exhibition Division 02-503-7124
Public Relation & Education Division
02-503-7125
Curatorial Office 02-503-9674

KOREAN TRADITIONAL PERFORMING ARTS CENTER

700, Seoch'o-dong, Seoch'o-gu, Seoul, 137-071,
Republic of Korea

Tel: 02-585-3151, Fax: 02-585-2485
General Affairs Division 02-585-0152
Performance Division 02-585-0153
Promotion Division 02-585-0154
Art Research Office 02-585-0155

Korean Folk Performing Arts Center 0671-626-0461

NATIONAL FOLK MUSEUM

1, Sejongno, Chongno-gu, Seoul, 110-050,
Republic of Korea
Tel: 02-734-1346, Fax: 02-723-2272

General Affairs Division 02-734-1345
Exhibition Division 02-739-9948
Folk Research Division 02-725-5965

HYOUNCHUNGSA SHRINE MANAGEMENT OFFICE

100, Baigam-ri, Youmchi-up, Asan-gun,
S. Ch'ungch'eong Prov., 337-815,
Republic of Korea
Tel: 0418-44-2161/3, Fax: 0418-44-0478

General Affairs Division 0418-44-2163
Maintenance Division 0418-44-2162
Eumbong Branch Office 0418-43-2819

KING SEJONG SHRINE MANAGEMENT OFFICE

San 83-1, Wangdae-ri, Nungso-myeon, Yeoju-gun,
Kyounggi Prov., 469-810, Republic of Korea
Tel: 0337-85-2606, Fax: 0337-84-0922

CHILBAEGUICHONG SHRINE MANAGEMENT OFFICE

166-1, Euchong-ri, Keumsong-myon,
Keumsan-gun, S. Ch'ungch'eong Prov., 312-910,
Republic of Korea
Tel: 0412-53-8701, Fax: 0412-53-5700

The National Academy of Arts, Republic of Korea

San-94, Panp'o-dong, Seoch'o-gu, Seoul, 137-042, Republic of Korea
Tel: 02-596-6213/5 Fax: 02-596-6209

Aims: The National Academy of Arts' objective is to contribute to the creation and development of national culture by guaranteeing the freedom of arts and promoting the status of artists.

Principal Activities
• Annual election of members of the National Academy of Arts, Republic of Korea
• Awards of the National Academy of Arts, Republic of Korea
• International Arts Symposium
• Members' Exhibition of the National Academy of Arts
• Members' Speeches
• Members' Seminar
• Publication of periodicals: "Bulletin of National Academy of Arts," "Collection of Treaties on Arts," "Korea Art," etc.
• Operation of Library and Art Gallery

Divisional Responsibilities

General Meeting
• Agreement to applicants for membership in the Academy
• Selection of prize-winners

4 Operations Divisions:
Literature Subdivision;
Fine Arts Subdivision;
Music Subdivision;
Theater, Cinema and Dance Subdivision
• Election of members
• Selection of prize-winners
• Deliberation on other matters relating to artistic events

Principal Facilities
• Art Gallery

The National Academy of the Korean language

Tôksu Palace, Chǒng-dong, Chung-gu,
Seoul, 100-120, Republic of Korea
Tel: 02-779-4810 Fax: 02-779-4819

Aims: Established by Presidential Decree No. 13163 (November 4, 1990) in order to contribute to development of Korean culture, the National Academy of the Korean Language provides basic materials for language policy through the scientific and systematic research of the Korean language, establishes norms for the Korean language on such matters as orthography, word spacing and speech, narration and proper forms of address, and publishes materials relating to the Korean language.

Major functions
- Systematization of the current Korean language
- Research regarding establishment of a national language policy
- Research on the current Korean language
- Research on historical changes in the Korean language
- Development of Korean language education
- Collection, arrangement, preservation and dissemination of research materials on the Korean language

Principal Activities
- Editing and publication of the quarterly "Sae Kugǒsaenghwal" (*New Korean Language Life*), the Academy's official organ
- Publication of collections of Koreanized or improved terms and expressions
- Standardization of language etiquette and proper forms of address

- Research on the current use of Chinese characters and foreign loan words
- Research on the use and teaching of the Korean language abroad
- Research on mistranslations into Korean appearing in publications
- Operation of *Kanada* telephone to answer questions on the Korean language, thereby helping improve people's linguistic awareness

Divisional Responsibilities

Department of Normative Studies
- Planning and coordination of research programs of the Korean language
- Research on computer processing of the Hangul, the Korea alphabetical script
- Research on Korean language norms including those on spelling
- Development and operation of computer system for processing Korean language materials
- Collection, development and management of computer-processed Korean language materials
- International academic exchanges including invitation of visiting researchers
- Editing and publishing of various

Korean language dictionaries
- Research matters not falling in the domains of other departments of the Academy

Department of Materials Studies
- Collection, management and publication of research materials of the Korean language
- Publication of collections of papers on the Korean language and Korean language policy
- Survey on use of Chinese characters in daily life and research on related matters
- Publication of bibliography of the Korean language and Korean language policy
- Research on errors occurring in translation into Korean
- Education and dissemination of the norms and standard pronunciation of the Korean language
- Operation of phonetic laboratory
- Translation of Korean and foreign publications
- Answering questions on the Korean language by the general public

Department of Despcriptive Studies
- Purification of the Korean language and standardization of language etiquette
- Studies on history of the Korean language and the Hangul
- Collection and research on dialects
- Research on the Korean language as used in north Korea
- Studies on language unification of South and North Korea
- Research on newspaper and Radio, TV language
- Research on Korean language as spoken in Korean communities abroad
- Matters concerning teaching of the Korean language in foreign countries

The Korean Culture and Arts Foundation

1-130, Dongsung-dong, Chongno-gu, Seoul, 110-510, Republic of Korea
Tel: 02-760-4500
Fax: 02-760-4700
Telex: TKCAF K29598

Aims: The Korean Culture and Arts Foundation (KCAF) was established with the goal of preserving and advancing Korea's national heritage through the promotion of culture and the arts in the form of support for academic research and creative activities as well as the widening of access to cultural and artistic events. Since its foundation in 1972, the KCAF has devoted itself to improving the quality of cultural life for all Koreans.

Principal Responsibilities

• Support for research and creative activities in the fields of literature, fine arts, photography, architecture, music, traditional music, drama, dance, film, entertainment and publishing
• Support for research, publication and distribution of works contributing to the development of Korea's unique national culture
• Support for international exchanges in the fields of culture and the arts
•Promotion of fund-raising projects and activities
• Undertaking other projects which contribute to the promotion of Korean culture and arts and the enrichment of the Culture and Arts Promotion Fund

Principal Activities

Support for creative activities
Literature, fine arts, music, drama, dance, performing arts, traditional arts

Additional support for culture and the arts
Publishing, film, popular culture

Subsidies for regional culture and arts
• Promotion of the arts and culture
• Establishment of the Provincial Culture and Arts Promotion Fund
• Improvement and expansion of regional cultural facilities
• Cultural festivals in regional areas

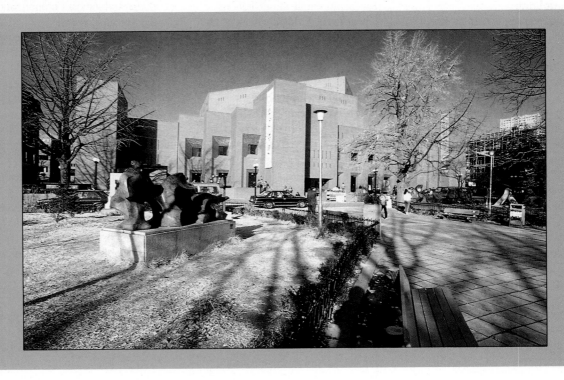

Improving the environment for
cultural and artistic creativity
- Arts scholarships
- Operation of the Stage Production
  and Training Center
- Operation of rehearsal facilities for
  the performing arts
- Subsidies for cultural and artistic
  organizations
- Welfare support for cultural and
  artistic figures

Introduction of
Korean culture and arts abroad
- International exchanges of artists
- Korean literary works overseas
- Support for participation in
  international art projects

Research and educational programs
- Development of long-and short-term
  cultural policy
- Analysis of cultural indicators
- Symposia and academic publications

Community outreach programs
- Lectures on culture and arts
- Performing arts academy
- Education for culture and arts
  specialists
- Culture lectures for young people

Publication and information services
- Culture and Arts yearbook
- "Culture and Arts" monthly journal
- Collection of culture and arts
- Performance and exhibition
  information
- Distribution of culture and arts
  information

The Art Center
The KCAF Art Center holds regular
art exhibitions and is responsible for

the acquisition and control of art
objects, as well as providing exhibition halls for artists.

The Munye Theater
The Munye Theater provides a valuable venue for a variety of performing arts. The Center consists of the
709-seat Main Hall, a smaller 200-seat
Small Hall, and spacious rehearsal
facilities.

Principal Facilities
- The Munye Theater
- The Art Center
- The Archives: research library, music
  library, film and video library,
  computer room for data control
- Stage Production and Training
  Center

National Committee for Copyright Deliberation and Conciliation

San 60-1, Panp'o-dong, Seoch'o-gu, Seoul, 137-042, Republic of Korea
Tel: 02-596-8405
Fax: 02-596-6053

Aims: As provided for under Article 81 of Korea's Copyright Act, the National Committee for Copyright Deliberation and Conciliation was established to perform a consultative role as well as to settle disputes over the rights protected under the Act. The Committee gives the government, the Ministry of Culture and sports expert opinions which have become more important since new frontiers of technological development have made copyright matters increasingly complicated and delicate.

Principal Activities
• Educational services
- Circuit lectures throughout the country
- Regular discussions with the general public on subjects which cover a wide range of topics as well as the holding of 3-month training courses for copyright industries
• Holding of seminars on current issues with particular reference to international trends in respect of copyright law and Korea's response to them
• Operation of the Copyright Information Center
• Publication of a quarterly journal

The Korean Public Performance Ethics Committee

Sanho Building, 1475-2, Seoch'o-dong, Seoch'o-gu, Seoul, 137-070, Republic of Korea
Tel: 02-522-6280/1, 02-522-2591/8
Fax: 02-522-2491

Aims: The Korea Ethics Committee for the Performing Arts was established in order to contribute to the development of national culture and the awakening of a healthy national spirit, by maintaining and enhancing the public interest in the performing arts and the order and dignity of performances.

Principal Activities
• Annual analysis of statistics for policy formulation
• Publication of consultative white book
• Campaign aimed at the eradication of pirate pornographic and violent video tapes
• Holding of symposia

The Korean Publication Ethics Committee

257-3, Gongdeok-dong, Map o-gu, Seoul, 121-020, Republic of Korea
Tel: 02-719-4897, 02-704-3360, Fax: 02-704-3735

Aims: The Korean Publication Ethics Committee was established in January 1970 in order to deliberate the contents of publications, such as books, journals, magazines and comic strips, and to promote various affairs for the sound development of prose and publication culture.

Principal Activities
• Selection of recommended books and their introduction to adolescents
• Distribution of cultural and educational books for the young generation
• Operation of seminars and social gatherings to foster ethical standards
• Study for the sound development of publication culture
• Award of the "Prize of Publication Ethics" to give prestige to the ethics of publication
• Publication of "Book-review"
• Publication of a bulletin "Publication Ethics"

The Federation of Artistic and Cultural Organizations of Korea

1-117, Dongsung-dong, Chongno-gu, Seoul,
110-510, Republic of Korea
Tel: 02-744-7870/3, Fax: 02-741-3372

Aims: The Federation of Artistic and Cultural Organizations of Korea, the main support body for artistic activities in Korea, was established to foster friendship among artists, to protect their interests, to promote the international exchange of folk art and, ultimately, to contribute to the development of the arts worldwide.

Principal Activities
- Protecting artists' rights
- Coping with problems of artistic groups at home and abroad

Divisional Responsibilities

The Korean Institute of Architects

The Korean Institute of Architects (KIA) was originally founded as the Korean Architectural Artists' Association in February 1957, in order to help achieve unity among Korean architects, to improve their welfare, and ultimately to contribute to the development of Korean architecture. KIA has been a regular participant in the Union of International Architects (UIA) General Assembly held once every three years, using each occasion as an opportunity to increase awareness of international architectural trends, enhance friendship with foreign architects and exchange information. KIA is also engaged in other activities, such as hosting the annual Korean Architectural Exhibition and publishing a bimonthly entitled "Architect Magazine".

The Korean Classical Music Association

This association was established with the primary goals of preserving, developing and promoting Korea's rich heritage of traditional music. It also aims to help its members exchange ideas and seeks to improve their collective welfare.
To achieve these ends, the association carries out the following activities:
- Studies of traditional Korean music and its promotion
- Education of traditional music performers
- International exchanges
- Promotion of traditional music performing groups and their performances
- Establishment of the National Traditional Music Award and its management

The Korean Dance Association

The Dance Association of Korea was established in 1961 to improve the status and rights of dancers by means of international exchanges and to develop the art of dance. This association organizes the National Dance Competition for students, the National Dance Competition for new dancers, and the Seoul Dance Festival. It also encourages leading dancers to perform throughout the nation, and holds symposia on dance-related topics.

The Korean Literary Writers' Association

The Korean Literary Writers' Association was formed on December 31, 1961, with the purposes of promoting Korean literature, enhancing friendship among writers, protecting writers' rights, and facilitating exchanges with foreign writers.

The organization's activities, in line with the above-mentioned purposes, include publication of a magazine, "Literature Monthly," which aims at promoting Korean literature abroad and supporting members by providing them with a forum for the exchange of ideas, and the biannual "Literature Symposium." KLWA's other activities include hosting the National Youth Essay Contest and the Exhibition of Pictures and Poems, running a youth reading club, providing scholarships for children of writers in difficult circumstances, and opening a literature and art college. In addition, the association is actively supporting the construction of writers' village and the Hyundai Culture Center.

The Korean Fine Arts Association

The Korean Fine Arts Association

(KFAA) held its inaugural meeting on December 18, 1961, with the aims of promoting Korea's fine arts, supporting the rights of artists, and bringing together artists inside the country and abroad.

Through its major activities of supporting creative art and promoting exchanges with foreign countries in the realm of fine arts, KFAA has been assisting the general development of Korean fine arts.

The Photo Artists' Society of Korea

Previous photography institutions, which had been dispersed around the country, including the Korean Artists' Association, the Korean Photography League and the Korean Association of Photographers, disbanded, and their membership merged to establish the Korean Photography Institute on December 17, 1960 at the National Information Center.

From May 1 through 19, 1962, PASK hosted the first New Artists Photography Contest at the Central Information Center. The contest was held seven times until 1968 and helped to promote many of today's leading photographers. Since 1982, PASK has hosted the Korean Photography Exhibition.

The Korean Theater Association

The Korean Theater Association of Korea was established in 1963 to promote the development of theatrical activities along with friendship and the welfare of actors. One of the biggest and the most important activities of this association is the "Seoul Drama Festival," which was run by the Korean Culture and Arts Foundation until 1988. It also organizes the National Drama Festival from late April to early June in which 14 major theatrical companies outside Seoul take part, performing in various cities. The Association has published a monthly magazine, "Korean Drama," since 1975, and holds an annual actors workshop and seminars twice a year. Lastly, it organizes various activities to promote friendship among its members, and in memory of various deceased actors.

The Korean Entertainment Association

The Korean Entertainment Association held its inaugural meeting on December 18, 1961, at the Hwarang Public Auditorium in Seoul, with 405 members from the fields of composition, musical performance, singing, and acting in attendance.

This association's main purposes are to support the development of the entertainment field, and to improve the welfare of its membership through active promotion of sound popular culture and unity among members of the association. In order to achieve these goals, it engages in the following activities:
• Education of entertainers
• Promotion of entertainment arts
• Participation in policy making for entertainment arts and assistance in enforcement of policies
• International entertainment exchanges
• Improvement of the welfare of its membership
• Establishing sound entertainment ethics and bringing order to performing activities in general
• Performances for soldiers and policemen

The Korean Motion Pictures Association

The Korean Motion Pictures Association was established in 1962 as an affiliate of the Federation of Artistic and Cultural Organizations of Korea. This association holds numerous annual events. The Golden Bell Film Awards, which were cosponsored by the Motion Picture Promotion Corporation and the Ministry of Culture and Information from their initiation in 1962, have been sponsored by KMPA since 1987. Together with the Motion Picture Promotion Corporation, KMPA has established a special movie endowment fund of 1 billion won, using it for pensions for movie workers, scholarships for the children of movie workers, and for supporting the bereaved families of deceased members.

The Korean Music Association

The Korean Music Association was established in 1961 to contribute to the development of Korean music and to promote the status and rights of musicians through international musical exchanges.

To fulfill its goals, the Korean Music Association carries out various activities:
• Holding the Seoul Music Festival annually since 1969
• Celebrating the anniversary of International Music Day on October 10 every year
• Holding a seminar on the development of music education in Korea
• Holding two major music contests annually: "Music Contest of Korea for Students" and "Korean Music Association Contest."

ART AND LITERATURE

Federation of Artistic and Cultural Organization of Korea
1-117, Tongsung-dong, Chongno-gu, Seoul
(02-744-7870)
Member Associations:
Korean Inst. of Architects (02-744-8050)
Korean Dance Assn. (02-744-8066)
Classical Music Assn. of Korea (02-744-8051)
Korean Writers Assn. (02-744-8046)
Photo Artistic's Soc. of Korea (02-744-8062)
Korean Fine Arts Assn. (02-744-8053)
Korean Theater Assn. (02-744-8055)
Motion Pictures Assn. of Korea (02-744-8064)
Korea Entertainment Assn. (02-744-8057)
Korea Music Assn. (02-744-8061)

Foundation for the Reservation of Cultural Properties
80-2, P'il-dong 2-ga, Chung-gu, Seoul
(02-266-9101)

Galleries' Assn. of Korea
182-2, Kwanhun-dong, Chongno-gu, Seoul
(02-733-3708)

Institute of Traditional Culture
284-6, Nakwon-dong, Chongno-gu, Seoul
(02-762-8401)

King Sejong the Great Memorial Society
San 1-157, Ch'ongnyangni-dong, Tongdaemun-gu, Seoul (02-966-2571)

Korea Arts Reviewer Society
128-23, Ch'angsin-dong, Chongno-gu, Seoul
(02-763-5985)

Korean Bongsan Mask Dance Drama
112-2, Samseong-dong, Kangnam-gu, Seoul
(02-566-6356)

Korean Culture and Arts Foundation
1-130, Tongsung-dong, Chongno-gu, Seoul
(02-760-4500)

Korea Foundation
526, Namdaemunro 5-ga, Chung-gu, Seoul
(02-753-6465)

Korea Mother of Pearl Lacquer Ware Art's Association
961-2, Tapsipni-dong, Tongdaemun-gu, Seoul
(02-247-4038)

Korean Ethics Committee of Public Performance
1475-2, Seoch'o-dong, Seoch'o-gu, Seoul
(02-522-6280)

Korean Library Association
San 60, Panp'o-2-dong, Seoch'o-gu, Seoul
(02-535-4868)

Korean Nationalistic Artists Federation
59-5, Nakwon-dong, Chongno-gu, Seoul
(02-743-5873)

Korea Phonogram and Video Association
255-56, Yongdu-dong, Tongdaemun-gu, Seoul
(02-922-6612)

Korean Poets Association
200-2, Hangangro 1-ga, Yongsan-gu, Seoul
(02-796-4521)

Korea Radio and TV Writers Association
17-1, Youido-dong, Yongdeungp'o-gu, Seoul
(02-782-1696)

Korea Writers Association
136-1, Map'o-dong, Map'o-gu, Seoul
(02-703-9837)

Research Institute of Korea Traditional Music (P'ansori)
944-22, Taech'i-dong, Kangnam-gu, Seoul
(02-566-9457)

FINE ARTS

Arario
354-1, Shinbu-dong, Ch'onan, S. Ch'ungch'ong Prov. (0417-62-9444)

Baik Song Art Gallery
197-9, Kwanhun-dong, Chongno-gu, Seoul
(02-730-5824)

Chohyung Gallery
198-1, Kwanhun-dong, Chongno-gu, Seoul
(02-733-4792)

Chosun Gallery
76-15, Ch'ongdam-dong, Kangnam-gu, Seoul
(02-516-3438)

Daelim Art Gallery
181, Kwanhun-dong, Chongno-gu, Seoul
(02-733-3738)

Dangong Gallery
70-2, Kongyung-dong, Chung-gu, Taegu
(053-423-0283)

Demi Gallery
192-18, Kwanhun-dong, Chung-gu, Seoul
(02-734-8826)

Dong San Bang Gallery
93, Kyonji-dong, Chongno-gu, Seoul
(02-733-5877)

Dong Soong Gallery
1-28, Tongsung-dong, Chongno-gu, Seoul
(02-745-0011)

Dongseo Gallery
192-18, Kwanhun-dong, Chongno-gu, Seoul
(02-733-9585)

Dongsuh Gallery
28, Ch'ang-dong, Masan, S. Kyongsang Prov.
(0551-44-2121)

Dongwon Gallery
223-16, Bongsan-dong, Chung-gu, Taegu
(053-423-1300)

Gallery Ami
566-30, Shinsa-dong, Kangnam-gu, Seoul
(02-514-5568)

Gallery Doll

192-18, Kwanhun-dong, Chongno-gu, Seoul
(02-739-1406)

Gallery Focus
62-35, Ch'ongdam-dong, Kangnam-gu, Seou
(02-516-3536)

Gallery Green
1694-4, Seoch'o4-dong, Seoch'o-gu, Seoul, Korea
(02-593-4243)

Gallery Hansol
263-15, Yeon-dong, Cheju Prov. (064-42-5364)

Gallery Mook
1-97, Tongsung-dong, Chongno-gu, Seoul
(02-745-3980)

Gallery Sangmoondang
189, Kwanhun-dong, Chongno-gu, Seoul
(02-732-4188)

Gallery World
179-11, Minlak-dong, Nam-gu, Pusan
(051-751-8855)

Gallery 63
8-1, Ch'ongdam-dong, Kangnam-gu, Seoul
(02-547-0735)

Gana Gallery
192-18, Kwanhun-dong, Chongno-gu, Seoul
(02-734-4093)

Garam Art Gallery
30-10, Kwanhun-dong, Chongno-gu, Seoul
(02-732-6170)

Gasan Gallery
9-2, Gasan Bldg., Ch'ongdam-dong,
Kangnam-gu, Seoul (02-516-8888)

Growrich Art Gallery
67-1, Sogyok-dong, Chongno-gu, Seoul
(02-737-8706)

Hansun Gallery
10, Insa-dong, Chongno-gu, Seoul
(02-725-5028)

Hansung Gallery
208-4, Samdok-dong 2-ga, Chung-gu, Taegu
(02-423-9933)

Hankgojae Gallery
100-5, Kwanhun-dong, Chongno-gu, Seoul

(02-739-4937)

Hyun Art Gallery
50, Kwanhun-dong, Chongno-gu, Seoul
(02-733-3339)

Gallery Hyundai
122, Sagan-dog, Chongno-gu, Seoul
(02-732-1736)

Ihn Gallery
302-64, Ich'on-dong, Yongsan-gu, Seoul
(02-797-2331)

Inkong Gallery
129, Samdok-dong 2-ga, Chung-gu, Taegu
(053-422-6538)

J & C Gallery
582-7, Shinsa-dong, Chongno-gu, Seoul
(02-514-7352)

Jean Art Gallery
7-38, T'ongui-dong, Chongno-gu, Seoul
(02-738-7570)

Joongang Gallery
217-8, Bongsan-dong, Chung-gu, Taegu
(053-425-0808)

Jungsong Gallery
62-2, Youido-dong, Yongdeungp'o-gu, Seoul
(02-783-2444)

Kongkan Gallery
179-11, Minlak-dong, Nam-gu, Pusan
(051-757-0031)

Kukje Gallery
59-1, Sogyok-dong, Chongno-gu, Seoul, Korea
(02-735-8449)

Korean Art Gallery
76-2, Ch'ongdam-dong, Kangnam-gu, Seoul
(02-549-9295)

Kum Gallery
30-1, Tonggwang-dong 3-ga, Chung-gu, Pusan
(051-246-4985)

Haenah-Kent Gallery
198-10, Kwanhun-dong, Chongno-gu,Seoul
(02-725-2602)

Gallery Gain
126-6, Sakan-dong, Chongno-gu, Seoul

(02-733-5010)

Gallery Agbae
200-176, Dongmyung 2-dong, Dong-gu, Kwangju
(062-228-4211)

Myoug Gallery
192-18, Kwanhun-dong, Chongno-gu, Seoul
(02-720-4716)

Gallery May
545-15, Shinsa-dong, Kangnam-gu, Seoul
(02-540-2911)

Galerie Bhak
80-6, Ch'ongdam-dong, Kangnam-gu, Seoul
(02-544-8481)

Gallery 2000
9, Insa-dong, Chongno-gu, Seoul
(02-720-4879)

Sae Gallery
6th Fl., Dongsuh Securities Bldg.,
51-11, Panp'o 4-dong, Seoch'o-Ku, Seoul
(02-599-9556)

Soomock Gallery
62-37, Ch'ongdam-dog, Kangnam-gu, Seoul
(02-518-5884)

Yejin Gallery
20-11, Deayan-dong, Chinju, S.Kyongsang Prov.
(0591-745-3366)

Maehyang Gallery
13-21, Daebong-ldong, Chung-gu, Taegu
(053-757-8436)

Mee Gallery
530-2, Shinsa-dong, Kangnam-gu, Seoul
(02-542-3004)

Miho Art Gallery
118-15, Ch'ongdam-dong, Kangnam-gu, Seoul
(02-540-1553)

Moin Gallery
192-11, Kwanhun-dong, Kangnam-gu, Seoul
(02-739-9291)

Na Gallery
197-9, Kwanhun-dong, Chongno-gu, Seoul
(02-732-8846)

Nabis Gallery

30-21, Shinsa-dong, Kangnam-gu, Seoul
(02-511-1511)

Namkyung Gallery

183, Insa-dong, Chongno-gu, Seoul
(02-733-1411)

Owon Gallery

471-1, Taehung 2-dong, Chung-gu, Taejon
(042-256-2225)

Park Ryu Sook Gallery

12, Ch'ongdam-dong, Kangnam-gu, Seoul
(02-544-7393)

Pyo Gallery

532-6, Shinsa-dong, Kangnam-gu, Seoul
(02-543-7337)

Saem Art Gallery

8-14, Nonhyun-dong, Kangnam-gu, Seoul
(02-545-1175)

Saemteo Gallery

118-12, Ch'ongdam-dong, Kangnam-gu, Seoul
(02-514-5121)

Seolim Art Gallery

63-2, Ch'ongdam-dong, Kangnam-gu, Seoul
(02-514-3377)

Seomi Gallery

79-15, Ch'ongdam-dong, Kangnam-gu, Seoul
(02-546-9740)

Song-a-dang Gallery

225-5, Bongsan-dong, Chung-gu, Taegu
(053-424-6713)

Songwon Gallery

198-32, Kwnhun-dong, Chongno-gu, Seoul
(02-732-3558)

Soo Gallery

159-1, Samseong-dong, Kangnam-gu, Seoul
(02-555-6756)

Ssanjin Gallery

51-26, Kung-dong, Dong-gu, Kwangju
(062-222-6655)

Sun Art Gallery

184 Insa-dong, Chongno-gu, Seoul
(02-734-0458)

Tho Art Space

Kwanglim Bldg., 570-2, Shinsa-dong,
Kangnam-gu, Seoul (02-511-3399)

Woong Gallery

635, Shinsa-dong, Kangnam-gu, Seoul
(02-548-7371)

World Art Gallery

80-6, Susong-dong, Chongno-gu, Seoul
(02-732-7755)

Yeemock Gallery

62-37, Ch'ongdam-dong, Kangnam-gu, Seoul
(02-514-8888)

Yeh Gallery

532-8, Shinsa-dong, Kangnam-gu, Seoul
(02-542-5543)

Yewon Gallery

931-25, Taechi-dong, Kangnam-gu, Seoul
(02-561-2170)

Yuna Gallery

118-15, Ch'ongdam-dong, Kangnam-gu, Seoul
(02-545-2151)

Samkyung Gallery

9, Insa-dong, Chongno-gu, Seoul
(02-735-1262)

Gallery Bing

258-7, Itaewon-2 dong, Yongsan-gu, Seoul
(02-796-7318)

Baik Jae

24, Kwanhun-dong, Chongno-gu, Seoul
(02-732-0218)

You Jin Gallery

2nd Fl., Kangnam Bldg., 49-3, Joongang-dong
Chung-gu, Pusan (051-247-5976/8)

Gallery Bon

Sunghwa Bldg., 192-18, Kwanhun-dong,
Chongno-gu, Seoul (02-732-2366)

Songha Gallery

179-11, Minlak-dong, Nam-gu, Pusan
(051-752-5289)

Woowon Gallery

24, Kwanhun-dong, Chongno-gu, Seoul
(02-738-0087)

Chung Art Gallery

62-24, Ch'ongdam-dong, Kangnam-gu, Seoul
(02-543-1663)

Indeco Gallery

615-4, Shinsa-dong, Kangnam-ku, Seoul
(02-511-0032)

MUSIC

KBS Symphony Orchestra

1, Youido-dong, Yongdeungp'o-gu, Seoul
(02-781-1550)

KBS TV Chorus

1, Youido-dong, Yongdeungp'o-gu, Seoul
(02-781-3462)

National Changguk Company

San 14-67, Changch'ung-dong 2-ga,
Chung-gu, Seoul (02-271-1742)

National Classical Music Institute

San 700, Seoch'o-dong, Seoch'o-gu, Seoul
(02-585-3151)

National Opera

San 14-67, Changch'ung-dong 2-ga, Chung-gu,
Seoul (02-271-1745)

National Chorus

San 14-67, Changch'ung-dong 2-ga,
Chung-gu, Seoul (02-271-1744)

Kim Cha Kyung Opera Company

24-3, Sinch'on-dong, Seodaemun-gu, Seoul
(02-392-3157)

Seoul Baroque Ensemble

208-18, Puam-dong, Chongno-gu, Seoul
(02-720-9266)

Seoul Opera Group

63-379, Hankangro 3-ga, Yongsan-gu, Seoul
(02-790-2831)

**Seoul Traditional Music
Orchestra**

81-3, Sejong-ro, Chongno-gu, Seoul (02-738-3082)

Little Angels

25, Neung-dong, Seongdong-gu, Seoul
(02-444-8221)

Seoul Municipal Orchestra

81-3, Sejong-ro, Chongno-gu, Seoul (02-735-0693)

World Vision Korean Children's Choir

711-11, Naebalsan-dong, Kangseo-gu, Seoul (02-662-1083)

Korean Traditional Performing Arts Centre

700, Seoch'o 3-dong, Seoch'o-gu, Seoul (02-585-0152/5)

Korean Folk Arts Center

807-3, Noam-dong, Namwon, N. Cholla Prov. (0671-626-0461/2)

Dong Ri National Music Institute

456-1, Upnae-ri, Kochang-eup, Kochang-gun, N. Cholla Prov. (0677-64-6949)

Nan-Kye Korean Music Orchestra

382, Puyong-ri, Yongdong-eup, Yongdong-gun, N. Ch'ungch'ong Prov. (0414-44-2101)

Chollabukdo Provincial Institution of Korean Traditional Music

184-1, Teokchin-dong 2-ga, Tokchin-gu, Chonju, N. Cholla Prov. (0652-252-1395)

Kyongnam Educational Institute for Korean Traditional Music

2-62, Jungang-dong 2-ga, Hap'o-gu, Masan, S. Kyongsang Prov. (0551-43-3663)

Pusan Municipal Traditional Music Orchestra

Cultural Center, San 213-4, Daeyeon4-dong, Nam-gu, Pusan (051-625-8130)

Taegu Municipal Korean Music Orchestra

Culture & Arts Hall, 187, Seodang-dong, Dalseo-gu, Taegu (053-652-0515)

Kwangju Municipal Kukguk Company

San 34-1, Unam-dong, Puk-gu, Kwangju (062-529-4466)

Yeonchong Institute of Taejeon Municipal for Korean

Traditional Music

214, Daehung 1-dong, Chung-gu, Taejeon (042-253-4024)

Ch'ungju Municipal Kayagum Orchestra

154-1, Sungnae-dong, Ch'ung ju, N. Ch'ungch'ong Prov. (0441-845-2855)

Ch'onan Municipal Traditional Music Orchestra

Dept. of Korean Traditional Music, Danguk Univ. , San29-1, Anseo-dong, Ch'onan, S. Ch'ungch'ong Prov. (0417-552-5336)

Chollanamdo Provincial Namdo Korean Music Orchestra

3nd Fl. , Naju Cultural Center, 1102, Songwol-dong, Naju, S. Cholla Prov. (0613-33-6928)

Kyongsangbukdo Provincial Korean Music Orchestra

Culture & Sports Div., Kyousangbukdo Provincial Hall, Samkyok-dong, Puk-gu, Taegu (053-943-0811)

Jinju Municipal Korean Music Orchestra

Sinan-dong, Jinju, S. Kyongsang Prov. (0591-41-5609)

Cheju Provincial Fork Arts Company

852, Ildo 2-dong, Cheju, Cheju-do (064-53-9597/8)

Corporation Korea Traditional Art Institute

339-1401, Hanshin 20ch'a APT, Chamwon-dong, Seoch'o-gu, Seoul (02-595-0146/7)

Woorisori

448-23, Sokyo-dong, Map'o-gu, Seoul (02-323-0170)

International Opera Company

912-30, Taechi-dong, Kangnam-gu, Seoul (02-558-2545/7)

Nochatsa (Peoples for Song)

4th Fl. , Kyungmun Bldg. , 184-17, Dongkyo-dong, Map'o-gu, Seoul (02-338-9948/9)

KBS Traditional Music Orchestra

18, Youido-dong, Yongdeungp'o-gu, Seoul (02-781-1558)

Central Traditional Music Orchestra

San 24-17, Shihung-dong, Kuro-gu, Seoul (02-896-2094)

Chonbuk Traditional Music Orchestra

22-1, Chungang-dong 1-ga, Chonju, N. Cholla Prov. (0652-88-0789)

Kwangju Traditional Music Orchestra

271-10, Chunghung-dong, Puk-gu, Kwargju (062-521-3201)

Sambo Traditional Chamber Orchestra

17-12, Yeokchon-dong, Eunpeong-gu, Seoul (02-352-6406)

Sejong Traditional Music Orchestra

4th Fl, Dongju Bldg., Samseon-dong 1-gu, Seongbuk-gu, Seoul (02-744-4315)

Orchestra Asia

San 24-17, Shihung-dong, Kuro-gu, Seoul (02-896-2094)

DANCE

National Ballet Company

San 14-67, Changch'ung-dong 2-ga, Chung-gu, Seoul (02-274-1151)

National Dance Company

San 14-67, Changch'ung-dong 2-ga, Chung-gu, Seoul (02-274-1151)

Seoul City Dance Theater

81-3, Sejong-ro, Chongno-gu, Seoul (02-738-1762)

Universal Ballet Company

25, Neung-dong, Seongdong-gu, Seoul (02-452-0035)

Taegu City Dance Company
187, Seongdang-dong, Talseo-gu, Taegu
(053-651-0435)

Taejon City Dance Company
1-2, Munwha-dong, Chung-gu, Taejon
(042-255-0310)

Kwangju City Dance Company
San 34-1, Wunam-dong, Puk-gu, Kwangju
(062-522-6807)

Mopkp'o City Dance Company
111-9, Citizen's Hall, Namgyo-dong, Mokp'o,
S.Cholla Prov. (0631-44-1604)

Chang Mu Dance Company
5-92, ch'angjeon-dong, Map'o-gu, Seoul
(02-337-5961/3)

Choi Sung Yi Ballet Academy
Suite 305, Hongsilsanga, 79, Samseong-dong,
Kangnam-gu, Seoul (02-511-4659)

Jung Je Man Dance Company
8-1307, Ssangyong Apt., Taech'i-dong,
Kangnam-gu, Seoul (02-566-6094)

Kim Bock Hee Dance Company
224-30, Yonnam-dong, Map'o-gu, Seoul
(02-333-4884)

**Kook, Soo-Ho Didim Dance
Company**
3th Fl, Young Bldg., 252-2, Chamsil-dong,
Songp'a-gu, Seoul (02-421-4797)

**Kui-In Chung & Pusan Modern
Dance Company**
Dance Dept., 30, Changjeon-dong, Kumjong-
gu, Pusan (051-510-1740)

Murrirang Ballet Theatre
978-32, Pangbae 2-dong, Seoch'o-gu, Seoul
(02-588-8112/9166)

Modern Dance Group Zoom
Dance Dept., Keungseong Univ., Daeyon-
dong, Nam-gu, Pusan (051-620-4961)

Modern Dance Shappo
Dance Dept., Wonkwang Univ., 344-2,
Shinyong-dong, Iri, N.Cholla Prov.
(0653-50-6213, 02-333-0057)

Real Dance Company
5th Fl., Baik-sang Bldg., 465-15, Jangan-dong,
Dongdaemun-gu, Seoul (02-213-7987)

Yum's Korean Dance Group
C-204, Seowoo Apt., Kaeshin-dong, Chung-gu,
Ch'ongju, N.Ch'ungch'ong Prov.
(0431-63-8687)

DRAMA

National Drama
San 14-67, Changch'ung-dong 2-ga, Chung-gu,
Seoul (02-274-1153)

Dongrang Repertory Company
8-19, Yejang-dong, Chung-gu, Seoul
(02-778-0261)

Ejoto Theater
70-19, Naesu-dong, Chongno-gu, Seoul
(02-738-6712)

Jayu Theater
62-69, Changch'ung-dong 2-ga, Chung-gu,
Seoul (02-267-5907)

Minjung Theater
93-85, Sinsu-dong, Map'o-gu, Seoul
(02-717-6936)

Minye Theater
130-47, Tongsung-dong, Chongno-gu, Seoul
(02-744-0686)

Roots
227-49, Myongryun-dong 2-ga, Chongno-gu,
Seoul (02-743-3675)

Shinhyup
756-6, Pangbae-dong, Seoch'o-gu, Seoul
(02-591-1023)

Songjwa
1-54, Tongsung-dong, Chongno-gu, Seoul
(02-745-3966)

Women's Theater
12-467, Kalhyon-dong, Unp'yong-gu, Seoul
(02-387-0529)

Boo Hwal

468-22, Mangwon-dong, Map'o-gu, Seoul
(02-336-4192)

Citizens Theatre
5th Fl, Yoo-Sung Bldg., 376-2, Yangjae-dong,
Seocho-gu, Seoul (02-529-7397)

Changgo Theatre
Yongsan P. O. Box 95 (032-341-6275)

Dae Ha Theater Group, the
432-1960, Shindang 2-dong, Chung-gu, Seoul
(02-238-4980)

Hyundai Art Theatre
481, Apgujong-dong, Kangnam-gu, Seoul
(02-540-6560)

Hyundai Theatre Company, the
64-1, Hyehwa-dong, Chongno-gu, Seoul
(02-762-6194)

Jejak Theater
110-10, Kuggi-dong, Chongno-gu, Seoul
(02-379-9824)

Kagyo Theater Group
74-16, Hyewha-dong, Chongno-gu, Seoul
(02-741-6705)

Kwangjang Theater Company
9-1, Ewha-dong, Chongno-gu Seoul
(02-743-8741)

Maek Toe
Daejin Bldg., 537-8, Pangbae-dong, Seoch'o-gu,
Seoul (02-584-4495/6)

Michoo Theatre Company
273, Yeongun-dong, Chongno-gu, Seoul
(02-743-7828/5911)

Royal Theatre
449-2, Kalhyon 2-dong, Unp'yong-gu, Seoul
(02-358-5449)

Sajo Theatre Company
Suite 507, Kyoungbo Bldg., 44-14 Youido-
dong, Yongdeungp'o-gu, Seoul (02-783-4050)

**Theatre Group
Shilhumgukchang**
Miseung Bldg., 808-1, Shinsa-dong, Kangnam-
gu, Seoul (02-515-7661/2)

Theatre Chun Choo

130-47, Tongsung-dong, Chongno-gu, Seoul
(02-766-7330)

Theatre Company Sanwoollim
327-9, Seokyo-dong, Map'o-gu, Seoul
(02-334-5915)

Theater Daejung
41-4, Myongryun-dong 2-ga, Chongno-gu,
Seoul (02-741-0251)

Theater Chen Mang
1th Fl. , 5-15, Ehwa-dong, Chongno-gu, Seoul
(02-352-7235)

Theater Se Mi
Suite 601, Baekam Bldg. , Tongsung-dong,
Chongno-gu, Seoul (02-743-8804)

Theatrical Company Arts House
4-108, Nogosan-dong, Map'o-gu, Seoul
(02-701-1978)

Third Stage Theatre, the
Suite 301, Hansung Bldg. , 112-21, Yongdu 2-
dong, Dongdaemoon-gu, Seoul
(02-929-6733)

Woo Ri Theater
14, Samseon-dong 4-ga, Seongbuk-gu, Seoul
(02-745-9710)

RELIGION

Christianity

Anglican Church in Korea
3, Chong-dong, Chung-gu, Seoul (02-738-6597)
Diocese of Seoul
3, Chong-dong, Chung-gu, Seoul (02-738-6597)
Diocese of Taejon
88-1, Seonhwa 2-dong, Chung-gu, Taejon
(042-256-9988)
Diocese of Pusan
1072-54, U 2-dong, Haeundae-gu, Pusan
(051-742-5742)
Catholic Conference of Korea
85-12, Neung-dong, Seongdong-gu, Seoul

(02-466-0123)
Archdiocese of Seoul
1, Myong-dong 2-ga, Chung-gu, Seoul
(02-771-7600)
Archdiocess of Taegu
225-1, Namsan 3-dong, Chung-gu, Taegu
(053-253-9440)
Archdiocese of Kwangju
5-32, Im-dong, Puk-gu, Kwangju (062-525-9004)
Catholic Priest Association for Justice
1, Myong-dong 2-ga, Chung-gu, Seoul
(02-777-0643)
Christian Academy
76, Suyu-dong, Tobong-gu, Seoul (02-900-3954)
Christian Literature Society of Korea
169-1, Samseong-dong, Kangnam-gu, Seoul
(02-553-0870)
Holy Spirit Association for the Unification of World Christianity
292-20, Dohwa-dong, Map'o-gu, Seoul
(02-711-5321)
Korea Assemblies of God
222, P'yong-dong, Chongno-gu, Seoul
(02-738-8711)
Korean Bible Society
1365-16, Seoch'o 2-dong, Seoch'o-gu, Seoul
(02-566-3061)
Korea Christian Cultural Institute
139-8, Taeshin-dong, Seodaemun-gu, Seoul
(02-392-2332)
Korea Evangelical Holiness Church
890-56, Taech'i-dong, Kangnam-gu, Seoul
(02-501-7085)
Korean Methodist Church
64-8, T'aep'yongro 1-ga, Chung-gu, Seoul
(02-399-2035)
National Council of Churches in

Korea
136-46, Yonji-dong, Chongno-gu, Seoul
(02-763-8427)
Prebyterian Church in Korea
136-56, Yonji-dong, Chongno-gu, Seoul
(02-743-8760)
Prebyterian Church of Korea
135, Yonji-dong, Chongno-gu, Seoul
(02-741-4350)
Salvation Army
58-1, Sinmunro 1-ga, Chongno-gu, Seoul
(02-732-1402)

Buddhism

Korean Buddhism Chogye Order
45, Kyonji-dong, Chongno-gu, Seoul
(02-735-5861)
Korea Buddhism Jingag Sect
22, Hawolgok-dong, Seongbuk-gu, Seoul
(02-913-0751)
Korean Buddhist Taego Order
292-1, Seongbuk-dong, Seongbuk-gu, Seoul
(02-745-2030)
Korean Buddist Ch'eontae Order
132-1, Baekja-ri, Danyong-gun,N. ch'ungchong
Prov.

Others

Association of Religion in Korea
1, Changkyo-dong, Chung-gu, Seoul
(02-756-3727)
Central Mission of Chondo-gyo
88, Kyongun-dong, Chongno-gu, Seoul
(02-732-3956)
Confucianism (Sungkyunkwan)
53, Myongryun-dong 3 ga,, Chongno-gu, Seoul
(02-765-0501)
Han-Ol Gyo
53-90, Ch'ongun-dong, Chongno-gu, Seoul
(02-777-2183)

Korea Muslim Federation
732-21, Hannam-dong, Yongsan-gu, Seoul
(02-794-7307)

Taejong-gyo
13-78, Hongeun 2-dong, Seodaemun-gu, Seoul
(02 389-8931)

Wonbul-gyo
344-2, Sinyong-dong, Iri, N. Cholla Prov.
(0653-50-3233, Seoul Office 02-813-2203)

NEWSPAPERS

Korean Language

Dong-A Ilbo
146-1, Ch'ungchongro 3-ga, Seodemun-gu,
Seoul (02-361-0114)

Chosun Ilbo
61, T'aep'yongro 1-ga, Chung-gu, Seoul
(02-724-5114)

Joong-ang Daily
7, Sunhwa-dong, Chung-gu, Seoul (02-7515-114)

Hankook Ilbo
14, Chunghak-dong, Chongno-gu, Seoul
(02-724-2114)

Hankyoreh Shinmun
116-25, Kongdok-dong, Map'o-gu, Seoul
(02-7100-114)

Kookmin Ilbo
371-6, Sinsu-dong, Map'o-gu, Seoul (02-7054-114)

Munhwa Ilbo
92, Mugyo-dong, Chung-gu, Seoul
(02-3108-114)

Daily Sports
14, Chunghak-dong, Chongno-gu, Seoul
(02-724-2114)

**Seoul Shinmun · Daily Sports
Seoul**
25, T'aep'yongro 1-ga, Chung-gu, Seoul
(02-735-7711)

Sports Chosun

61, T'aep'yongro 1-ga, Chung-gu, Seoul
(02-724-6114)

Kyunghyang Daily News
22, Cheong-dong, Chung-gu, Seoul
(02-730-5151)

Segye Times
63-1, Hangangro 3-ga, Yongsan-gu, Seoul
(02-799-4114)

RADIO & TELEVISION STATIONS

**Korean Broadcasting System
(KBS)**
18, Youido-dong, Yongdeungp'o-gu, Seoul
(02-781-1000)
Local Network: Pusan, Taegu, Taejon,
Kwangju, Ch'angwon, Chonju, Ch'unch'on,
Ch'ongju, Mokp'o, Yosu, Namwon, P'ohang,
Kongju, Kangnung, Sokch'o, Wonju, Cheju,
Chinju, Yongwol, Andong, Sunch'on, Kunsan,
Ch'ungju, Taebaek, Ulsan, Kongju

**Munhwa TV-Radio Broadcasting
Corp. (MBC)**
31, Youido-dong, Yongdeungp'o-gu, Seoul
(02-780-0114)

**Christian Broadcasting System
(CBS)**
917-1, Mok-dong, Yangch'on-gu, Seoul
(02-650-7000)

**Seoul Broadcasting System
(sbs)**
10-2, Youido-dong, Yongdeungp'o-gu, Seoul
(02-780-0006)

**Asia Broadcasting Company
(ABC)**
89, Sangsu-dong, Map'o-gu, Seoul (02-3200-114)

**Buddhist Broadcasting System
(BBS)**
140, Map'o-dong, Map'o-gu, Seoul (02-705-5114)

Education Broadcasting System

(EBS)
92-6, Umyon-dong, Seoch'o-gu, Seoul
(02-572-5021)

**Far-East Broadcasting Company
(FEBC)**
89, Sangsu-dong, Map'o-gu, Seoul
(02-3200-114)

**Pyonghwa Broadcasting Corp.
(PBC)**
2-3, Cho-dong 1-ga, Chung-gu, Seoul
(02-2702-114)

**Traffic Broadcasting System
(TBC)**
45, Toryom-dong, Chongno-gu, Seoul
(02-724-7114)

NEWS AGENCIES

Naewoe Press
42-2, Chuja-dong, Chung-gu, Seoul
(02-267-0439)

Yonhap News Agency
485-1, Susong-dong, Chongno-gu, Seoul
(02-3983-114)

PUBLISHERS

Daekyo Ltd.
446-3, Pangbae-dong, Seoch'o-gu, Seoul
(02-523-0909)
Children's Books, Reference Books

**Dong-A Publishing & Printing
Co. , Ltd.**
295-15, Toksan-dong, Kuro-gu, Seoul
(02-866-8800)
General Works, Philosophy, Religion, Social
Science, Pure Science, Technology, Art,
Language, Literature, History, Children's
Books, Periodicals, School References
English, Japanese, French, German, Spanish,

Chinese, Arabic

Eulyoo Publishing Co., Lid.
46-1, Susong-dong, Chongno-gu, Seoul,
K. P. O. Box 362 (02-732-4745)
Cable. EUL-YOO
Philosophy, Social Science, Language,
Literature, History
English, French, German

Han Gil Publishing Company
506, Shinsa-dong, Kangnam-gu, Seoul,
(02-515-4811/5)
Philosophy, Social Science, History, Periodicals

Han Shin Publishing
Suite 402, Yuson Bldg., 326-4, Kunja-dong,
Songdong-gu, Seoul (02-244-1520)
Philosophy, Language, Literature
English

Il Cho Kak
9, Kongp'yong-dong, Chongno-gu, Seoul
K. P. O. Box 279 (02-734-3545)
Cable. ILCHOPUBLICO
Philosophy, Religion, Social Science, Pure
Science, Technology, Art, Language,
Literature, History, Periodicals
English, Japanese

Il Ji-Sa
46-1, Chunghak-dong, Chongno-gu, Seoul
(02-732-3980/9320)
Philosophy, Religion, Social Science, Pure
Science, Art, Language, Literature, History,
Children's Books, Periodicals
English

Jisik Sanup Publications Co. , Ltd.
35-18, Tonguidong, Chongno-gu, Seoul
K. P. O. Box 1809
(02-734-1978/1958)
Religion, Social Science, Art, Literature
History, Children's Books
English, Japanese, Chinese

Ke Mong Sa
772, Yoksam-dong, Kangnam-gu, Seoul
(02-552-5500)

Children's Books, Periodicals

Kum Sung Publishing Co. , Ltd.
242-63, Kongdok-dong, Map'o-gu, Seoul
Map'o P. O. Box 92
(02-713-9651/8)
General Works, Philosophy, Religion, Social
Science, Art, Language, Literature, History,
Children's Books
English, Japanese

Si-sa-yong-o-sa, Inc.
55-1, Chongno 2-ga, Chongno-gu, Seoul
K. P. O. Box 148 (02-274-0509)
Tlx. SLSASEL K34193
General Works, Language, Literature,
Periodicals, School References
English

Tai Hak Dang
45-1, Tonui-dong, Chongno-gu, Seoul
(02-745-1336)
Art, Language, History

Sam Seong Publishing Co. , Ltd.
5th Fl. , Daeo Bldg., 26-5, Youido-Dong,
Yongdeungp'o-gu, Seoul (02-761-2907)
General Works, Philosophy, Social Science,
Pure Science, Art, Language, Literature,
Children's Books, Periodicals, English, French,
German, Japanese

Hollym Corporation; Publishers
14-5, Kwanchol-dong, Chongno-gu, Seoul
(02-735-7551/4)
Art, Language, Literature, History, Children's
Books
English, Japanese, German

Korea Froebel Co. , Ltd.
Nocksack Jipanii Bldg., 649-5, Yeoksam-dong,
Kangnam-gu, Seoul (02-345-4000)
Children's Books

Hyun-Am Publishing Co.
627-5, Ahyon-dong, Map'o-gu, Seoul
(02-365-5051)
Literature, Social Science, Philosophy
Periodicals

Youl Hwa Dang
506, Shinsa-dong, Kangnam-gu, Seoul
(02-515-3141/3)
Art, Literature
English, Japanese, French

Chip Moon Dang
251-1, Shindang 1-dong, Chung-gu, Seoul,
(02-234-2227, 232-3461)
Social Science, Pure Science, Technology, Art,
Language, General Works

Mi Jin Sa
327-10, Sogyo-dong, Map'o-gu, Seoul
(02-336-6085/3121)
Art

Kuk Min Seo Gwan Publishing Co. , Ltd.
257-3, Kongdok-dong, Map'o-gu, Seoul
C. P. O. Box 8519 (02-710-7777)
General Works, Philosophy, Religion, Social
Science, Pure Science, Art, Language,
Literature, Children's Books, Periodicals

COPYRIGHT AGENCIES

DRT International
Graden Tower Bldg., 98-78, Unni-dong,
Chongno-gu, Seoul
C. P. O. Box 290 (02-745-3350)
Literary Works, Art Works, Children's Works

IPS Copyright Agency
Kongp'yong Bldg. , 5-1, Kongp'yong-dong,
Chongno-gu, Seoul K. P. O. Box 469
(02-734-2666, 738-5432)
Literary Works

Korea Music Copyright Association
2nd Fl. , Samjon Chemical Bldg., 236-3,
Nonhyon-dong, Kangnam-gu, Seoul, 135-010
(02-547-7080)
Music Works

Korea Radio & TV Right

Association

Suite 401, Kumsam Bldg. , 17-1, Youido-dong, Yongdeungp'o-gu, Seoul
(02-782-1696)
Literary Works

Korea Society of Authers

Suite 1007, Sungwoo Bldg. , 51-1, Dowha-dong, Map'o-gu, Seoul (02-704-2325)
Literary Works, Photographic Works

Pan Korea Book Corp.

1-222, Shinmunro 2-ga, Chongno-gu, Seoul
(02- 733-2014)
Literary Works

Shin Won Agency Co.

147-44, Dongkyo-dong, Map'o-gu, Seoul
(02-335-6388)
Literary Works

Shinhan Publishing Media Co. , Ltd.

Suite 707, Hanaro Bldg. , 194-4, Insa-dong, Chongno-gu, Seoul (02-732-5573)
Literary Works

Yeong Mun Copyright Agency

69-1, Samseong-dong, Kangnam-gu, Seoul
(02- 756-8944/5)
Literary Works

OVERSEAS BOOKS TRADE AGENCY

Art and Design Book Center

8-6, Ehwa-dong, Chongno-gu, Seoul
(02-741-2557)

Chongno Book Center Co. , Ltd.

84-9, Chongno 2-ga, Chongno-gu, Seoul
(02-732-2331)

Dong Hwa Books

727-2, Yongdu 2-dong, Tongdaemun-gu, Seoul
(02-928-2784)

Eul-Yoo Publishing Co. , Ltd.
46-1, Susong-dong, Chongno-gu, Seoul
(02-734-3515)

Jin-Myong International Inc.

Suite 201, Kyungkee Bldg. , 170-10, Pangi-dong, Songp'a-gu, Seoul (02- 424-3860/1)

Korea Britannica Corporation

5th Fl. , Shanglim Bldg. , 151-11, Shanglim-dong, Chung-gu, Seoul (02- 275-2151/5)

Korea Overseas Publication Inc.

1-160, Shinmunno 2-ga, Chongno-gu, Seoul
K. P. O. Box 2558 (02-735-5401/4)

Kukje Books Co.

23-8, Ch'ungmuro 1-ga, Chung-gu, Seoul
(02-775-4851/2)

Kumi Trading Co. , Ltd.
983-41, Pangbae 3-dong, Seoch'o-gu, Seoul
(02-588-6667)

Kyobo Book Center Co. , Ltd.

1rt Fl. , Kyobo Bldg. , Chongno 1-ga, Chongno-gu, Seoul, Kwang Hwa Moon P. O. Box 1658
(02-739-2710)

Nae Woe Publishing Co. , Ltd.

1rt Fl. , Jaewoong Bldg, 176-11, Nonhyon-dong, Kangnam-gu, Seoul (02-518-7866/7)

Pan Korea Book Corporation

1-222, Shinmunro 2-ga, Chongno-gu, Seoul
(02-733-2001/8)

Panmun Book Co. , Ltd.

40, Chongno 1-ga, Chongno-gu, Seoul, 110-121
(02-732-5131/3)

Science Publication Center

Suite 201, Taekyong Bldg. , Hapchong-dong, Map'o-gu, Seoul P. O. Box 101 (02-325-4015/6)

Sejong Book Center Inc.

2nd Fl. , Shopping Mall, Lotte World, 40-1, Chamshil-dong, Songp'a-gu, Seoul
(02- 423-8551)

Shin Ho Trading Co.

Suite 303, Yangch'on Bldg. , 1338-27, Seoch'o-dong, Seoch'o-gu, Seoul (02-556-0734)

Shinhan Publishing Media Co. , Ltd.

Suite 707, Hanaro Bldg. , 194-4, Insa-dong,
Chjongno-gu, Seoul (02-732-5573)

STM Marketing Korea Inc.

337-15, Taehung-dong, Map'o-gu, Seoul
(02-718-5343)

Tongbang Publication Service Inc.

1589-5, Century Officetel, Seoch'o-dong, Seoch'o-gu, Seoul (02-778-3960)

Ulchi Book Center

6, Ulchiro 2-ga, Chung-gu, Seoul (02-757-8991/5)

PUBLISHING RELATED ORGANIZATIONS

Ilsan Publishing City Cooperative

506, Shinsa-dong, Kangnam-gu, Seoul
(02-511-9566/8)

Korea Electronic Publishing Association

150, P'alpa'n-dong, Chongno-gu, Seoul
(02-722-6486)

Korea Foreign Book Importers Association

Kumi-Bldg., 983-41, Pangbae 3-dong, Seoch'o-gu, Seoul (02-582-8908)

Korea Magazine Association

174-1, Ch'ongjin-dong, Chongno-gu, Seoul
(02-735-9464)

Korean Library Association

San 60-1, Panp'o 2-dong, Seoch'o-gu, Seoul
(02-535-4868)

Korean National Commission for UNESCO

10th Fl, Sungwoon Bldg., 141, Samseong-dong, Kangnam-gu, Seoul (02-776-2661/7)

Korean Publishers Association

105-2, Sagan-dong, Chongno-gu, Seoul
(02-735-2701/3)

Korean Printing Cultural Association

352-26, Sokyo-dong, Map'o-gu, Seoul
(02-335-5881/3)

Korean Publishing Cooperatve

448-6, Shinsu-dong, Map'o-gu, Seoul
(02-716-5621/3)

The Korea Publishing Fund

105-2, Sagan-dong, Chongno-gu, Seoul
(02-732-1434/5)

Korean Publishing Research Institute

105-2, Sagan-dong, Chongno-gu, Seoul
(02-739-9040)

Korean Study Materials Association

105-111, Gongdok-dong, Map'o-gu, Seoul
(02-718-4050)

National Booksellers Association

Suite 403, Hangul-Center, 58-14, Sinmunro 1-ga,
Chongno-gu, Seoul (02-733-3997/8)

National Centural Library

San 60-1, Panp'o-dong, Seoch'o-gu, Seoul
(02-535-4142/5)

Copyright Deliberation and Conciliation Committee

San 60-1, Panp'o-dong, Seoch'o-gu, Seoul
(02-596-8404/5)

INTERNATIONAL ORGANIZATIONS

Counsel of International Organization of Folklore Festival(CIOFF) Korean National Committee

526, Namdaemunro 5-ga, Chung-gu, Seoul
(02-753-6554)

Cultural and Social Center for the Asian and Pacific Region(ASPAC)

94-267, Yongdeungp'o-dong, Yongdeungp'o-gu, Seoul (02-679-7835)

Federation International des Editeurs de Journaux et Publications(FIEJ)

13F., Korea Press Center Bldg., 25, T'aep'yongro
1-ga, Chung-gu, Seoul (02-733-2251)

International Human Rights League of Korea

340-2,T'aep'yongro 2-ga, Chung-gu, Seoul
(02-717-9611)

International Press Institute(IPI) Korean National Committee

25, T'aep'yongro 1-ga, Chung-gu, Seoul
(02-732-6005)

Korean-American Education Commission(KAEC)

89-4, Kyongun-dong, Chongno-gu, Seoul
(02-732-7926)

Korean National Commission for United Nations Educational, Scientific and Cultural Organization(UNESCO)

50-16, Myong-dong 2-ga, Chung-gu, Seoul
(02-776-2661)

Korea Northeran Relations Council

58, Hyoch'ang-dong, Yongsan-gu, Seoul
(02-711-5520)

Korean PEN Center

238, Sinmunro 1-ga, Chongno-gu, Seoul
(02-720-8897)

Moral Re-Armament(MRA) Korea Headquarters

139-45, Hongje-dong, Seodaemun-gu, Seoul
(02-690-3620)

Press Foundation of Asia(PFA) Korean National Committee

25, T'aep'yongro 1-ga, Chung-gu, Seoul
(02-732-6005)

Professors World Peace Academy

63-1, Hangangro 3-ga, Yongsan-gu, Seoul
(02-792-8911)

United Nations

Association of Korea

115-3, Kwonnong-dong, Chongno-gu, Seoul
(02-764-8998)

United Nations Children's Fund(UNICEF) Seoul Office

17-1, Ch'angseong-dong, Chongno-gu, Seoul
(02-736-7862)

United Nations Development Program(UNDP) Seoul Office

353-8, Sindang-dong, Chung-gu, Seoul
(02-237-9563)

United Nations Korean War Allies Association

11-11, Youido-dong, Yongdeungp'o-gu, Seoul
(02-785-4088)

World Health Organization (WHO) Representative in Korea

1, Chungang-dong, Kwach'on, Kyonggi Prov.
(02-503-7533)

World Taekwondo Federation (WTF)

San 635, Yeoksam-dong, Kangnam-gu, Seoul
(02-557-5446)

Korea Esperanto Association

20, Sinch'eon-dong, Songp'a-gu, Seoul
(02-419-4081)

GENERAL

Association of Commenorative Services for Patriot Kim Koo

5-38, Hyoch'ang-dong, Yongsan-gu, Seoul
(02-719-1312)

Association of Meritorious Supporters of Korea Independence

194, Wonnam-dong, Chongno-gu, Seoul
(02-745-3155)

Central Committee for National Unification of Korea

824-21, Yeoksam-dong, Kangnam-gu, Seoul

(02-557-7771)

Dosan Memorial Foundation
Tongsung-dong, Chongno-gu, Seoul
(02-737-2078)

Hung Sa Dan
(Young Korean Academy)
1-28, Tongsung-dong, Chongno-gu, Seoul
(02-743-2511)

Information Culture Center
645-11, Deungch'on-dong, Kangseo-gu, Seoul
(02-606-4032)

International Youth Culture Exchange Association
12-37, Namdaemunro 5-ga, Chung-gu, Seoul
(02-752-7383)

Korea Foundation
526, Namdaemunro 5-ga, Chung-gu, Seoul
(02-753-6461)

Korean Association for Conservation of Nature
280-17, Pullkwang-dong, Unp'yong-gu, Seoul
(02-383-0694)

Korean Council on Foreign Relation
710, Yeoksam 2-dong, Kangnam-gu, Seoul
(02-566-8025)

Korean National Red Cross
32, Namsan-dong 3-ga, Chung-gu, Seoul
(02-755-9301)

Korea Survey(Gallup) Polls Ltd.
221, Sajik-dong, Chongno-gu, Seoul
(02-736-8448)

National Parks Association of Korea
19, Naeja-dong, Chongno-gu, Seoul
(02-736-9656)

RESEARCH INSTITUTES

Academy of Korean Studies (AKS)
50, Unjung-dong, Seongnam, Kyonggi Prov.
(0342-234-8111)

Institute for East Asian Studies
508-143, Chongneung 2-dong, Seongbuk-gu, Seoul (02-917-4462)

Institute for North Korea Studies
431-4, Changan-dong, Tongdaemun-gu, Seoul
(02-248-2392)

Institute of Asian Studies
814, Yeoksam-dong, Kangnam-gu, Seoul
(02-563-9911)

Institute of Modern Society
San 26-4, Hasanun-dong, Seongnam, Kyonggi Prov. (0342-236-2000)

International Religions Research Institute
137-15, Sangbong-dong, Chungrang-gu, Seoul
(02-434-9683)

National Academy of Arts (NAA)
San 94, Panp'o-dong, Seoch'o-gu, Seoul
(02-591-8166)

National History Compilation Committee(NHCC)
2-6, Chungang-dong, Kwach'on, Kyonggi Prov.
(02-503-8811)

ACADEMIC SOCIETIES

American Studies Association of Korea
Seoul Nat'l Univ., San 56-1, Sillim9-dong, Kwanak-gu, Seoul (02-880-6224)

Architectural Institute of Korea
635-4, Yeoksam-dong, Kangnam-gu, Seoul
(02-553-4715)

Geological Society of Korea
Kangwon Nat'l Univ., San 192-1, Hyoja 2-dong, Ch'unch'on, Kangwon Prov. (0361-50-6114)

Korea Academic Society of Tourism
Kyonggi Univ.; San 94-6, Iui-dong, Changan-gu, Suwon, Kyonggi Prov. (0331-6-2175)

Korea Advanced Farmers Association
301-87, Ich'on-dong, Yongsan-gu, Seoul
(02-795-1748)

Korean Association for Public Administration
304-28, Sajik-dong, Chongno-gu, Seoul
(02-736-4977)

Korean Association of Buddhist Studies
Dongguk Univ., 26, P'il-dong 3-ga, Chung-gu, Seoul (02-260-3096)

Korean Folklore Society
Chungang Univ.; 221, Huksok-dong, Tongjak-gu, Seoul (02-810-2057 Ext. 2065)

Korean Geographical Society
Korea Univ.; 1-2, Anam-dong 5-ga, Seongbuk-gu, Seoul (02-926-2641)

Korean History Association
P'yong-dong, Chongno-gu, Seoul (02-739-0036)

Korean Language Society
Seoul Nat'l Univ.; San 56-1, Sillim-9-dong, Kwanak-gu, Seoul (02-880-6034)

Korean Society for Journalism and Communication Studies
Chungang Univ., 221, Huksok-dong, Tongjak-gu, Seoul (02-810-2114)

Korean Society for the Study of Education
San 92-6, Umyon-dong, Seoch'o-gu, Seoul
(02-572-4696)

Korean Society of Food Science and Technology
635-4, Yeoksam-dong, Kangnam-gu, Seoul
(02-566-9937)

Society for Korean Archaeology
Korea Univ., 1-2, Anam-dong 5-ga, Seongbuk-gu, Seoul (02-920-1717)

EDUCATION AND SCHOLARSHIP FOUNDATIONS

Asan Foundation
388-1, P'ungnap-dong, Songp'a-gu, Seoul
(02-480-3114)

Association for Fostering Korea Children
7-12, Sinch'eon-dong, Songp'a-gu, Seoul
(02-413-1010)

Daewoo Foundation
526, Namdaemunro 5-ga, Chung-gu, Seoul
(02-779-3741)

FKTU (Federation of Korean Trade Union)
Scholarship Foundation 35, Seoul
(02-815-0181 Ext. 242)

Heung Han Foundation
1337-34, Seoch'o-dong, Seoch'o-gu, Seoul
(02-557-8628)

International Cultural Foundation
185, Kahoe-dong, Chongno-gu, Seoul
(02-763-1347)

Jungsan Scholarship Foundation
11-293, Hannam-dong, Yongsan-gu, Seoul
(02-795-3457)

Jungsu Scholarship Foundation
22, Chong-dong, Chung-gu, Seoul (02-738-0132)

Korean Association of Private Secondary School Principals
19, Naeja-dong, Chongno-gu, Seoul (02-739-5613)

Korea Coal Scholarship Foundation
80-6, Susong-dong, Chongno-gu, Seoul
(02-734-1204)

Korean Council for University Education
27-2, Youido-dong, Yongdeungp'o-gu, Seoul
(02-783-3065)

Korean Cultural Foundation Inc.
25, Neung-dong, Seongdong-gu, Seoul
(02-452-0002)

Korea Heart Foundation
11-9, Sinch'eon-dong, Songp'a-gu, Seoul
(02-414-5321)

Korea Institute of Life-long Education
198-1, Kwanhun-dong, Chongno-gu, Seoul
(02-732-1196)

Korea Literature Foundation
292-1, Ch'ungjongro 3-ga, Seodaemun-gu, Seoul
(02-313-3013)

Korean Private Educational Foundation Association
44-15, Youido-dong, Yongdeungp'o-gu, Seoul
(02-783-8418)

Korea Research Foundation
199-1, Tongsung-dong, Chongno-gu, Seoul
(02-741-4631)

Korea Scholarship Foundation
539-6, Teungch'on-dong, Kangseo-gu, Seoul
(02-602-6141)

Korea Science and Engineering Foundation
181, Kachong-dong, Yusong-gu, Taejon
(042-869-6114 Seoul Office 02-525-4491)

Korea Science Foundation
960-12, Taech'i-dong, Kangnam-gu, Seoul
(02-555-0701)

Korea Teachers Mutual Fund
35-3, Youido-dong, Yongdeungp'o-gu, Seoul
(02-783-0131)

Korea Tourism Scholarship Foundation
10, Ta-dong, Chung-gu, Seoul (02-757-2345)

Korean Traders Scholarship Foundation
1337-31, Seoch'o-dong, Seoch'o-gu, Seoul
(02-568-6196)

May 16 National Awards Foundation
538, Tohwa-dong, Map'o-gu, Seoul
(02-716-7672)

Paek Sang Foundation
14, Chunghak-dong, Chongro-gu, Seoul
(02-724-2241)

Samsung Foundation of Art and Culture
250, T'aep'yongro 2-ga, Chung-gu, Seoul
(02-752-0767)

Samil Cultural Foundation
169-3, Wonhyoro 4-ga, Yongsan-gu, Seoul
(02-712-6573)

Sammi Cultural Foundation
1004, Taech'i-dong, Kangnam-gu, Seoul
(02-557-8302-

Sungkok Academic Cultural Foundation
24-1, Ch'o-dong 2-ga, Chung-gu, Seoul
(02-273-4823)

Yonam Foundation
20, Youido-dong, Yongdeungp'o-gu, Seoul
(02-785-7142)

Yonkang Foundation
13, Chongro 4-ga, Chongno-gu, Seoul
(02-763-8151)

Yook Young Foundation
San 3-39, Neung-dong, Seongdong-gu, Seoul
(02-458-2007)

PRESS SOCIETIES

Announcer Association of Korea
31, Youido-dong, Yongdeungp'o-gu, Seoul
(02-789-3493)

Broadcasting Producer Association of Korea
61-3, Youido-dong, Yongdeungp'o-gu, Seoul
(02-782-2814)

Foundation for the Broadcast Culture
168-9, Yomri-dong, Map'o-gu, Seoul (02-714-6181)

Journalists Association of Korea
25, T'aep'yongro 1-ga, Chung-gu, Seoul

(02-734-9321)

Korean Broadcasters Association

25, T'aep'yongro 1-ga, Chung-gu, Seoul

(02-735-7117)

Korean Broadcasting Deliberations Committee

25, T'aep'yongro 1-ga, Chung-gu, Seoul

(02-735-2641)

Korea Copy Editors Association

25, T'aep'yongro 1-ga, Chung-gu, Seoul

(02-732-1267)

Korea Journalists Club

25, T'aep'yongro 1-ga, Chung-gu, Seoul

(02-732-4797)

Korea Journalists Fund

25, T'aep'yongro 1-ga, Chung-gu, Seoul

(02-733-7011)

Korean Newspaper Editors Association

25, T'aep'yongro 1-ga, Chung-gu, Seoul

(02-733-2251)

Korea Photo Journalists Association

25, T'aep'yongro 1-ga, Chung-gu, Seoul

(02-733-9576)

Korea Press Center

25, T'aep'yongro 1-ga, Chung-gu, Seoul

(02-733-7011)

Korean Press Ethics Commission

25, T'aep'yongro 1-ga, Chung-gu, Seoul

(02-734-3081)

Korean Press Institute

25, T'aep'yongro 1-ga, Chung-gu, Seoul

(02-733-9434)

Korea Proof Readers Association

25, T'aep'yongro 1-ga, Chung-gu, Seoul

(02-732-7368)

Korea Women Journalists Club

61, T'aep'yongro 1-ga, Chung-gu, Seoul

(02-724-5381)

Kwanhun Club

25, T'aep'yongro 1-ga, Chung-gu, Seoul

(02-732-0876)

Press Arbitration Commission

25, T'aep'yongro 1-ga, Chung-gu, Seoul

(02-732-6031)

Press Foundation of Asia Korean National Committee

25, T'aep'yongro 1-ga, Chung-gu, Seoul

(02-732-6005)

Seoul Foreign Correspondents' Club

25, T'aep'yongro 1-ga, Chung-gu, Seoul

(02-734-3272)

Seoul Press Foundation

541, Namdaemunro 5-ga, Chung-gu, Seoul

(02-778-1707)

Shinyong Journalism Fund of Kwanhun Club

25, T'aep'yongro 1-ga, Chung-gu, Seoul

(02-732-0876)

Sungkok Foundation for Journalism

188, Ch'ongjin-dong, Chongno-gu, Seoul

(02-734-0342)

SPORTS

Korea Amateur Sports Association (KASA)

88, Oryun-dong, Songp'a-gu, Seoul

(02-420-3333)

Membership of KASA: Athletics, Swimming, Football, Baseball, Tennis, Softball Tennis, Basketball, Volleyball, Table Tennis, Handball, Rugby Football, Cycle, Boxing, Wrestling, Weight Lifting, Judo, Archery, National Archery, Shooting, Gymnastics, Hockey, Fencing, Badminton, Taekwondo, Skating, Ski, Ice Hockey, Sirum(Korean Wrestling), Yacht, Bowling, Golf, Canoeing, Modern Pentathlon iñ Biathlon Union, Kumdo, Equestrian, Roller Skating, Rowing, Water Ski, Alpine, Body Building, Sepaktakraw, Wu-Shu, Softball, Under Water

Korean Olympic Committee(KOC)

88, Oryun-dong, Songp'a-gu, Seoul

(02-420-4214)

Korea Baseball Organization(KBO)

946-16, Togok-dong, Kangnam-gu, Seoul

(02-557-7887)

Korea Boxing Commission

40-171, Hangangro 3-ga, Yongsan-gu, Seoul

(02-792-2244)

Kuk Ki Won

635, Yeoksam-dong, Kangnam-gu, Seoul

(02-567-3024)

Seoul Olympic Sports Promotion Foundation

88, Oryun-dong, Songp'a-gu, Seoul(02-4101-114)

WOMEN AND YOUTH

Boy Scouts of Korea

18-3, Youido-dong, Yongdeungp'o-gu, Seoul

(02-782-1867)

Consumers Union of Korea

272-1, Hannam-dong, Yongsan-gu, Seoul

(02-795-1042)

Girl Scouts of Korea

163, Anguk-dong, Chongno-gu, Seoul

(02-733-4347)

Holt Children's Services, Inc

382-14, Hapjong-dong, Map'o-gu, Seoul

(02-332-7501)

Joongang Women's Association

7, Pomun-dong 2-ga, Seongbuk-gu, Seoul

(02-928-2107)

Korean Association of University Women

423-44, Ss'angmun-dong, Tobong-gu, Seoul (02-995-7811)

Korean Businesswomen's Association

16-2, Youido-dong, Yongdeungp'o-gu, Seoul (02-783-4952)

Korea Catholic Women's Organization

1, Myong-dong 2-ga, Chung-gu, Seoul (02-776-5618)

Korean Children's Center

San 3-39, Neung-dong, Seongdong-gu, Seoul (02-458-0541)

Korean Federation of Business Professional Women's Culb

408, Apgujong-dong, Kangnam Seoul (02-514-5200)

Korea Federation of House-Wives' Clubs

1-2, Namch'ang-dong, Chung-gu, Seoul (02-752-4227)

Korean League of Women Voters

11-9, Sinch'eon-dong, Songp'a-gu, Seoul (02-423-5355)

Korean National Council of Women

40-427, Hankangro 3-ga, Yongsan-gu, Seoul (02-793-5196)

Korea National Federation of Women's Welfare Service

427-5, Kongdeok-dong, Map'o-gu, Seoul (02-712-0713)

Korean National Mothers' Association

100-4, Nonhyon-dong, Kangnam-gu, Seoul (02-512-0488)

Korean Women's Association

105-191, Kongdeok-dong, Map'o-gu, Seoul

(02-701-7321)

Korean Women's Development Institute

1-363, Pulgwang-dong, Unpyong-gu, Seoul (02-356-0070)

Korea Youth Hostel Association

80, Cheokseon-dong, Chongno-gu, Seoul (02-725-3031)

Korea Youth League

396, Sindaebang-dong, Tongjak-gu, Seoul (02-841-9291)

National Council of Consumer Protection Organization

40-427, Hankangro 3-ga, Yongsan-gu, Seoul (02-790-4050)

National Council of Housewives Classes

19-3, Ch'ungmuro 5-ga, Chung-gu, Seoul (02-265-3627)

National Council YMCAs of Korea

112-34, Sogong-dong, Chung-gu, Seoul (02-754-7891)

National Council of Youth Organization in Korea

396, Sindaebang-dong, Tongjak-gu, Seoul (02-841-8548)

National YWCA

1-3, Myong-dong 1-ga, Chung-gu, Seoul (02-774-9702-

Saemaul Women's Federation

1093, Hwagok-5-dong, Kangseo-gu, Seoul (02-605-7000)

Saesak Society

541, Namdaemunro 5-ga, Chung-gu, Seoul (02-752-0907)

Women's Research Association

18, Mukchong-dong, Chung-gu, Seoul (02-273-7645)

RECREATION AND SOCIAL CLUBS

Corean Alpine Club

4F.,Taein Bldg., Yeoksam-dong Kangnam-gu, Seoul (02-539-1781)

Hankuk Kiwon(Go)

13-4, Kwanch'ol-dong, Chongno-gu, Seoul (02-734-9819)

Korean Alpine Federation

3F.,Duwon Bldg., 840-9,Yeoksam-dong, Kangnam-gu (02-539-8851)

Korea Fishing Association

57-1, Inui-dong, Chongno-gu, Seoul (02-747-0501)

Korea Golf Association

36-2, Youido-dong, Yongdeungp'o-gu, Seoul (02-783-4748)

Korea Gliding Association

11-9, Sinch'eon-dong, Songp'a-gu, Seoul (02-423-3405)

Korea Professional Golfers Association

315, Hongik-dong, Seongdong-gu, Seoul (02-294-9988)

Lions Clubs International Multiple District 309 Korea

80, Cheokseon-dong, Chongno-gu, Seoul (02-734-5111)

Rotary International (Korea)

5, Tangju-dong, Chongno-gu, Seoul (02-736-8550)

Current Status of Public Museums

Public Museums & Specialty Museums Founded by the Central Government

Museum	Address	Characteristics of Museum and No. of items in Collection
The National Museum	1, Sejongno, Chongno-gu, Seoul (02-738-3800) *Date of Foundation* : 1908 *Area(p'yŏng)* : 3,091	119,690 pieces from of Three Kingdoms to Chosŏn period including Buddhist statues, paintings, ceramics, and cultural relics of the pre-historic era. A museum of archaeology,history and art based on the Chosŏn royal art collection
Kyongju Nationl Museum	76, Inwang-dong, Kyongju, N. Kyongsang Prov. (0561-772-5192) *Date of Foundation* : Sept. 1913 *Area(p'yŏng)* : 923	14,632 pieces of relics excavated from Anapchi, and various relics of Silla period and prehistoric era-such as gold crown, goldware, glassware earthenware, and stoneware.
Kwangju National Museum	San 83-3, Maegok- dong, Puk-gu, Kwangju (062-571-1419) *Date of Foundation* : Dec. 6, 1978 *Area(p'yŏng)* : 583	34,024 pieces of stoneware, earthenware, tiles, Buddhist statues, metal artifacts from prehistoric to Koryo period centered on Honam district, celadons of Koryo and Chosŏn periods, relics salvaged from Shinan and Wando seabed, and paintings & writings from Chosŏn period
Chonju National Museum	893-1, Hyoja-dong, Wansan-gu, Chonju N. Cholla Prov. (0652-223-5650) *Date of Foundation* : Oct. 26, 1990 *Area(p'yŏng)* : 799	3,087 pieces of Koryo celadon, metal artifacts and folk data that reveal the cultural life of prehistoric era in Cholla Province

Museum	Address	Characteristics of Museum and No. of items in Collection
Ch'ongju National Museum	San 81, Myongam-dong, Ch'ongju N. Ch'ungch'ong Prov. (0431-55-1631) *Date of Foundation* : Oct. 30, 1987 *Area(p'yŏng)* : 437	A systematic and educational display of cultural relics excavated from the Chungwon cultural district, farly printing relics from Three Kingdoms to Chosŏn period, 3, 602 objects

Museum	Address	Characteristics
Chinju National Museum	171-1, Namseong- dong, Chinju, S. Kyongsang Prov. (0591-42-5950) *Date of Foundation* : Nov. 2, 1984 *Area(p'yŏng)* : 715	1,096 relics from the Kaya Period and cultural objects from the Japanese Invasion of 1592

Current Status of Public Museums

Public Museums & Specialty Museums Founded by the Central Government

Museum	Address	Characteristics of Museum and No. of items in Collection
Puyo National Museum	San 16-1, Tongnam-ri, Puyo-up, Puyo-gun, S. Ch'ungch'ong Prov. (0463-33-8561) *Date of Foundation* : 1929 *Area(p'yŏng)* : 680	7,867 objects of various Paekche relics such as metalwork, precious stones, earthenware & ceramics, bone & horn-made instruments, wooden & bamboo products, silk products, textile products, writings & paintings excavated from Paekche relic sites
Kongju National Museum	284-1, Chung-dong, Kongju, S. Ch'ungch'ong Prov. (0416-54-2205) *Date of Foundation* : 1934 *Area(p'yŏng)* : 230	7,981 objects excavated from King Muryong's tomb in 1971 and etc.

Kyongju National Museum

Museum	Address	Characteristics of Museum and No. of items in Collection
The National Folk Museum	1, Sejongno, Chongno-gu, Seoul (02-734-1346) *Date of Foundation* : 1946 *Area(p'yŏng)* : 1,515	17,453 pieces that provide a glimpse of Korean folk life displayed in 3 halls, 15 permanent exhibition rooms and a specialty exhibition hall
The National Museum of Contemporary Art	San 58-1, Makgye- dong, Kwach'eon, Kyonggi Prov. (02-503-7744) *Date of Foundation* : Aug. 26, 1986 *Area(p'yŏng)* : Indoor 4,278, Outdoor 10,000	Systematical collection, preservation and exhibition of modern arts of historic value. The museum sponsors various programs such as modern art classes and youth art classes through its Modern Art Hall Association. Introduction of Korean culture overseas through art exchanges. 3, 450 objects
Chosŏn Period's Court Relics Exhibition Hall	5-1, Cheong-dong, Chung-gu, Seoul (02-752-0735) *Date of Foundation* : Dec. 23, 1992 *Area(p'yŏng)* : 752	5,872 court relics, such as sculpture, wrapping cloths, personal ornaments and clothes
Admiral Lee Ch'ung-mu's Relics Exhibition Hall	Premises of Hyeonch'ungsa, Paekam-ri, Yomch'i-up, Asan- gun, S. Ch'ungch'ong Prov. (0418-44-2161) *Date of Foundation* : April. 28, 1960 *Area(p'yŏng)* : 106	153 relics of Admiral Lee Sun-sin (including 9 examples of 3 kinds of relics designated National Treasures, 6 examples of 4 kinds of treasures)

Current Status of Public Museums

Public Museums & Specialty Museums Founded by the Central Government

Museum	Address	Characteristics of Museum and No. of items in Collection
National Science Museum	32-2, Kuseong- dong, Yuseong-gu, Taejeon (042-861-2524) *Date of Foundation* : Oct. 9, 1990 *Area(p'yŏng)* : 1,728	5,570 pieces related to space & mankind, Korean nature and history of science & technology, the understanding & adaptation of nature, and harmony between nature, man and science
Seoul National Science Museum	2, Waryong-dong, Chongno-gu, Seoul (02-762-5204) *Date of Foundation* : April. 27, 1990 *Area(p'yŏng)* : 2,695	Data on the history of nature, science & technology, natural science and technology. 2,920 objects on 133 themes
Diplomacy Museum	1376-2, Seoch'o 2-dong, Seoch'o- gu, Seoul.Foreign Affairs Security Research Center (02-571-1020) *Date of Foundation* : Feb. 16, 1993 *Area(p'yŏng)* : 30	About 140 pieces related to foreign affairs since late Chosŏn period
Postal Museum	21, Ch'ungmuro 1-ga, Chung-gu, Seoul (02-756-2858) *Date of Foundation* : May. 1, 1985 *Area(p'yŏng)* : 500	Approximately 160,000 objects, such as postal documents and data from the era of the Postal Ch'ongguk period which first introduced the postal system until the modern times
Communications Museum	39-7, Kyonji- dong, Chongno-gu, Seoul (02-734-8369) *Date of Foundation* : Dec. 4, 1972 *Area(p'yŏng)* : 30	The Ministry of Communication acquired the building used as *Cheoneuigam* around 1600 and the Postal Ch'ongguk in 1884 after Korea's Independence, and copied part of the data in the Postal Museum in 1972 and put about 300 of them on display

Museum	Address	Characteristics of Museum and No. of items in Collection
Forestry Museum	Chikdong-ri, Soheol-myon, P'och'on-gun, Kyonggi Prov. (0357-32-1448). *Date of Foundation* : April. 20, 1987 *Area(p'yŏng)* : 1,400	25,000 examples of 10,832 species of trees, such as coniferous and broadleaf trees, animals, plants, fossils, and forestry tools
Chinju Forestry Museum	South Forestry Testing Site, Forestry Research Center, Kajwa-dong Chinju, S. Kyongsang Prov. (0591-759-8231) *Date of Foundation* : Sep. 1, 1992 *Area(p'yŏng)* : 196	6,082 examples of 3,000 species of academic forestry specimens from the southern region
Railroad Museum	31-4, Wolam-dong, Euiwangshi, Kyonggi Prov. (0343-61-3610) *Date of Foundation* : Jan. 26, 1988 *Area(p'yŏng)* : Indoor-686, outdoor-585	1,877 relics of railroad history, 509 vehicles, 295 pieces of electric, signal and communication equipment, 168 facility, line maintenance, construction & construction products, 858 pieces of drive equipment, 3,986 pieces of railroad-related data.

Current Registry Status of Museums and Art Museums

Museums(Art Museums) Registered under the Museum & Art Museum Promotion Law

Museum	Address	Collection, No. of objects
Agricultural Museum	75, Ch'ungjeongno 1-ga, Chung-gu, Seoul (02-397-5673/7)	Farming tools, 457
Andong Folklore Museum	784-1, Seongkok-dong, Andong, N.Kyongsang Prov. (0571-3-0649)	Folklore relics, 232
Ch'amsori Phonograph Audio Museum	216-15, Songjeong-dong, Kangneung, Kangwon Prov. (0391-41-2500)	Phonographs, etc. 105
Changgikap Beacon Museum	Taebo-ri, Taebo- myon, Yongil-gun, N. Kyongsang Prov. (0562-84-9376)	Information related to Horses
Chungmun Folklore Museum	2563-1, Chungmun-dong, Seokwip'o, Cheju Prov. (064-32-5511)	Folklore relics, 232
Cheju Folklore Museum	2505, Samyang 3-dong, Cheju, Cheju Prov. (064-55-1976)	Folklore relics, 203
Cheju Folklore & Natural History Museum	996-1, Ildo 2-dong, Cheju, Cheju Prov. (064-22-2465)	Archaeological and folklore data, 2,383
Cheju Sculpture Park, Shin-ch'onji Art Museum	Kwangryong 2-ri, Aewol-up, Pukcheju-gun, Cheju Prov. (064-48-2137)	Sculptures, 430

Museum	Address	Collection
Ch'ongju Early Printing Museum	866, Unch'on-dong, Ch'ongju, N. Ch'ungch'ong Prov. (0431-69-0556)	Ancient publications, 110
Ch'ungju Museum	190-1, Songnae-dong, Ch'ungju, N. Ch'ungch'ong Prov. (0441-43-7702)	Folklore data, 973
Currency Museum	35, Kacheong-dong, Yuseong-gu, Taejeon (042-861-5201)	Currency, 499
Haekang Porcelain Museum	330-1, Sukwang-ri, Shindun-myon, Ich'on-gun, Kyonggi Prov. (0336-34-2266)	Porcelains, 112
Hanpat Educational Museum	113-1, Samsong-dong, Tong-gu, Taejeon (042-622-5399, 042-626-5394)	Educational affairs data, 604
Hanwon Art Museum	1449-12, Seoch'o- dong, Seoch'o-gu, Seoul (02-588-5642)	Paintings, 123
History of Straw & Grass Life Museum	97-9, Ch'ongdam-dong, Kangnam-gu, Seoul (02-516-5585)	Straw artifacts, 100

Current Registry Status of Museums and Art Museums

Museums(Art Museums) Registered under the Museum & Art Museum Promotion Law

Museum	Address	Collection
Ho-Am Art Museum	204, Kashil-ri, P'okok-myon, Yongin-gun, Kyonggi Prov. (0335-30-3553)	Archaeological data, paintings, 350
Hongsan Museum	67-5,Yangjae-dong, Seoch'o-gu, Seoul (02-572-7496)	Earthenwares, 862
Horim Museum	903-27, Taech'i-dong, Kangnam-gu, Seoul (02-566-8329)	Earthenwares, 532
Hwangi Art Museum	210-8, Puam-dong, Chongno-gu, Seoul (02-725-7701)	Paintings, 130
Inch'on Municipal Museum	San 525, Okryon- dong, Nam-gu, Inch'on (032-865-2570)	Porcelains, 200
Independence Memorial Hall	230, Namhwa-ri, Mokch'on-myon, Ch'onan-gun, S. Ch'ungch'ong Prov. (0417-60-0114)	Publications, 1046
Kangneung Folk Historical Records	177-4, Chukheon-dong, Kangneung, Kangwon Prov. (0391-40- 4499) 330-1, Sukwang-ri,	Folklore data, 612
Keoch'ang Museum	216-5, Kimch'on-ri, Keoch'ang-up, Keoch'ang-gun, S. Kyongsang Prov. (0598-944-8218)	Archaeological data, 170

Museum	Address	Collection
Keojae Museum	1565, Okp'o 2-dong, Changseungp'o S. Kyongsang Prov. (0558-687-6790)	Archaeological relics, 204
Kondulbau Museum	733-4, Taebong-dong Chung-gu, Taegu (053-421-6677)	Shamanism data, 478
Korean Magazine Museum	174-1, Ch'ongjin-dong, Chongno-gu, Seoul (02-735-9464, 02-738-7326/9)	Magazines, 120
Korean Art Museum	P'ungseong Bldg., 7th F, 51-12, Panp'o 4-dong, Seoch'o-gu, Seoul (537-6413/4)	Korean paintings, 130
Korean Buddhist Art Museum	108-4, Wonseo-dong, Chongno-gu, Seoul (02-747-3000)	Buddhist art, 200
Korean Furniture Museum	9-11, Seongbuk-dong, Seongbuk-gu, Seoul (02-766-0168)	Furnitures, 222
Korea Museum of Modern Costome	13-1, Nam san-dong 3-ga, chung-gu, Seoul (02-319-5497)	Clothes, 1,500
Korean Ski Museum	106-28, Hun-ri, Kanseong-up, Koseong-gun, Kangwon Prov. (0392-681-5030, 0392-681-2788)	Ski data, 224
Kwangju Municipal Art Museum	San 34-1, Unam-dong, Puk-gu, Kwangju (062-521-7556)	Western paintings, 142
Kwangju Municipal Folklore Museum	1005, Yongbong-dong, Puk-gu, Kwangju (062-521-9041)	Folklore relics, 105
Kyonggi Province Folk HistoricalRecordsRoom	1, Maesan-ro 3-ga, Kwonseon-gu, Suwon, Kyonggi Prov. (042-42-6161)	Archaeological and folklore data, 696
Lotte World Folk Village	40-1, Chamshil-dong, Songp'a-gu, Seoul (02-411-4762, 02-419-4454)	Earthenwares, 217
Masa Museum	685, Chuam-dong, Kwach'on, Kyonggi Prov. (02-500-1283, 02-500-1818)	Information related to Horses
Miryang Municipal Museum	318-1, Naeil-dong, Miryang, S. Kyongsang Prov. (0527-354-3294)	Paintings & writings, 224

Current Registry Status of Museums and Art Museums

Museums(Art Museums) Registered under the Museum & Art Museum Promotion Law

Museum	Address	Collection
Mokam Art Museum	30-3, Pyokjae-dong, Koyang, Kyonggi Prov. (0344-62-9214)	Sculptures, 166
Mok-a Buddhism Museum	395-2, Iho 1-ri, Kangch'on-myon, Yoju-gun, Kyonggi Prov. (0337-85-9954)	Artifacts, 1,033
Moran Art Museum	246-1, Wolsan-ri, Hwado-up, Namyangju-gun, Kyonggi Prov. (0346-594-8001)	Sculptures, 106
Munshin Art Museum	51-1,Chusan-dong, Happ'o-gu,Masan, S.Kyonsang Prov. (0551-21-5050)	Sculptures, 290

Museum	Address	Collection
Museum of Korean Embroidery	89-4, Nonhyon-dong, Kangnam-gu, Seoul (02-515-5114/7)	Clothes, 121
Myongga Kimch'i Museum	159-1, Samseong-dong, Kangnam-gu, Seoul (02-562-1075)	Food dishes, 263
Naju Pear Museum	384-5, Seokcheon-ri, Kumch'on-myon, Naju-gun, S. Cholla Prov. (0613-31-5038)	Farming tools, 219
Namjin Art Museum	477-1, Sammak-ri, Yimhoe-myon, Chindo-gun, S. Cholla Prov. (0632-43-0777)	Oriental paintings, 110
Onggi Folklore Museum	497-15, Ssangmun-dong, Tobong-gu, Seoul (02-900-0399)	Earthenwares, 300

Current Registry Status of Museums and Art Museums

Museums(Art Museums) Registered under the Museum & Art Museum Promotion Law

Museum	Address	Collection
Onyang Folklore Museum Horim Museum	403-1, Kwonkok-dong, Onyang, S. Ch'ungch'ong Prov. (0418-42-6001)	Folklore data, 410
Pusan Municipal Museum	948-1, Taeyon 4- dong, Nam-gu, Pusan (051-624-6341)	Archaeological data, 211
Samsung Publishing Museum	340-2, Tangsan-dong, 6-ga, Yongdeungp'o-gu, Seoul (679-4597)	Publications, 105
Seoul Design Museum	757-1, Pangbae-dong, Seoch'o-gu, Seoul (02-590-3473)	Daily appliances, 146
Sonjae Art Museum	370, Shinp'yong- dong, Kyongju, N. Kyongsang Prov. (0561-745-7075)	Western paintings, 120
Song-am Art Museum	587-145, Hakik-dong, Nam-gu, Inch'on (032-869-2602)	Porcelain, 149
South Cholla Yongsanho Agricultural Museum	307, Nabul-ri, Samho-myon, Yongam-gun, S. Cholla Prov. (0631-78-2796)	Farming tools, 120
Taejeon Folk Historical Records Hall	145-3, Munhwa-dong, Chung-gu, Taejeon (042-580-4359)	Folklore data, 214
T'ae-p'yongyang Chemicals Museum	686-5, Sindaebang-dong, Tongjak-gu, Seoul (02-832-3486)	Metalwares, 890
Taekwanryong Museum	374-3, Eoheul-ri, Seongsan-myon, Myongju-gun, Kangwon Prov. (0391-41-4683)	Folklore data, 230
T'ongdosa Seungbo Museum	583, Chisan-ri, Hapuk-myon, Yangsan-gun, S. Kyongsang Prov. (0523-82-7195)	Buddhist paintings, 650
Tongjinsuri Folklore Museum	105, Yoch'on-dong, Kimjae, N. Cholla Prov. (0658-547-3121)	Farming tools, 725
Total Outdoor Art Museum	10-2, Ilyong-ri, Changheung-myon, Yangju-gun, Kyonggi Prov. (0351-40-5791)	Sculptures, 104

Museum	Address	Collection
Uiryong County Museum	8-24, Tong-dong, Uiryong-up, Uiryong-gun, S. Kyongsang Prov. (0555-73- 6800)	Folklore data, 252
Walker Hill Art Museum	Cheju Sculpture Park, Shin-ch'onji Art Museum	Paintings, 150
Woljon Art Museum	35-1, P'alp'an-dong Chongno-gu, Seoul (02-732-3777)	Paintings & writings, 140
Yong-il Folklore Museum	39-8, Songnae-ri, Hunghae-up, Yongil-gun, N. Kyongsang Prov. (0562-40-0224)	Daily appliances, 2,371

Data Provided by University Museum Association (University: 72/ Industrial University: 1/ Junior College: 2)

Museum (Managing Department)
Address (Tel.)
Date of Foundation (Area-pyong)
Characteristics of Museum and No. of
Collections

Konkuk University Museum
93-1, Mojin-dong, Seongdong-gu, Seoul
(02-450-3880/2)
March 1, 1963 (450, outdoor 100)
4,854 pieces such as jades, bone &
horn made instruments, paintings &
writings, old documents, including 6
volumes of National Treasure No.142
(Tongkuk Chŏng-un)

Kyunghee University Museum
1, Hoegi-dong, Tongdaemun-gu, Seoul
(02-961-0141)
Oct 1955 (2,921)
5,841 pieces of metalware, earthenware, ceramics, rubbing of paintings &
writings from prehistoric era to modern times

Korea University Museum
1, Anam-dong 5-ga, Seongbuk-gu, Seoul
(02-920-1114)
1934 (1,808)
95,000 pieces of archaeological and
historical relics, folklore, ceramics,
paintings & writings, traditional
industrial equipment, and modern art

Kookmin University Museum
861-1, Chongneung-dong, Seongbuk-gu, Seoul
(02-910-4212)
July 5, 1973 (778)
12,107 pieces of stoneware, earthenware, ceramics, metal artifacts, paintings, rubbing, folklore items from prehistoric era to modern times

Dankook University Museum
San 8, Hannam-dong, Yongsan-gu, Seoul
(02-709-2186)
July 3, 1967 (114.92, outdoor 200)
9,907 pieces of relics of archaeological
art, measuring instruments, learning
tools used in traditional schools of
Three Kingdoms period to Chosŏn
period

Dongguk University Museum
26, P'il-dong 3-ga, Chung-gu, Seoul
(02-260-3462)

Sep 3, 1963 (371.2)
2,613 pieces of archaeological and art
data related to Buddhism (including
13 National Treasures)

Dongduk Women's College Museum
23-1, Hawolgok- dong, Seongbuk-gu, Seoul
(02-913-2001)
May 27, 1977 (523.4)
179 objects, including 18 pieces of
earthenware & ceramics, 11 paintings
& writings, 20 wooden & bamboo
products

Duksung Women's College Museum
419, Ssangmun-dong, Tobong-gu, Seoul
(02-901-8131)
1971 (255)
2,189 objects, including 323 pieces of
earthenware & ceramics, 403 metalware, 100 precious stones, 162 paintings & writings

Sogang University Museum
1, Sinsu-dong, Map'o-gu, Seoul
(02-705-8215)
1973 (99.174)
1,500 objects, mainly paintings and
writings, and folklore artifacts from
Chosŏn period

Seoul National University Museum
San 56-1, Sillim 2-dong, Kwanak-gu, Seoul
(02-874-5693)
1940 (1,980)
6000 objects (including 3 treasure),
earthenware, ceramics, metal artifacts,
paintings & writings, bone & horn
instruments, and data on archaeology,
art history and folklore

Seoul Municipal University Museum

8-3, Cheonnong-dong, Tongdaemun-gu, Seoul
(02-210-2285)
1984 (352.9)
1,035 objects, including 317 pieces of earthenware & ceramics, 107 pieces of metalware, 45 precious stones, 227 paintings & writings

Sungkyunkwan University Museum

San 53, Myongryun-dong 3-ga, Chongno-gu Seoul
(02-760-1217)
June 22, 1964 (290.5)
11,210 objects(including one treasure), earthenware, ceramics, metalware, old documents, paintings & writings, relics of Buddhism culture.

Sungshin Woman's University Museum

249-1, Tongseon-dong 3-ga, Seongbuk-gu, Seoul (02-920-7325)
Sep 1, 1966 (277)
2,155 objects(including 1 treasure), including 322 earthenware & ceramics, 393 precious stones, 500 paintings & writings, 392 wooden & bamboo products, 219 pieces of metalware

King Sejong University Museum

98 Kunja-dong, Seongdong-gu, Seoul
(02-460-0075-6)
May 5, 1973 (2,160)
4,058 pieces of clothing and personal ornaments from late Chosŏn period

Sookmyung Women's University Museum

53-12, Ch'ongp'a-dong 2-ga, Yong-san-gu, Seoul
(02-710-9134)

June 10, 1971 (3,636)
4,035 pieces related to female customs, old documents, metalware, earthenware, wooden & bamboo products, rubbings of paintings & writings (including 65 National Treasures & treasures)

Soongsil University Museum (Korean Christian Museum)

1-1, Sangdo 1-dong, Tongjak-gu, Seoul
(02-820-0751)
Oct 10, 1967 (1,233)

6,695 objects(including 19 National Treasures and treasures), such as data on Catholicism & Protestantism and *Tanyusaemunkyong*

Yonsei University Museum

134, Sinch'on-dong, Seodaemun-gu, Seoul
(02-361-3335/43)
March 15, 1965 (2720.7, outdoor 1,360.4)
143,360 objects (including 1 treasure) including data on prehistoric era, history, art, folklore, medicine, geology, fossils and old documents

Data Provided by University Museum Association (University: 72/ Industrial University: 1/ Junior College: 2)

Military Academy Museum

P.O.Box 77-1, Kongneung-dong, Nowon-gu, Seoul (02-970-2571)
May 1, 1985 (2,966, outdoor 2,364)
A museum specializing in various military data, from prehistoric era to present. 7,963 pieces (12 treasures) of military data, such as *Ch'onja T'ongt'ong* and *Pusanjin-sunjeoldo.*

Ewha Woman's University Museum

11-1, Taehyon-dong, Seodaemun-gu, Seoul
(02-360-3152)
1935 (1,542)
Earthenware, blue celadon, white celadon, paintings & writings from Three Kingdoms to Chosŏn Period (1 National Treasure, 11 treasures)

Ewha Woman's University Museum of Natural History

11-1, Taehyon-dong, Seodaemun-gu, Seoul
(02-360-3155)
Nov 20, 1969 (495)
55,000 examples of 5,000 species of fossils, animals & plants, and minerals.

Presbyterian Theological College Museum

353, Kwangjang-dong, Seongdong- gu, Seoul
(02-453-3101)
July 1983 (194.4)
450 objects, including religious paintings, ceramics, folklore artifacts and paintings.

Hanyang University Museum

17, Haengdang-dong, Seongdong-gu, Seoul (02-290-1394)
Dec 1978 (780, outdoor 100)
4,980 objects, including earthenware & ceramics, paintings & writings, folk-lore items, wooden artifacts, steel-ware, and traditional industrial manufacturing tools

Hongik University Museum

72-1, Sangsu-dong, Map'o-gu, Seoul
(02-320-1322)
Feb 1, 1967 (2,854)
2,500 objects, including ancient art pieces such as paintings & writings, Buddhist statues, earthenware, ceramics, woodenware, sculptures and modern art pieces

Hankuk University of Foreign Studies Museum

270, Imun-dong, Tongdaemun-gu, Seoul
(02-961-4124)
To be opened
3,000 objects (including 12 treasures) including 909 pieces of earthenware & ceramics, 242 metalware, 77 precious stones, 511 paintings & writings, 492 wooden & bamboo products

Dong-a University Museum

1, Tongdaeshin-dong 3 ga, Seo-gu, Pusan
(051-240-2671~4)
Nov 1, 1959 (620, outdoor 300)
21,792 objects (including 12 National Treasure & treasures), mainly relics excavated from Pusan, S. Kyongsang Province

Tongeui University Museum

San 24, Kaya-dong, Chin-gu, Pusan
(051-890-1412-3)
May7, 1986 (734.006)
2,714 objects, including 1,223 pieces of earthenware & ceramics, 1,181 metalware, 224 precious stones, 72 paintings & writings

Pusan National University Museum

San 30, Changjeon-dong, Keumjeong-gu, Pusan (051-510-1835-9)
May 1964 (594, outdoor 396)
17,002 objects such as the relics of the Nedilhic era, the Bronze Age and Kaya period excavated from Pusan, S. Kyongsang Province.

Pusan Women's College Museum

1528, Yonsan-dong, Tongnae-gu, Pusan
(051-860-5281)
Dec 1984 (141)
1,248 objects. Relics from the Three Kingdoms and Kaya period

Kyongseong University Museum

110-1, Taeyon-dong, Nam-gu, Pusan
(051-622-5331)
May 1971 (200, outdoor 10)
6,251 objects, including ceramics, personal ornaments, rubbings of paintings & writings, books and paintings

Pusan Fisheries College Museum

599-1, Taeyon 3-dong, Nam-gu, Pusan (051-622-3951)
March5, 1984 (898.5)
582 objects of marine data, such as fishery eqipment, various kinds of fish, stuffed specimens, and a fish donated by the President of Morocco

Pusan Women's College (Seolsong) Museum

74, Yangjeong-dong, Chin-gu, Pusan
(051-82-0081)
July 20, 1983 (99)
500 pieces on Tado

Kyemyong University Museum

2139, Taemyong-dong, Nam-gu, Taegu
(053-620-2171)

May 20, 1978 (657)
2,078 objects, including metalware, precious stones, earthenware, ceramics from prehistoric to Choson Period

Kyongbuk University Museum
1370, Sankyok- dong, Puk-gu, Taegu
(053-952-2996)
May 28, 1959 (2,485, outdoor 13,824)
6,709 objects(including 7 treasures) including earthenware and ceramics from Three Kingdoms, Koryo, and Chosŏn period

Taegu University Museum
15, Naeri-ri, Chinryang-myon, Kyongsan-gun, N. Kyongsang Prov. (0541-50-5216)
1994 (planned)
2,552 objects related to Korean history, culture, art and folklore

Taegu Teachers' College Museum
1797-6, Taemyong-dong, Nam-gu, Taegu
(053-620-1471/2)
Sep, 1975 (173, outdoor 90)
1,937 objects, including 1,100 examples of earthenware & ceramics, 320 metalware, 171 paintings & writings, etc.

Inha University Museum
253, Yonghyon-dong, Nam-gu, Inch'on
(032-860-7861, 8260)
1982 (264)
130 objects, including 80 examples of earthenware & ceramics, 50 wooden & bamboo products, etc.

Chonnam National University Museum
300, Yongbong-dong, Puk-gu, Kwangju
(062-520-7785)
May 7, 1957 (400)
5,772 objects, including earthenware,

ceramics, metal artifacts, paintings & writings, copies of weapons, data on archaeology, folklore and art

Tongsin College Museum
177, Tuam-dong, Puk-gu, Kwangju
(062-512-2010)
1983 (1,320)
2,600 objects, including earthenware, blue & white celadon, paintings & writings, folklore paintings from Kaya to Chosŏn period

Chosun University Museum
375, Seoseok-dong, Tong-gu, Kwangju
(062-230-6333)
May 15, 1992 (100)
213 objects including 43 examples of earthenware & ceramics, 45 pieces of metalware, 2 precious stones, 8 paintings & writings, 90 wooden & bamboo products

Chosun University Art Museum
375, Seoseok-dong, Tong-gu, Kwangju
(062-230-7832)
Nov 20, 1989 (766)
220 Western & Korean paintings, sculptures and artifacts

Kwangju Teachers' College Museum
1-1, P'ungyang-dong, Puk-gu, Kwangju
(062-55-8506)
1987 (247, outdoor 49)
936 objects including 336 pieces of earthenware & ceramics, 227 pieces of metalware, 25 precious stones, 63 paintings & writings, 231 wooden & bamboo products

Chungnam National University Museum

220, Kung-dong, Yusong-gu, Taejeon
(042-821-6040/2)
April 28, 1968 (7293 outdoor 660)
1,799 objects, including such as Paekche earthenware, paintings & writings, metalware, wooden & stoneware

Hannam University Museum
133, Ojeong-dong, Tong-gu, Taejeon
(042-629-7696)
June 1982 (600)
Folklore products, including earthenware, paintings & writings and books, animals and plants

Taejon University Museum
96-3, Yongun-dong, Tong-gu, Taejon
(042-280-2800)
Oct 27, 1984 (275)
913 objects, including 318 pieces of ceramics, 307 paintings & writings, 116 pieces of earthenware, 49 pieces of bronzeware, 34 books, 14 Buddhist statues, etc.

Kyonggi University Museum
San 94-6, Iui-dong, Changan-gu, Suwon
(0331-40-7141/1)
Oct 27, 1983 (500)
1,000 pieces of earthenware & ceramics, metalware, etc.

Myongji University Museum
San 38-2, Nam-ri, Yongin-gun, Kyonggi Province (0335-35-4001)
1979 (1,574.8)
4,327 items mainly paintings & writings, and earthenware. Personal handwriting of King Sunjo and a screen which belonged to Chang Sŭng-ŏp

Data Provided by University Museum Association (University: 72/ Industrial University: 1/ Junior College: 2)

Hanshin University Museum

411, Yangsan-dong, Osan, Kyonggi Province
(0339-72-3341/2)
March 1991 (93)
565 objects of earthenware & ceramics, paintings & writings, folklore data

Chungang University Museum

Nae-ri, Taedok-myon, Ansong-gun,
Kyonggi Province (0334-675-3101/9)
June 1954 (904)
936 objects, including 296 piece of earthenware & ceramics, 166 pieces of metalware, 27 precious stones ,62 paintings & writings, 228 wooden & bamboo products, 130 leather items, 24 ancient clothes, 3 other items

Kwandong University Museum

San 72-1, Naekok-dong, Kangneung, Kangwon Province (0391-497-480)
1973 (1,290)
6,578 relics related to on the archaeology, history, culture, folklore art of the Yŏngdong district

Kangneung College Museum

San 1, Chibyon-dong, Kangneung,
Kangwon Province (0391-640-2596)
1974 (92)
2,500 pieces of relics belonging to the New Stone Age and Bronze Age found mainly in Yongdong district

Kangwon National University Museum

192-1, Hyoja 2- dong, Ch'unch'on,
Kangwon Province (0361-50-8025/7)
1979 (684)
7,593 pieces of earthenware & ceramics, metalware, paintings & writings from prehistoric era to modern times

Hallim University Museum

1, Okch'on-dong Ch'unch'on,
Kangwon Province
(0361-58-1825/8)
May 18, 1988 (150)
1,374 objects including 621 pieces of earthenware & ceramics, 89 metalware, 5 paintings & writings, etc.

Air Force Academy Museum

Ssangsu-ri, Namil-myon, Ch'ongwon-gun,
N. Ch'ungch'ong Province
(0431-53-9164/6)
Dec 21, 1985 (2,178, outdoor 16,500)
1,915 objects

Ch'ongju Teachers' College Museum

15, Sukok-dong, Ch'ongju,
N. Ch'ungch'ong Province (0431-68-6340)
March 1, 1981 (91, outdoor 187)
446 pieces of stoneware, ceramics, folklore items, old documents, paintings & writings, rubbings, copies, etc.

Ch'ongju University Museum

36, Naedok-dong, Ch'ongju,
N. Ch'ungch'ong Province (0444-51-8666)
1968 (720, outdoor 700)
852 items including relics from the area submerged by Ch'ungju Dam (Chungwon Mirŭk Temple site, and Hŭngdok Temple site)

Chungbuk National University Museum

San 18, Kaeshin-dong, Ch'ongju,
N. Ch'ungch'ong Province (0431-61-2901/2)
Sep 27, 1970 (589)
3,164 objects

Ch'ungju Industrial College Museum

123, Komdan-ri, Iyu-myon, Chungwon-gun,
N. Ch'ungch'ong Province (0441-841-5114)
Apri 1, 1980 (30)
350 objects including historical, archaeological, artistic artifacts and folklore data

Hanguk Teachers' College Museum

San 7, Tarak-ri, Kangnae-myon, Ch'ongwon-gun, N. Ch'ungch'ong Province
(0431-60-3821)
April 1, 1987 (413)
221 objects including 85 pieces of earthenware & ceramics, 10 pieces of metalware, 1 precious stone, 55 paintings & writings, 1 wooden & bamboo product

Kongju Teachers' College Museum

376, Ponghwang-dong, Kongju,
S. Ch'ungch'ong Province (0416-50-1351)
1975 (292)
799 objects of historical, archaeological art, artifacts and folklore data, etc.

Kongju University Museum

182, Shinkwan-dong, Kongju,
S. Ch'ungch'ong Province (0346-53-2151)
March 1, 1970 (235)
Mainly research and collection of on relics from Paekche period. 660 relics from prehistoric to modern times

Chonbuk National University Museum

Teokchin-dong 1-ga, Teokchin-gu, Chonju,
N. Cholla Province (0652-70-3488)
May 1, 1961 (258)
12,000 items such as farming tools, metalcrafts from prehistoric to modern times

Chonju Teachers' College Museum

128, Tongsohak-dong, Wansan-gu, Chonju, N. Cholla Province (0652-85-7102)
July 25, 1974 (325.54)
1,044 objects including 267 pieces of earthenware & ceramics, 229 pieces of metalware, 118 precious stones, and 465 wooden & bamboo products

Chonju University Museum

Hyoja-dong 3-ga, Chonju,
N. Cholla Province (0652-220-2159)
1984 (1,500)
2,305 objects, including earthenware, ceramics, metalware, old art pieces, Korean paintings, sculptures, artifacts, and modern art

Wonkwang University Museum

344-2, Shinyong-dong, Iri, N. Cholla Province (0653-50-5482/3)
Jan 1968 (2,310)
8,721 objects related to folklore and folk religion, mainly of N. Cholla Province from prehistoric to modern times

Kunsan University Museum

San 68, Mirong-dong, Kunsan
N. Cholla Province (0654-60-1184)
May 17, 1984 (190.9)
1,116 objects including 484 pieces of earthenware & ceramics, 242 pieces of metalware, 61 precious stones, 22 paintings & writings, 198 wooden & bamboo products

Mokp'o University Museum

61, Torim-ri, Ch'onggye-myon, Muan-gun,
S. Cholla Province (0631-52-4774/83)
1982 (132)
3,941 prehistoric relics, folklore objects, and old documents that reveal glimpses of cultural life in Southwest coastal region

Tongguk University Kyongju Museum

Kumjang-ri, Hyonkok-myon, Kyongju-gun
N. Kyongsang Province (0561-770-2462)
April 10, 1983 (280.5)
1,260 pieces of earthenware & ceramics

Andong University Museum

P.O.Box 200, Andong, N. Kyongsang Province (0571-50-5247/8)
March 12, 1979 (2,083.49)
2,888 historical relics and folklore data from Andong area

Yongnam University Museum

214-1, Tae-dong, Kyongsan, N. Kyongsang Province (053-810-3622)
Nov 1989 (2,348.7, outdoor 200,000)
12,317 objects such as old documents, clothes and metalware excavated from Yongnam area, mainly from pre-historic to Chosŏn era

Hyosong Woman's College Museum

330, Kumrak 1-ri, Hwayang-up, Kyongsan-gun
N. Kyongsang Province (0541-50-3281/4)
May 1977 (2,480.7)
2,942 objects including 1,459 piece of earthenware & ceramics, 636 pieces of metalware, 90 precious stones, 183 paintings & writings, 307 wooden & bamboo products

Kyongnam University Museum

449, Wolyong-dong, Happ'o-gu, Masan
S. Kyongsang Province (0551-49-2921)
Nov 18, 1976 (179)
4,648 objects including 1,359 pieces of earthenware & ceramics, 196 pieces of metalware, 2,607 paintings & writings

Ch'angwon University Museum

9, Sarim-dong, Ch'angwon
S. Kyongsang Province (0551-68-7815/6)
1986 (183.6)
6,340 objects including 4,119 pieces of earthenware & ceramics, 1,793 pieces of metalware, 166 precious stones, 3 paintings & writings, 243 wooden & bamboo products

Kyongsang University Museum

900, Kajwa-dong, Chinju,
S. Kyongsang Province (0591-751-5120/4)
1984 (490)
2,966 objects including 1,289 pieces of earthenware & ceramics, 1,488 pieces of metalware, 95 precious stones.

Naval Academy Museum

P.O.Box 88-1, #2, Aenggok-dong, Chinhae,
S. Kyongsang Province (0553-49-5015, 5816)
Jan 17, 1976 (1,270, outdoor 3,300)
3,943 pieces of data on Yi Sun-shin, navy and naval force, weapons and equipment, uniforms, medals, war records and souvenirs

Cheju University Museum

1, Ara 1-dong, Cheju, Cheju Province (064-55-8065)
March 20, 1967 (450)
5,000 pieces of folklore cultural data on Cheju Island

Current Status of Theaters

Name	Address	Seating Capacity	Lighting Facilities	Sound Facilities	Projection Facilities
Sejong Cultural Center	81-3, Sejongno, Chongno-gu, Seoul 02-736-2720	3,895 522	✦	🔊	🎥
Korean Culture and Arts Foundation, Munye Center	1-130, Tongsung-dong, Chongno-gu, Seoul 02-740-4520	709 200	✦	🔊	
Hoam Art Hall	7, Sunhwa-dong, Chung-gu, Seoul 02-751-5114	950	✦	🔊	🎥
National Theatre	San 14-67, Changch'ung-dong 2-ga, Chung-gu, Seoul 02-274-1151	1,518 454 300 1200	✦	🔊	
Sookmyung Women's Univ. Grand Auditorium	53-12, Ch'ongp'a-dong 2-ga, Yongsan-gu, Seoul 02-710-9045	1,500			

Sejong Cultural Center

Name	Address	Seating Capacity	Lighting Facilities	Sound Facilities	Projection Facilities
Little Angels Performing Arts Center	25, Neung-dong, Seongdong-gu, Seoul 02-450-0035	1,280	🔦	🔊	
Seoul Arts Center	700, Seoch'o-dong, Seoch'o-gu, Seoul 02-580-1114	2,346 711 2,608 400	🔦	🔊	📷
Children's Hall, Mujigae Theatre	San 3-39, Neung-dong, Seongdong-gu, Seoul 02-446-6062	1,035	🔦	🔊	📷
Seoul Education Cultural Center	202, Yangjae-dong, Seoch'o-gu, Seoul 02-571-8100	1,085	🔦	🔊	
Seoul Nori Madang	47, Chamshil-dong, Songp'a-gu, Seoul 02-414-1985	3,000			
Citizens' Hall	830-31, Peomil-dong, Tong-gu, Pusan 051-645-4951	2,020 450	🔦	🔊	📷
Cultural Hall	San 213-4, Taeyon 4-dong, Nam-gu, Pusan 051-625-8130	1,656 886 249	🔦	🔊	📷

Seoul Nori Madang

Current Status of Theaters

Name	Address	Seating Capacity	Lighting Facilities	Sound Facilities	Projection Facilities
KBS Pusan Hall	63, Namch'on 1-dong, Nam-gu, Pusan 051-620-7591	4,022	✓	✓	
Taegu Cultural Arts Center	187, Seongdang-dong, Talseo-gu, Taegu 053-652-0515	1,118 320	✓	✓	✓
Taegu Citizens' Hall	1, T'aep'yongno 2-ga, Chung-gu, Taegu 053-23-7441	1,654 396	✓	✓	✓
Inch'on Citizens' Hall	190-4, Chuan 1-dong, Nam-gu, Inch'on 032-82-3760	1,350	✓	✓	
Inch'on Composite Cultural Arts Center	965, Kuwol-dong, Namdong-gu, Inch'on 032-427-8401	1,612 568 440	✓	✓	
Kwangju Cultural Arts Center, Grand Theatre	San 34-1, Unam-dong, Puk-gu, Kwangju 062-528-3840	1,800	✓	✓	
Kwangju Citizens' Hall	21-1, Ku-dong, Seo-gu, Kwangju 062-675-3280	758	✓	✓	✓
Taejeon Citizens' Hall	1-27, Munhwa-dong, Chung-gu, Taejeon 042-253-4015	956 310	✓	✓	✓
Usong Art Hall	226, Chayang-dong, Tong-gu, Taejeon 042-628-3631	1,248	✓	✓	✓
Kyonggi-do Cultural Arts Hall	1117, Inkye-dong, Kwonseon-gu, Suwon, Kyonggi Province 0331-36-4121	1,904 554	✓	✓	✓
Suwon Citizens' Hall	San 2-1, Maesanno 3-ga, Kwonseon-gu, Suwon, Kyonggi Province 0331-42-5284	538	✓	✓	✓
Seongnam Citizens' Hall	3309-425, T'aep'yong 2-dong, Sujeong-gu, Seongnam, Kyonggi Prov. 0342-755-2267	1,084 296	✓	✓	

Name	Address	Seating Capacity	Lighting Facilities	Sound Facilities	Projection Facilities
Anyang Munye Center	550, Anyang 8-dong, Anyang, Kyonggi Province 0343-48-3006	1,500 527	🔦	🔊	📹
Puchon Citizens' Hall	788, Chung-dong, Wonmi-gu, Puch'on, Kyonggi Province	1,254 416	🔦	🔊	📹
Ch'unch'on Composite Munye Center	San 40-2, Hyoja 1-dong, Ch'unch'on, Kangwon Province 0361-50-3534	1,104	🔦	🔊	📹
Wonju Ch'iak Art Hall	589, Myongryun-dong, Wonju, Kangwon Province 0371-731-4042	720	🔦	🔊	
Kangneung Cultural Arts Center	408, Kyo 2-dong, Kangneung, Kangwon Province 0391-647-2005	550 200	🔦	🔊	
Sokch'o Cultural Center	570-5, Yongnang-dong, Sokch'o, Kangwon Province 0392-31-1173	750	🔦	🔊	📹
Ch'onan Citizens' Hall	471-1, Shinbu-dong, Ch'onan, S. Ch'ungch'ong Province 0417-63-6017	1,016 200	🔦	🔊	📹
Kongju Citizens' Hall	283, Ungjin-dong, Kongju, S. Ch'ungch'ong Province 0416-50-4467	645 190	🔦		
Seosan Cultural Center	514, Eupnae-dong, Seosan, S. Ch'ungch'ong Province 0455-60-2561	718	🔦	🔊	📹
Cheonbuk Art Hall	104-5, Kyongwon-dong 1-ga, Wansan-gu, Cheonju, N. Cholla Province 0652-84-4445	780	🔦	🔊	
Cheonbuk Students' Hall	301-70, Chinbuk-dong, Teokchin-gu, Cheonju, N. Cholla Province 0652-74-0131	1,503	🔦	🔊	📹
Cheongeup-shi Art Hall	87, Shigi-dong, Cheongju, N. Cholla Province 0681-535-9339	824	🔦	🔊	

Current Status of Theaters

Name	Address	Seating Capacity	Lighting Facilities	Sound Facilities	Projection Facilities
Chinp'o Cultural Center	790-3, Naun-dong, Kunsan, N. Cholla Province 0654-62-9308	1,001	✓	✓	✓
Iri Cultural Center	86, Namjung-dong 1-ga, Iri, N. Cholla Province 0653-53-3151	1,036	✓	✓	✓
Sunch'on Munye Center	183, Seokhyon-dong, Sunch'on, S. Cholla Province 0661-51-1722	728	✓	✓	
Kwangyang Iron & Steel Keumho Music Hall	674, Keumho-dong, Tongkwangyang, S. Cholla Province 0667-770-2667	1,088	✓		
Andong Citizens' Composite Hall	344, Myongryun-dong, Andong, N. Kyongsang Province 0571-50-0540	884 / 438	✓	✓	
Kumi Composite Cultural Arts Center	75, Songjeong-dong, Kumi, N. Kyongsang Province 0546-51-2707	1,364 / 386	✓	✓	✓
S. Kyongsang Prov. Cultural Arts Center	500-15, Ch'ilam-dong, Chinju, S. Kyongsang Province 0591-759-1501	1,469 / 280	✓	✓	✓
KBS Ch'angwon Hall	97-1, Shinwol-dong, Ch'angwon, S. Kyongsang Province 0551-80-7100	1,973	✓	✓	
KBS Ulsan Hall	416-7, Tal-dong, Nam-gu, Ulsan, S. Kyongsang Province 0552-70-7100	2,563	✓	✓	
Cheju-do Munye Center	852, Ildo 2-dong, Cheju, Cheju Province 064-53-9597	902 / 200	✓	✓	✓
Drama Center	8-19, Yejang-dong, Chung-gu, Seoul 02-778-0261	430	✓	✓	
Sungeui Music Hall	8-3, Yejang-dong, Chung-gu, Seoul 02-752-8924	1,990	✓	✓	
Yeongang Hall	270, Yeonji-dong, Chongno-gu, Seoul 02-708-5001	500	✓	✓	✓

Name	Address	Seating Capacity	Lighting Facilities	Sound Facilities	Projection Facilities
Nanp'a Music Hall	San 8, Hannam-dong, Yongsan-gu, Seoul	814 200	🔦	🔊	
Yonsei University Centennial Hall	134, Shinch'on-dong, Seodaemun-gu, Seoul 02-361-3818	904	🔦	🔊	
Viva Art Hall	736-1, Hannam-dong, Yongsan-gu, Seoul	359	🔦	🔊	
Kyemong Art Hall	772, Yeoksam-dong, Kangnam-gu, Seoul 02-559-5560	601	🔦		📽
Samp'ung Art Hall	San 192-4, Seoch'o-dong, Seoch'o-gu, Seoul 02-535-0002	700	🔦		
Hoban Stage	40-1, Chamshil-dong, Songp'a-gu, Seoul 02-411-2000	498	🔦	🔊	
Garden Stage	40-1, Chamshil-dong, Songp'a-dong, Seoul 02-411-2000	600	🔦	🔊	
Madang Cecil Theatre	3-7, Cheong-dong, Chung-gu, Seoul 02-737-5773	280	🔦	🔊	
Yeum Hall	58-1, Ch'ungjeongno 1-ga, Chung-gu, Seoul 02-736-3200	150	🔦	🔊	📽
Comedy Art Hall	50-44, Tongsung-dong, Chongno-gu, Seoul 02-743-8804	200	🔦	🔊	
Seongjwa Small Theatre	1-54, Tongsung-dong, Chongno-gu, Seoul 02-745-1214	150	🔦	🔊	
Hakjeon Small Theatre	1-79, Tongsung-dong, Chongno-gu, Seoul 02-763-8233	170	🔦	🔊	
Ch'ungdol 2 Theatre	1-97, Tongsung-dong, Chongno-gu, Seoul 02-764-5715	160	🔦	🔊	
Saemt'o Parangsae Theatre	1-115, Tongsung-dong, Chongno-gu, Seoul 02-763-8964	200	🔦	🔊	

Current Status of Theaters

Name	Address	Seating Capacity	Lighting Facilities	Sound Facilities	Projection Facilities
Tongsung Art Center, Small Theatre	1-130, Tongsung-dong, Chongno-gu, Seoul 02-740-4520	200	✦		
Semi Small Theatre	1-153, Tongsung-dong, Chongno-gu, Seoul 02-741-6069	170	✦	◀)	
Taehakno Theatre	178-1, Yongeon-dong, Chongno-gu, Seoul 02-764-6052	155	✦	◀)	
Pat'anggol Small Theatre	1-60, Tongsung-dong, Chongno-gu, Seoul 02-765-6681	220	✦	◀)	
Naksan Theatre	179-4, Hehwa-dong, Chongno-gu, Seoul 02-742-4848	180	✦	◀)	
Inkel Art Hall	41-4, Myongryun 2-ga, Chongno-gu, Seoul 02-741-0251	215	✦	◀)	

Name	Address	Seating Capacity	Lighting Facilities	Sound Facilities	Projection Facilities
Han Madang	109-1, Hehwa-dong, Chongno-gu, Seoul 02-743-1266	150	✓	✓	
Metro Hall	713, Sangkye 2-dong, Nowon-gu, Seoul 02-933-8344	200	✓	✓	
Keukdan Yedang	31-87, Nogosan-dong, Map'o-gu, Seoul 02-701-1978	120	✓	✓	✓
The Post Theatre	5-92, Ch'angjeon-dong, Map'o-gu, Seoul 02-337-5961	200	✓	✓	
Onnuri Art Hall	368-6, Hongeun-dong, Seodaemun-gu, Seoul 02-307-2900	220	✓	✓	
Hyundai To-Art Small Theatre	Hyundai Department Store, Trade Center, 159-7, Samseong-dong, Kangnam-gu, Seoul 02-552-2775	280	✓	✓	✓
Yurim Art Hall	584-1, Shinsa-dong, Kangnam-gu, Seoul 02-514-9600	252	✓	✓	
Hyundai Cultural Theatre	584-1, Shinsa-dong, Kangnam-gu, Seoul 02-514-9600	260	✓	✓	
Neunkkae Drama Hall	1487-3, Seoch'o-dong, Seoch'o-gu, Seoul 02-586-9863	200	✓	✓	
Lotte Art Theatre	40-1, Chamshil-dong, Songp'a-gu, Seoul	397	✓	✓	
Mukunghwa Hall	75, Keoje 1-dong, Tongnae-gu, Pusan 051-503-2484	1,784	✓		
Kyongseong University Concert Hall	70-1, Taeyon 3-dong, Nam-gu, Pusan 051-622-5331	600	✓	✓	✓
Nulwon Art Hall	825-3, Peomil-dong, Tong-gu, Pusan 051-631-0660	250	✓	✓	✓

Current Status of Theaters

Name	Address	Seating Capacity	Lighting Facilities	Sound Facilities	Projection Facilities
Fisheries University Auditorium	599-1, Taeyon 3-dong, Nam-gu, Pusan 051-622-3951	1,205	⚲		
Pusan Catholic Center, Small Theatre	29-1, Taech'ong-dong 4-ga, Pusan 051-462-1870	234	⚲	◀))	🎥
Chaeneung Educational Small Theatre	1240-12, Onchon 3-dong, Tongnae-gu, Pusan 051-505-6006	150	⚲	◀))	
Olympics Memorial People's Living Hall	1127-37, U 2-dong, Nam-gu, Pusan 051-744-1181	200	⚲		🎥
Kkoekkori Theatre	San 136-2, Hwangkeum-dong, Suseong-gu, Taegu 053-763-5693	710	⚲	◀))	🎥
Dong-a Cultural Center	53-3, Teoksan-dong, Chung-gu, Taegu 053-252-3364	410	⚲	◀))	

Name	Address	Seating Capacity	Lighting Facilities	Sound Facilities	Projection Facilities
Inch'on Cultural Center	7-4, Sungeui 4-dong, Nam-gu, Inchon 032-866-2019	184	●	●	
Olympics Memorial People's Living Hall	1246, Kuwol 2-dong, Namdong-gu, Inch'on 032-438-8182	188	●	●	●
Tolch'e Small Theatre	187, Kyong-dong, Chung-gu, Inch'on 032-72-7361	515	●	●	
Music Cultural Center	80-1, Chuan 1-dong, Nam-gu, Inch'on 032-429-0248	300		●	
Kkumnamu Small Theatre	572, Pup'yong 3-dong, Puk-gu, Inch'on 032-513-6364	150	●	●	
Kwangju Cultural Arts Center, Small Theatre	San 34-1, Unam-dong, Puk-gu, Kwangju 062-528-3840	515	●	●	
Kwangju Students' Independence Movement Memorial Hall, Student Theatre	56-1, Hwangkeum-dong, Tong-gu, Kwangju	600	●	●	●
Keumho Cultural Center	154-64, Tongmyong 1-dong, Tong-gu, Kwangju 062-22-2775	150	●	●	
Korea Advanced Institute for Science and Technology, Grand Auditorium	373-1, Kuseong-dong, Yuseong-gu, Taejeon 042-869-5114	1,000	●	●	●
Science Munye Center, Concert Hall	328, Toryong-dong, Yuseong-gu, Taejeon 042-869-6610	848	●	●	●

Current Status of Theaters

Name	Address	Seating Capacity	Lighting Facilities	Sound Facilities	Projection Facilities
Hannam University Small Theatre	133, Ojeong-dong, Taedeok-gu, Taejeon 042-629-7114	396	✓	✓	
Hannam University Open-Air Theatre	133, Ojeong-dong, Taedeok-gu, Taejeon 042-629-7114	300	✓		
Hannam University Seongji Hall	133, Ojeong-dong, Taedeok-gu, Taejeon 042-629-7114	1,612	✓	✓	
Catholic Cultural Center	189, Taeheung 1-dong, Chung-gu, Taejeon 042-257-0190	330	✓		
Christian Union, Service Center	1-13, Munhwa-dong, Chung-gu, Taejeon 042-254-2323	600	✓	✓	✓
Hanbat Library Performance Area	145-3, Munhwa 1-dong, Chung-gu, Taejeon 042-580-4215	428	✓	✓	✓
Yesul Madang Ukeumch'i	202-19, Seonhwa 3-dong, Chung-gu, Taejeon 042-254-2620	250	✓	✓	
Taejeon Cultural Institute, Cultural Love	1-166, Munhwa-dong, Chung-gu, Taejeon 042-256-3684	187	✓	✓	✓
Euijeongbu Citizens' Hall	678, Kaneong 1-dong, Euijeongbu, Kyonggi Province 0351-872-1755	477	✓	✓	
Olympic Memorial People's Living Hall	604, Kojan-dong, Ansan, Kyonggi Province 0351-83-6761	1,614	✓	✓	✓
Suwon Art Theatre	29-1, Namch'ang-dong, P'aldal-gu, Suwon, Kyonggi Province 0331-44-9800	150	✓	✓	
Keukdan Hanuri	1123-8, Inkye-dong, P'aldal-gu, Suwon, Kyonggi Province 0331-33-4063	250	✓	✓	
Keukdan Seongjeon	Samseong Electronics, P'aldal-gu, Suwon, Kyonggi Province	300	✓	✓	

Name	Address	Seating Capacity	Lighting Facilities	Sound Facilities	Projection Facilities
Yongwol-gun Munye Center	961-2, Yongheung 4-ri, Yongwol-up, Yongwol-gun, Kangwon Province 0373-70-2545	538	🔦	🔊	
Kongjichon Open-Air Stage	Samch'on-dong, Ch'unch'on, Kangwon Province	3,000			
Ch'unch'on Municipal Cultural Center	2-12, Yoseon-dong, Ch'unch'on, Kangwon Province 0361-54-3159	471	🔦	🔊	📹
Wonju Catholic Center	242-16, In-dong, Wonju, Kangwon Province 0371-42-2946	270	🔦		
Ch'ungbuk Art Cultural Center	861, Sajik-dong, Ch'ongju, N. Ch'ungch'ong Province 0431-67-7333	998	🔦	🔊	📹
Ch'ungju Cultural Center	190-1, Seongnae-dong, Ch'ungju, N. Ch'ungch'ong Province 0441-847-7228	1,000	🔦	🔊	
Chech'on Cultural Center	103, Hwasan-dong, Chech'on, N. Ch'ungch'ong Province 0443-42-6411	830	🔦	🔊	
Ch'ongsa Art Hall	459, Pongmyong-dong, Ch'ongju, N. Ch'ungch'ong Province 0431-275-0226	250	🔦	🔊	
Neoreumsae	598, Sajik-dong, Ch'ongju, N. Ch'ungch'ong Province 0431-69-1881	200	🔦	🔊	
Olympics Memorial People's Living Hall	423-17, Onch'on-dong, Onyang, S. Ch'ungch'ong Province 0418-546-4800	532 300	🔦	🔊	📹
Namdo Art Hall	53, Taeeui-dong, Tong-gu, Kwangju 062-227-1136	572	🔦	🔊	📹

Current Status of Theaters

Name	Address	Seating Capacity	Lighting Facilities	Sound Facilities	Projection Facilities
Hongju Cultural Center	152-1, Okam-ri, Hongseong-up, Hongseong-gun, S. Ch'ungch'ong Province 0451-32-0021	722	●	●	
Kimje Cultural Arts Center	399-5, Seoam-dong, Kimje, N. Cholla Province 0658-540-3499	478	●	●	
Teokchin Composite Hall	190-1, Teokchin-dong 2-ga, Teokchin-gu, Cheonju, N. Cholla Province 0652-254-4354	280	●	●	●
Yosu Chinnam Munye Center	42-4, Kwangmu-dong, Yosu, S. Cholla Province 0662-41-4350	366	●	●	●
Mokp'o Citizens' Hall	111, Namkyo-dong, Mokp'o, S. Cholla Province 0631-72-2171	1,220	●	●	●
Yosu Citizens' Hall	Kwangbu-dong, Yosu, S. Cholla Province 0662-41-3150	1,014	●	●	●
Sunch'on Citizens' Hall	79-5, Changch'on-dong, Sunch'on, S. Cholla Province 0661-744-8111	512	●	●	●
P'ohang Citizens' Hall	113-12, Teoksan-dong, P'ohang, N. Kyongsang Province 0562-46-0018	668	●	●	●
Seorabeol Cultural Center	1-26, Sajeong-dong, Kyongju, N. Kyongsang Province 0561-2-2578	574	●	●	●
Andong Cultural Center	123-1, Tongbu-dong, Andong, N. Kyongsang Province 0571-2-6101	460 200	●	●	
Sangju Cultural Center	118-1, Namseong-dong, Sangju, N. Kyongsang Province 0582-32-1059	644 100	●	●	●
Art Space	129-1, Noseo-dong, Kyongju, N. Kyongsang Province 0561-43-3855	200	●	●	
Teulsori Small Theatre	156-4, Chuyak-dong, Chinju, S. Kyongsang Province 0591-52-9050	150	●	●	

Name	Address	Seating Capacity	Lighting Facilities	Sound Facilities	Projection Facilities
Olympics Memorial People's Living Hall, Small Theatre	964-451, Wonp'yong-dong, Kumi, N. Kyongsang Province 0546-51-6025	168	✓	✓	
Ulsan Hanmaeum Hall	290-6, Cheonhwa-dong, Chung-gu, Ulsan, S. Kyongsang Province 0522-36-5111	478	✓	✓	✓
Hyundai Cultural Center	523, Yangjeong-dong, Chung-gu, Ulsan, S. Kyongsang Province 0522-80-8715	367		✓	✓
Ulsan Chamber of Commerce & Industry Theatre	589-1, Shinjeong 3-dong, Nam-gu, Ulsan, S. Kyongsang Province 0522-74-2111	456	✓	✓	✓
Chinhae Citizens' Hall	San 55-1, T'aebaek-dong, Chinhae, S. Kyongsang Province 0553-40-4560	442	✓	✓	
Iksan Cultural Center	726-3, Shincheong 4-dong, Nam-gu, Ulsan, S. Kyongsang Province 0522-76-6722	180	✓	✓	
Jointer Hall	722-5, Hapseong-dong, Hoewon-gu, Masan, S. Kyongsang Province 0551-55-6688	120	✓	✓	
Peoksugol Small Theatre	68-5, Chungang-dong, Ch'ungmu, S. Kyongsang Province 0557-645-6379	200	✓	✓	
Dong-a Life Insurance Cultural Center	282-3, Yon-dong, Cheju, Cheju Province 064-42-4511	180	✓	✓	

THEATERS

Asea Theater
156-1, Changsa-dong, Chongno-gu, Seoul
(02-276-1011)

Cine complex Lumiere
164-7, Nonhyon-dong, Kangnam-gu, Seoul
(02-545-3800)

Cine House
91-6, Nonhyon-dong, Kangnam-gu, Seoul
(02-544-7171)

City Theater
City Bldg, 816, Yeoksam-dong, Kangnam-gu,
Seoul (02-561-3388)

Core Art Hall
13-13, Kwanch'ol-dong, Chongno-gu, Seoul
(02-739-9932)

Daehan Theater
125, Ch'ungmu-ro 4-ga, Chung-gu, Seoul
(02-278-8171/2)

Dansung-sa
56, Myo-dong, Chongno-gu, Seoul
(02-764-3745)

Dong-A Theater
714-6, Yeoksam-dong, Kangnam-gu, Seoul
(02-552-6111)

Dongsung Art Center
1-5, Tongsung-dong, Chongno-gu, Seoul
(7414-3391/4)

Grandprix Theater
501-2, Shinsa-dong, Kangnam-gu, Seoul
(02-518-9191)

Hollywood Theater
284-6, Nakwon-dong, Chongno-gu, Seoul
(02-742-1481)

Jungang Theater
1-48, Ch'o-dong, Chung-gu, Seoul
(02-776-7004)

Korea Theater
50-16, Myong-dong 2-ga, Chung-gu, Seoul
(02-776-4273)

Kukdo Theater
310, Ulchi-ro 4-ga, Chung-gu, Seoul
(02-266-1444)

Lotte World Cinema
40-1, Chamsil-dong, Songp'a-gu, Seoul
(02-417-0211)

Myongbo Theater
18-5, Ch'o-dong, Chung-gu, Seoul (02-274-2121)

Piccadilly Theater
139, Tonui-dong, Chongno-gu, Seoul
(02-765-2245)

Piccaso Theater
139, Tonui-dong, Chongno-gu, Seoul
(02-745-8427)

Scala Theater
41, Ch'o-dong, Chung-gu, Seoul (02-266-6333)

Seoul Cinema Town
59-7, Kwansu-dong, Chongno-gu, Seoul
(02-277-3011)

PRODUCTION COMPANIES

AHN'S WORLD PRODUCTION
4F., Hannam Plaza, 707-36, Hannam-dong,
Yongsan-gu, Seoul
Pres. Ahn Dong-Kyu
(02-792-6743)

DA NAM ENTERPRISE INC.
602, Younghan Bldg., 59-23, Changch'ung-
dong 3-ga, Chung-gu, Seoul
Pres. Lee Ji-ryong
(02-275-9870, F. 277-5550)

DAE DONG HEUNG UP CO., LTD.
51-15, Ch'ungmuro 2-ga, Chung-gu, Seoul
Pres. Do Dong-Whan
(02-278-0696/8, 266-4259)

DAE IL FILM CO., LTD.
63-1, Insa-dong, Chongno-gu, Seoul
Pres. Kook Ki-ho
(02-720-7701/3, F. 277-7029)

DAE JONG FILM CO., LTD.
Renaissance Bldg., 8, Mikeun-dong,
Seodaemun-gu, Seoul
Pres. Byun Jang-ho
(02-365-1701/3)

DAE WON DONGHWA CO., LTD.
40-456, Hangangro 3-ga, Yongsan-gu, Seoul
Pres. Ahn Hyun-dong
(02-796/7131)

DONG-A CINEMA CORP.
284-6, Nakwon-dong, Chongno-gu, Seoul
Pres. Lee Chang-mu
(02-744-4013/4)

DONG-A EXPORTS CO., LTD.
56-16, Changch'ung-dong 1-ga,
Chung-gu, Seoul
Pres. Lee Woo-suk
(02-273-3181/6)

DOO SON FILM CO., LTD.
1-28, Tongsung-dong, Chongno-gu, Seoul
Pres. Chung Yong-sik
(02-744-3026, 7361)

DOOSUNG FILM CO., LTD.
Y65, Lotteworld Young Plaza, 40, Chamsil-
dong, Songp'a-gu, Seoul
Pres. Lee Doo-yong
(02-417-0213, 02-412-5884)

**HAH MYUNG JOONG FILM CO.,
LTD.**
703-7, Yeoksam-dong, Kangnam-gu, Seoul
Pres. Park Kyoung-ae
(02-565-7800)

HAN JIN ENTERPRISES CO., LTD.
62-15, P'il-dong 3-ga, Chung-gu, Seoul
Pres. Han Kap-chin
(02-267-2723, 2346)

HAP DONG FILM CO., LTD.
59-7, Kwansoo-dong, Chongno-gu, Seoul
Pres. Kwak Jung-hwan
(02-277-3011/3)

HWA CHUN FILM CO., LTD.
8th Fl, Dong-A Bldg, 88, Da-dong, Chung-gu,
Seoul
Pres. Park Jong-chan
(02-753-0391/4)

HWANG KI SUNG FILM CO., LTD.
54, 1-ga, Dongseomoon-dong, Seongbuk-gu,
Seoul
Pres. Hwang Ki-sung

(02-279-5691)

JIMI FILMS CO., LTD.
1-97, Dongsung-dong, Chongno-gu, Seoul
Pres. Jin Sung-man
(02-741-5141)

**KANG WOO-SUK PRODUCTION
CO., LTD.**
65-1, Unni-dong, Chongno-gu, Seoul
Pres. Kang Woo-suk
(02-747-7916)

KIWAEK SIDAE
3Fl, Art House, 158-1, Wonseo-dong,
Chongno-gu, Seoul
Pres. Yu In-taek
(02-747-5091)

KUK DONG SCREEN CO., LTD.
38-23, Ch'ungmuro 1-ga, Chung-gu, Seoul
Pres. Kim Sung
(02-266-0869, 02-267-3911)

NAM-A JINHEUNG CO., LTD.
98-78, Unni-dong, Chongno-gu, Seoul
Pres. Suh Chong-ho
(02-756-4950/1)

PAN FILM CO., LTD.
111-5, Banp'o-dong, Seoch'o-gu, Seoul
Pres. Park Hun-soo
(02-535-9146, 536-2516)

**PARK KWANG-SOO FILM CO.,
LTD.**
140-67, Kye-dong, Chongno-ku, Seoul
Pres. Park Kwang-soo
(02-762-4675)

SEI HAN PROMOTION CO., LTD.
125, Ch'ungmuro 4-ga, Chung-gu, Seoul
Pres. Kook Jung-bon

(02-279-1090)

SAM HO FILM CO., LTD.
3Fl, Dookyung Bldg., 64-1, Hannam-dong
Yongsan-gu, Seoul
Pres. Park Hyo-sung
(02-749-2060/7)

SCREEN LINE CO., LTD.
#105, Seijin Bldg., 797-27, Yeoksam-dong,
Kangnam-gu, Seoul
Pres. Chung Ji-hoon
(02-517-5631/4)

SHINCINE FILM CO., LTD.
31-28, Myungryun-dong 1-ga,
Chongno-gu, Seoul
Pres. Shin Cheol
(02-766-6105)

SUNG YIL CINEMART CO., LTD.
#815, Daewon Bldg., 43, Ch'ungmuro 3-ga,
Chung-gu, Seoul
Pres. Kang Sim-yong
(02-278-9344)

**TAE HUNG PRODUCTION CO.,
LTD.**
3-1, Hannam-dong, Yongsan-gu, Seoul
Pres. Lee Tae-won
(02-797-5121/4)

WOO JIN FILM CO., LTD.
37-26, Nonhyon-dong, Kangnam-gu, Seoul
Pres. Han Hyun-sook
(02-540-4637/8)

YE FILMS CO., LTD.
2012, Korea Business Center, 138-21,
Seoch'o-dong, Seoch'o-gu, Seoul
Pres. Go Gyu-sub
(02-565-6167/8)

Summary of Major Regional Cultural Arts Festivals held Nation-wide

National Folklore Arts Contest
❶ Ministry of Culture & Sports, Korean Culture and Arts Foundation ❷ 1958 ❸ October ❹ Traditional Farmers' Band Music, Folk Music, Folklore Dramas & Games, etc. ❺ Nationwide Tour

National Youth Composite Arts Festival
❶ Korean Culture and Arts Foundation, Youth Federation ❷ 1984 ❸ October ❹ Folklore Festival, Chorus Festival, *Sijo* (short lyric poem) Contest, Sketch Contest, Painting Contest ❺ Held in 13 Provinces

Seoul

General Nam I Grand Festival
❶ General Nam I Grand Festival Committee ❷ April, July, October ❸ Street Exorcisms, Flower Lantern Parade, Shaman Rituals, General Nam I Celebration, Shaman Exorcism, Taedong Festival, Feast in honor of the aged ❸ Shaman Exorcism is held on April 1st every other year.

Shamanistic Arts Festival
❶ Korean Shamanistic Arts Preservation Committee ❷ 1981 ❸ August ❹ Performance of Exorcisms of Various Regions

Intangible Cultural Assets Grand Festival
❶ Korean Cultural Protection Committee ❷ 1970 ❸ Irregular ❹ Performances by those designated as National Treasure in Each Category

Pusan

Pusan Stage Arts Festival
❶ Yech'ong Pusan Branch Committee ❷ 1978 ❸ August ❹ National Sijo Contest, Literary Arts Events, etc.

Suyong Traditional Folklore Festival
❶ Suyong Traditional Folklore Preservation Committee ❷ 1972 ❸ August ❹ Mask Dance Drama from Suyong, Fishing Play of Chwasuyong, Traditional Farming and Working Songs of Suyong Nongch'ong

Inch'on

Seohaean P'ungŏje
❶ Inch'on Folklore Culture Preservation Committee ❷ 1983 ❸ Irregular ❹ Dragon King Exorcism, Kotch'ang Exorcism, Paeyonshin Exorcism, etc. ❺ Designated as Important Intangible Cultural Asset No.82

Chemulp'o Arts Festival
❶Inch'on Arts Organization Union ❷ 1983 ❸ October ❹ Ŭnyul Mask Dance, Shaman Ritual for Bountiful Harvest from the Sea of Puksongp'o

Taegu

Talgubul Festival
❶ Taegu City ❷ 1982 ❸ October ❹ Celebrations, Literary Arts Events, Tug-of-War

Kwangju

Namdo Cultural Festival
❶ South Cholla Province ❷ 1972 ❸ November ❹ Folklore Arts Performance, P'ansori Performance, Folklore Games Contest

Kyŏnggi Province

Kangdo Cultural Festival

❶ Kangdo Cultural Festival Committee ❷ 1984 ❸ October ❹ Ch'amsongdan Founding Celebration, Yongdujil Song Presentation, Miss Hwamunseok Contest, Traditional Farmers' Band Music Contest ❺ The Name of the Festival derived from Kangdo, the former name of Kanghwa

Tasan Cultural Festival

❶ Namyangju Cultural Institute ❷ 1986 ❸ October ❹ Traditional Farmers' Band Music, Folklore Dramas, Writing Contest, Sketch Contest, Orchestra Performance, Painting Contest

Tonggu Cultural Festival

❶ Namyangju Cultural Institute ❷ 1983 ❸ October ❹ Memorial Services for T'aejo Kohwangje, Sketch Contest, Writing Contest, etc. ❺ The State Memorial Service Performed in Tonggurung

Intangible Cultural Assets Regular Performance

❶ *Yangjubyolsandae Nori* Preservation Committee and *Yangjusonorigut* Preservation Committee ❷ 1980 ❸ May ❹ Mask Dance Drama from Yangju, Shaman Cow Ritual of Yangju

Sejong Culture Grand Festival

❶ Yoju Cultural Institute ❷ 1961 ❸ October ❹ Traditional Farmers' Band Music, Hwangma and Yoma Nori, Mask Dance Drama from Yohung, Wonburi Bridge Treading to Ward off Misfortune, Twin Dragon Chariot Tug-of-War

Hwahong Cultural Festival

❶ Suwon Cultural Institute ❷ 1964 ❸ October ❹ Literary Arts Festival, Folklore Events, Sports Contest ❺ Festival to Pay Tribute to King Chongjo

Kangwon Province

Kangnŭng Tano Festival

❶ Kangnŭng Tano Festival Committee ❷ Around May 5 (Lunar Calendar) ❸ Government Servants' Mask Drama, Wrestling Match, Riding Swings, Sports Contest, Sacrificial Rituals and Shaman Exorcisms ❺ Important Intangible Cultural Asset No.13 (Designated in '66)

Kangwon Composite Arts Festival

❶ Yech'ong Kangwon Province Branch Committee ❷ 1983 ❸ October ❹ Hwach'on Turtle Game, Music Festival, Drama Festival, All sorts of Exhibitions, Chorus Contest, A Water Pail and Mortar Game of Hongch'ŏn, Arts Festival

Tanjong Festival

❶ Yŏngwol Tanjong Festival Committee ❷ 1967 ❸ April (Held Simultaneously on County Residents' Day) ❹ National Classical Music Performance, Flower Festvival, Changnŭng Sacrificial Rite, Chinese Poetry and Korean Writing Contest

Taehyon Yi Yul-kok Festival

❶ Yi Yul-kok Festival Committee ❷ 1962 ❸ October ❹ Grand Lectures on the Philosophy of Yi Yul-kok, Writing Contest, Archery Contest, Calligraphy Contest, Photography Exhibition, Sacrificial Rites

Soyang Festival
❶ Soyang Festival Committee
❷ 1983 ❸ May ❹ Ceremony held
on the Eve of the Festival, Traditional
Farmers' Band Music, Wagon Pushing
Contest, Floating Oil Lanterns on
River, Raft Making, Folklore Contest,
Literary Arts Events, Wrestling Match,
Tug-of-War

Chŏngsŏn Arirang Festival
❶ Chŏngsŏn Arirang Festival
Committee ❷ 1986 ❸ September
❹ Traditional Farmers' Band Music,
Folklore Games Contest, Folklore
Games, Sacrificial Rite for Loyal
Subjects, Chŏngsŏn Arirang *Sijo*
Presentation and Contest

Chukseo Cultural Festival
❶ Samch'ok Chukseo Cultural Festival
Committee ❷ 1973 ❸ January (Lunar
Calender) ❹ Traditional Farmers'
Band Music Contest, Tug-of-War
(Kangwon Province's Intangible
Cultural Asset No. 2) ❺ *Sulbi Nori*,
Folklore Games, Archery Contest,
Sacrificial Rite to Sky, Earth and
Water

Ch'iak Grand Festival
❶ Kuryong Temple ❷ 1967 ❸ April
8 (Lunar Calender) ❹ Sacrificial Rites
to Mountain Gods ❺ A Festival
Performed since Chosŏn Period and
Revived in '67

Ch'iak Cultural Festival
❶ Ch'iak Cultural Festival Committee
❷ 1982 ❸ September ❺ *Sijo* Contest,
Chinese Poetry and Korean Writing
Contest, Riding Swings, Tongak
Sacrificial Rite

Hyunsan Cultural Festival
❶ Hyunsan Cultural Festival
Committee ❷ 1979 ❸ April (Held
Simultaneously with Yangyang
County Residents' Grand Festival)
❹ Literary Arts Events, Tug-of-War,
Wrestling Match, Jumping on Seesaw
Boards, Riding Swings, Traditional
Farmers' Band Music Contest

N.Ch'ungch'ŏng Province

Nankye Arts Festival
❶ Yech'ong Yongdong Branch Committee ❷ 1969 ❸ October ❹ National Classical Music Contest, *Sijo* Contest, A Presentation of Traditional Farming and Working Songs of Solkyeri, Folklore Games, Cultural Arts Exhibition, etc. ❺ A Festival to Pay Tribute to the Spirit of Nankye Park Yŏn

Songni Celebration Festival
❶ Poŭn Cultural Institute ❷ 1978 ❸ April ❹ Sacrificial Rite to Mountain Gods, Wagon Pushing Contest, Traditional Farmers' Band Music, Wrestling Match, Tug-of-War, Ceremonies for Mask Dance, Paper Lantern Festival

Urŭk Cultural Festival
❶ Yech'ong Ch'ungju Branch Committee ❷ 1971 ❸ October ❹ *Kanggangsuwŏlle* (Circle Dance and Song by Women), National Kayakûm Contest, *Sijo* Contest, T'ankumdaebang-a Song, Yangjinmyongso Oryong Exorcism, Shamanistic Village-Ritual of Okkye,

Traditional Farmers' Band Music of Chongwon ❺ A Festival to Pay Tribute to the Spirit of Uruk

Chungbong Ch'ungryol Festival
❶ Okch'on Cultural Institute ❷ 1976 ❸ October ❹ A Ceremony to Cherish the Memory of Chungbong, Loyal Army March, Wagon Pushing Game, Traditional Farmers' Band Music Contest, *Kanggangsuwŏlle*, Tug-of-

War, Riding Swings, Wrestling Match ❺ A Festival to Pay Tribute to the Patriotic Martyrdom of Chungbong Cho Hŏn

Ch'ongwon Nongja Festival
❶ Yech'ong North Ch'ungch'ong Province Branch Committee ❷ 1983 ❸ October ❹ *Nongjanori*, Riding Swings, Four-stick Game Contest, Wrestling Match

Ch'ungbuk Arts Festival
❶ Yech'ong North Ch'ungch'ong Branch Committee ❷ 1959 ❸ October ❹ Cultural Exhibition, Aesthetics Committee Exhibition, Folklore Arts Festival, Construction Arts Festival, Drama Performances, Mask Dance of Kangnyong

S. Ch'ungch'ŏng Province

Kŭmsan Ginseng Festival

❶ Kŭmsan Ginseng Festival Planning Committee ❷ 1981 ❸ October ❹ Ginseng Festival, Ginseng Production Contest, Cultural Events, Miss Ginseng Contest, Fireworks, Fancy Parade, Traditional Farmers' Band Music Contest, etc.

Kiji-shi Tug-of-War Folklore Festival

❶ Kiji-shi Tug-of-War Preservation Committee ❷ March ❸ Shaman Ritual, Sacrificial Rite to Dragon King, Tug-of-War Contest, Miss Queen

Oknyo Contest, Traditional Farmers' Band Music Contest, Hemp Cloth Weaving Contest, Archery Contest, *Sijo* Contest, Litter Sweeping Contest ❺ First began about 400 years ago

Maehŭn Cultural Festival

❶ Yesan-County ❷ 1974 ❸ April ❹ Diabolo Game, Traditional Rope Walking, Four-stick Game, All Sorts of Dance, Chorus, *Samulnori*, Maehun Farmer's Award Ceremony ❺ A Festival to Pay Tribute to the Spirit of Maehŭn Yun Pong-gil, the National Patriot

Paekche Cultural Festival

❶ Paekche Cultural Enhancement Committee ❷ 1955 ❸ October ❹ National *Sijo* Contest, Archery Contest, Fireworks, Totem Pole Festival, Regional Folklore Games, Cultural Events, Rituals ❺ Held in Kongju and Puyo every other Year

Sangnok Cultural Festival

❶ Sangnok Cultural Festival Planning Committee ❷ 1977 ❸ October ❹ Traditional Farmers' Band Music, Swing Riding Contest, *Sijo* Contest, Archery Contest, A Ceremony to Cherish the Memory of Sangnok ❺ A Festival to Pay Tribute to the Spirit of Sangnoksu of Shim Hun

Seosan Cultural Festival

❶ Seosan Cultural Festival Committee ❷ 1987 ❸ October ❹ Hanging Lanterns of Blue Gauze, Traditional Official Dance, Traditional Farming and Working Songs, Rituals to Ask for a Bountiful Harvest from the Sea, Fiery Darts Game, Traditional Farmers' Band Music for Harvesting Rice, *Samulnori*

Onyang Cultural Festival

❶ Onyang Cultural Festival Committee ❷ 1962 ❸ April ❹ Fancy Parade of the Loyal Army of Admiral Yi Sun-sin, Wrestling Match, Riding Swings ❺ Held on the Birthday of Admiral Yi Sun-sin

Ŭnsan Pyolshinje

❶ *Ŭnsan Pyolshinje* Preservation Committee ❷ 1947 ❸ January (Lunar Calendar) ❹ Chindae Cutting, Flower Catching, Shaman Sacrificial Rites, *Sangsongjehu, Mulbonghagi,* Chorasul Event, Folklore Contest, All sorts of Contests ❺ Designated as Important Intangible Cultural Asset No.9 in 1965

N. Chŏlla Province

Mahan Folklore Festival

❶ Iksan County ❷ 1971 ❸ October ❹ Traditional Farmers' Band Music Contest, Traditional Farming and Working Songs of Samgi, *Iksangisaebae*, Traditional Dance, Monks' Drum Playing, *Sŭngmu* (Dance to Represent the Teachings of Buddhism Performed by Layman), Tug-of-War, *Takgaebinori*, Mr. Miruk Contest

Moyangsong Festival

❶ Koch'ang Cultural Institute ❷ 1974 ❸ October ❹ Tapseungnori, P'ansori, *Ogeori Tangsannori*, Regional Folklore Contest, Tug-of-War,

Traditional Farmers' Band Music, Archery Contest ❺ The only Songkwak Cultural Festival held in Korea

Pyokgol Cultural Festival

❶ Yech'ong Kimje Branch Committee ❷ 1961 ❸ April ❹ Ritual for a Bountiful Harvest, Twin Dragon Game, Ipsŏk Tug-of-War, Traditional Farmers' Band Music, National Male & Female *Sijo* Contest, Chinese Poetry Composing Contest, Calligraphy Contest, Traditional Farmers' Band Music Contest, All Sorts of Folklore Plays & Cultural Events

Wido P'ungŏje

❶ Wido P'ungŏje Committee ❷ January (Lunar Calendar) ❸ Shaman Sacrificial Rites, *Ttuibatnori*

Ŭiam Ju Non-gae Festival

❶ Ŭiam Ju Non-gae Festival Committee ❷ 1968 ❸ September 3 (Lunar Calendar) ❹ Traditional Farmers' Band Music Contest and Folklore Events, Cultural Events

Chŏlla Arts Festival

❶ Yech'ong North Cholla Province Branch Committee ❷ 1962 ❸ October ❹ Arts Exhibition, Photography Exhibition, Twin Dragon Game, *Samdonggutnori*, National Classical Music, Dance & Films

Chŏnju *Taesasupnori* National Contest

❶ Chŏnju Munhwa Broadcasting Station, Chŏnju City ❷ 1975 ❸ June ❹ Performance and Contest in 9 categories including P'ansori, Traditional Farmers' Band Music, Instrumental Music, Folk Song, *Sijo*, Archery, General P'ansori, *Kayagŭm* Accompanied by Singing and Dance

Ch'unhyang Festival

❶ Ch'unhyang Cultural Enhancement Committee ❷ 1937 ❸ April 8 (Lunar Calendar) ❹ Memorial Service for Ch'unhyang, *Ch'unhyangjon* Drama, *Yongma* Nori, *Samdonggutnori*, Cultural Events, Miss Ch'unhyang Contest

P'ungnam Festival

❶ Chŏnju City ❷ 1959 ❸ June ❹ Group Dance, Seoch'on Bridge Treading, Writing Contest, *Nanjang* Opening ❺ Chŏnju *Taesasupnori* National Contest is also held during the same period

S. Chŏlla Province

Kossaŭm Festival
(Rice Straw Loop Game of Kwangsan)
❶ Kossaŭm Preservation Committee
❷ 1983 ❸ May ❹ Kossaum Nori,
Wrestling Match, Tug-of-War,
Traditional Farmers' Band Music,
Older Peoples' Festival ❺ Important
Intangible Cultural Asset No.33,
Kossaŭmnori Presentation

Kŭmnŭng Cultural Festival
❶ Kangjin Cultural Institute ❷ 1974
❸ May ❹ Tug-of-War, Field Games,
Riding Swings, Sangyonori, General
Yomgol Drama

Tahyang Festival
❶ Posŏng Tea-drinkers' Committee
❷ 1985 ❸ May ❹ Miss Green Tea
Contest, Writing Contest on the
Subject of Tea, Calligraphy,
Photography Exhibition

Yongdŭng Festival
❶ Yongdŭng Festival Preservation
Committee ❷ 1975 ❸ May ❹
Kanggangsuwŏlle, Farming Song of
Chindo, Shaman Exorcism and other
Folklore Events ❺ Held when the Silt

between Hoedong Village of Kogun-
myon and Modo Village of Ûishin-
myon is Exposed

Chirisan Medicinal Water Festival
❶ Kurye Cultural Institute ❷ 1962
❸ April ❹ Medicinal Water Sacrificial
Rite, National *Sijo* Recital Contest,
National Archery Contest, Traditional
Farmers' Band Music Contest,
Wrestling Match, etc.

Chinnam Festival
❶ Chinnam Festival Preservation
Committee, Chinnam Festival
Committee ❷ 1967 ❸ May
❹ Yongshinmat-i Exorcism to ask for
a Bountiful Harvest from the Sea,
Sodongp'aenori, Traditional Farmers'
Band Music Contest, Archery Contest

Haenam *Kanggangsuwŏlle* Regional Festival
❶ *Kanggangsuwŏlle* Regional Festival
Committee ❷ 1983 ❸ October (Event
Held After County Residents' Day)
❹ *Myŏngryangdaech'ŏp* Celebration,
Dragon Capturing Exorcism,
Kanggangsuwŏlle Contest, Field Stone
Lifting Game, Riding Swings,
Traditional Farmers' Band Music,
Wrestling Match, etc.

N. Kyŏngsang Province

Taekaya Cultural Arts Festival
❶ Koryŏng Cultural Institute ❷ 1974
❸ October ❹ Traditional Farmers' Band Music Presentation, Kayakum Performance, Fan Dance, Folklore Games ❺ An Event to Pay Tribute to a Great Musician, Urŭk

Silla Cultural Festival
❶ Silla Cultural Enhancement Committee ❷ 1967 ❸ October ❹ Silla's Processional Music for the Royal Military Band, Restoration of P'alkwan Grand Sacrificial Ritual, Silla Nanjang, Hwarang and Wonhwa Selecting Contest, Hwarang Wrestling Match

Andong Folklore Festival
❶ Andong Cultural Institute ❷ 1971
❸ September ❹ *Notdari* Treading, Shamanistic Ritual of Hahoe, T'apdol-i, Wagon Pushing Contest, Archery

Yongyang Cultural Festival
❶ Yongyang Cultural Institute ❷ 1983
❸ October ❹ Traditional Farmers' Band Music Contest, Tug-of-War, etc.

S. Kyŏngsang Province

Karak Cultural Festival
❶ Karak Cultural Festival Planning Committee ❷ 1967 ❸ March 15-17 (Lunar Calendar) ❹ King Kim Su-ro's Coronation, Tug-of-War, Wrestling

Match, *Sijo* Contest ❺ An Event to Continue the Traditions of Kaya Culture

Kaech'on Arts Festival

❶ Kaech'on Arts Foundation ❷ 1950 ❸ October ❹ Arts Cultural Event, Mask Dance Drama from Kosong, Exhibitions, Traditional Farmers' Band Music Contest, National Archery Contest, Riding Swings

Miryang Arang Festival

❶ Arang Festival Planning Committee ❷ 1957 ❸ May ❹ Servants' Festival of Miryang, Lighting and Carrying Torches at Each Traditional School, Dragon and Tiger Drama ❺ A Festival to Pay Tribute to the Integrity of Arang and the Knowledge and Virtue of Kim Chong-jik

Sach'ŏn Cultural Festival

❶ Sach'ŏn Cultural Institute ❷ 1958 ❸ October ❹ Mask Dance Drama from Kasan, P'ansori Performance, Kite Flying Contest

March 1 : Independence Movement Folklore Cultural Festival

❶ March 1 : Independence Movement National Cultural Enhancement Committee ❷ 1961 ❸ From February to March ❹ Battle Between Cow-head Shaped Wood Structures Born on Human Shoulders Played in Yŏngsan, Yŏngsan Tug-of-War, Archery Contest, Traditional Farmers' Band Music Contest, *Sijo* Contest

Sokaya Cultural Festival

❶ Kosong Cultural Institute ❷ 1975 ❸ September ❹ Mask Dance Drama from Kosong, Traditional Farming and Working Songs of Kosong, Tug-of-War, Archery Contest

Ŭibyŏng Festival

❶ Ŭibyŏng Festival Committee ❷ 1973 ❸ April ❹ Fireworks, Cow Fights, Mask Dance, Wagon Pushing Game, Large Rope Pulling, *Sijo* Contest, Folklore Games Contest, etc ❺ Event to Pay Tribute to General Hongŭi, Kwak Chae-u.

Ch'ŏ yong Festival

❶ Ulsan Cultural Institute ❷ 1985 ❸ October ❹ Sacrificial Rite for Ch'ŏyong, A Presentation of Mask Dance Honoring the Spirit of Ch'ŏyong, Writing Contest

Ch'onryong Cultural Festival

❶ Hamyang-gun ❷ 1963 ❸ May ❹ Cultural Events such as Literature, Art, Dance, Music, Drama, Photography, and Folklore Events such as Sansongnori, Traditional Farmers' Band Music, etc. ❺ A Festival to Pay Tribute to the Spirit of Koun, Ch'oe Ch'i-won

Hansandaech'op Memorial Festival

❶ *Hansandaech'op* Memorial Festival Committee ❷ 1962 ❸ October ❹ Military Ritual of Chosŏn Period, Satto's Outing Parade, Grand Ritual to Ask for a Bountiful Harvest from the Sea, Victory Dance, Mask Dance from T'ongyong, Sword Dance of Tongyong ❺ A Festival to Celebrate the Exploits of Admiral Yi Sun-sin during *Hansandaech'op* Battle

Cheju Island

Cheju Yŏngdŭnggut

❶ *Cheju Ch'ilmŏridanggut* Preservation Committee ❸ February (Lunar Calendar) ❹ *Yŏngdŭnggut Nori*

Halla Cultural Festival

❶ Yech'ong Cheju Island Branch Committee ❷ 1962 ❸ October ❹ A Contest of Carrying Loads on Back, Wrapping and Unwrapping of Straw Mats, Pony Contest

Current Status of Cultural Institutes Nation-wide

Province	Name	Address
Kyonggi Province	**Anseong Cultural Institute**	690, Nakwon-dong, Anseong-up, Anseong-gun (0334)73-2625
	Inch'on Cultural Institute	(Former Museum) 1-11, Songhak-dong, Chung-gu, Inch'on (032)761-2778
	Suwon Cultural Institute	74, Kyo-dong, Kwonseon-gu, Suwon (0331)44-2161/3
	Puch'on Cultural Institute	(Puch'on Citizens' Hall) 788, Chung-dong, Nam-gu, Puch'on (032) 62-3739
	Anyang Cultural Institute	550, Anyang 8-dong, Anyang (0343) 49-4451
	Seongnam Cultural Institute	3309-425, T'aep'yong 2-dong, Sujeong-gu, Seongnam (0342) 756-5245
	Songt'an Cultural Institute	176-1, Seojeong-dong, Songt'an (0333) 62-6300, 65-2923
	Tongduch'on Cultural Institute	(Citizens' Hall) 124, Sangp'ae-dong, Tongduch'on (0351) 865-2933
	P'yongt'aek Cultural Institute	847, Bijeon-dong, P'yongt'aek (0333) 655-2184
	Namyangju Cultural Institute	(Namyangju-gun Public Health Center) 20-16, Chikeum-dong, Mikeum (0346) 62-0666
	Hwaseong Cultural Institute	871, Osan-dong, Osan (0339) 374-2526
	Kanghwa Cultural Institute	523-3, Kwanch'ong-ri, Kanghwa-up, Kanghwa-gun (0349) 32-0011
	Yongin Cultural Institute	346, Kimryangjang-ri, Yongin-up, Yongin-gun (0335) 35-2033
	Ich'on Cultural Institute	San 1, Ch'angjeon-ri, Ich'on-up, Ich'on-gun (0336) 635-2316

CULTURAL INSTITUTES ASSOCIATION : 11-6, Ch'ongjin-dong, Chongno-gu, Seoul (02)732-7656-7

Current Status of Cultural Institutes Nation-wide

Province	Name	Address
Kyonggi Province	**Yoju Cultural Institute**	74-2, Hongmun-ri, Yoju-up, Yoju-gun (0337) 83-3450
	P'aju Cultural Institute	56-9, Keumch'on-ri, Keumch'on-up, P'aju-gun (0348) 941-2425
	Yangp'yong Cultural Institute	343-2, Yangkeun-ri, Yangp'yong-up, Yangp'yong-gun (0338) 71-3866,
	Koyang Cultural Institute	600, Chukyo-dong, Koyang (0344) 63-0600
	Kimp'o Cultural Institute	Sau-ri, Kimp'o-up, Kimp'o-gun (0341) 84-6550
	P'och'on Cultural Institute	33-45, Shineup-ri, P'och'on-up, P'och'on-gun (0357) 32-5055
	Kap'yong Cultural Institute	505-2, Eupnae-ri, Kap'yong-up, Kap'yong-gun (0356) 82-2016
	Kwangju Cultural Institute	120, Songjeong-ri, Kwangju-up, Kwangju-gun (0347) 64-0686
	Yonch'on Cultural Institute	44-1, Oksan-ri, Yonch'on-up, Yonch'on-gun (0355) 34-2350
	Ansan Cultural Institute	604, Kojan-dong, Ansan (0345) 494-1524
	Yangju Cultural Institute	738-61, Kanap-ri, Kwangjeuk-myon, Yangju-gun (0351) 40-6467
	Euijeongbu Cultural Institute	326-1, Euijeohgbu 2-dong, Euijeongbu (0351) 872-5678
	P'yongt'aek-gun Cultural Institute	299-10, Anjung-ri, Anjung-myon, P'yongt'aek-gun (0333) 81-1800
	Kwach'on Cultural Institute	45, Pyolyang-dong, Kwach'on (02) 504-6513

Province	Name	Address
	Kuri Cultural Institute	374-1, Sut'aek-dong, Kuri (0346) 553-3993
	Kwangmyong Cultural Institute	222-1, Ch'olsan-dong, Kwangmyong (02) 687-6669, 688-7245
	Kwanak Cultural Institute	1589-13, Pongch'on 4-dong, Kwanak-gu, Seoul (02) 885-5975
Kangwon Province	**Ch'unch'on Cultural Institute**	(Former Ch'unch'on Municipal Library) San 12, Pongeui-dong, Ch'unch'on (0361) 54-5105
	Wonju Cultural Institute	127, Won-dong, Wonju (0371) 42-3794
	Kangneung Cultural Institute	15-2, Hongje-dong, Kangneung (0391) 648-3014
	Sokch'o Cultural Institute	570-5, Yongrang-dong, Sokch'o (0392) 32-1231
	Tonghae Cultural Institute	240, Palhan-dong, Tonghae (0394) 31-3298
	T'aebaek Cultural Institute	62-3, Hwangji 1-dong, T'aebaek (0395) 53-3161
	Samch'ok Cultural Institute	(Premises of Chukseoru) 9-3, Seongnae-dong, Samch'ok (0397) 73-2882
	Yangyang Cultural Institute	4-8, Nammun 3-ri, Yangyang-up, Yangyang-gun (0396) 671-8762
	Yongwol Cultural Institute	894, Yongheung-ri, Yongwol-up, Yongwol-gun (0373) 73-1443
	Hongch'on Cultural Institute	51-20, Shinjangdae-ri, Hongch'on-up, Hongch'on-gun (0366) 434-2080
	Yanggu Cultural Institute	265-4, Sang 4-ri, Yanggu-up, Yanggu-gun (0364) 481-2681

Current Status of Cultural Institutes Nation-wide

Province	Name	Address
	Hoengseong Cultural Institute	68, Ha-ri, Hoengseong-up, Hoengseong-gun (0372) 43-2271
	Hwach'on Cultural Institute	A-ri, Hwach'on-up, Hwach'on-gun (0363) 442-2607
	Inje Cultural Institute	3-ri, Sang-dong, Inje-up, Inje-gun (0365) 461-6678
	Koseong Cultural Institute	12, Ha 2-ri, Kanseong-up, Koseong-gun (0392) 681-2922
	Cheongseon Cultural Institute	354-1, Pongyang 2-ri, Cheongseon-up, Cheongseon-gun (0398) 62-5471
	Ch'olwon Cultural Institute	649, 4-ri, Shinch'olwon, Kalmal-up, Ch'olwon-gun (0535) 50-5385, 5574
	P'yongch'ang Cultural Institute	355-2, Chung-ri, P'yongch'ang-up, P'yongch'ang-gun (0374) 32-3546
South Ch'ung-ch'ong Province	**Taejeon Cultural Institute**	1-166, Munhwa-dong, Chung-gu, Taejeon (042) 256-3684
	Ch'onan Cultural Institute	694-9, Seongjeong-dong, Ch'onan (0417) 551-3004
	Kongju Cultural Institute	184-2, Panjuk-dong, Kongju (0416) 52-9005
	Onyang Cultural Institute	57, Onch'on-dong, Onyang (0418) 545-2222
	Taech'on Cultural Institute	983-16, Tongdae-dong, Taech'on (0452) 34-3061
	Seosan Cultural Institute	268, Eupnae-dong, Seosan (0455) 65-5050
	Yesan Cultural Institute	433, Yesan-ri, Yesan-up, Yesan-gun (0458) 35-2441, 34-2441

Province	Name	Address
	Hongseong Cultural Institute	412-13, Okwan-ri, Hongseong-up, Hongseong-gun (0451) 32-3613
	Seoch'on Cultural Institute	(County Residents' Hall) 176-2, Kunsa-ri, Seoch'on-up, Seoch'on-gun (0459) 953-0123
	Keumsan Cultural Institute	176-43, Sang-ri, Keumsan-up, Keumsan-gun (0412) 2-2724
	Seonghwan Cultural Institute	449, Seonghwan-ri, Seonghwan-up, Ch'onan-gun (0417) 581-2101
	Nonsan Cultural Institute	279-1, Nae-dong 2-ri, Nonsan-up, Nonsan-gun (0461) 32-2395
	Ch'onan-gun Cultural Institute	172, Pyongch'on-ri, Pyongch'on-myon, Ch'onan-gun (0417) 64-1022
	Choch'iwon Cultural Institute	21-1, Kyo-dong, Choch'iwon-up, Yonki-gun (0415) 865-2411
	Tangjin Cultural Institute	528-3, Eupnae-ri, Tangjin-up, Tangjin-gun (0457) 54-2367
	Puyo Cultural Institute	722, Tongnam-ri, Puyo-up, Puyo-gun (0463) 835-3318
	Ch'ongyang Cultural Institute	202-5, Eupnae-ri, Ch'ongyang-up, Ch'ongyang-gun (0454) 43-4774
	T'aean Cultural Institute	637-9, Nammun-ri, T'aean-up, T'aean-gun (0455) 674-2192
North Ch'ung-ch'ong Province	**Ch'ongju Cultural Institute**	92, Nammunno 2-ga, Ch'ongju (0431) 56-3624
	Ch'ungju Cultural Institute	San 1, Ch'ilkeum-dong, Ch'ungju (0441) 847-3906
	Chech'on Cultural Institute	(Cultural Center) 26-1, Jungangno 2-ga, Chech'on (0443) 46-3646

Current Status of Cultural Institutes Nation-wide

Province	Name	Address
	Chinch'on Cultural Institute	435-11, Eupnae-ri, Chinch'on-up, Chinch'on-gun (0434) 33-2744
	Eumseong Cultural Institute	817, Namch'on-dong, Eumseong-up, Eumseong-gun (0446) 72-4084
	Poeon Cultural Institute	67-1, Changshin-ri, Poeun-up, Poeun-gun (0433) 2-2314
	Koesan Cultural Institute	751-10, Tongbu-ri, Koesan-up, Koesan-gun (0445) 32-3588
	Okch'on Cultural Institute	222-177, Samyang-ri, Okch'on-up, Okch'eun-gun (0475) 33-5588
	Yongdong Cultural Institute	675-1, Kyesan-ri, Yongdong-up, Yongdong-gun (0414) 42-2215
	Tanyang Cultural Institute	(County Residents' Hall) 315, Pyolkok-ri, Tanyang-up, Tanyang-gun (0444) 423-0701
	Ch'ongwon Cultural Institute	(County Residents' Hall) 144-1, Chibuk-dong, Ch'ongju (0431) 57-2858
	Chech'on-gun Cultural Institute	(Old Peoples' Welfare Center) 25-35, Uirim-dong, Chech'on (0443) 45-5252
	Chungwon-gun Cultural Institute	(Chungwon County Office) 53-3, Keumneung-dong, Ch'ungju (0441) 848-2211
	Cheungp'yong Cultural Institute	239, Yontan-ri, Cheungp'yong-up, Koesan-gun (0445) 36-3400
South Kyŏng-sang Province	**Masan Cultural Institute**	531-2, Sanho-dong, Happ'o-gu, Masan (0551) 46-5840
	Chinju Cultural Institute	(Premises of Cultural Tourism Center) 10-4, Ponseong-dong, Chinju (0591) 746-5001,
	Ulsan Cultural Institute	518, Tal-dong, Nam-gu, Ulsan (0522) 72-3438

Province	Name	Address
	Samch'onp'o Cultural Institute	254-5, Seongu-dong, Samch'onp'o (0593) 33-3163
	Chinhae Cultural Institute	28-6, Chaehwangsan-dong, Chinhae (0553) 44-8880
	Kimhae Cultural Institute	159-20, Oe-dong, Kimhae (0525) 36-2646
	Yangsan Cultural Institute	327-2, Pukbu-dong, Yangsan-up, Yangsan-gun (0523) 386-0890~1
	Miryang Cultural Institute	81, Naeil-dong, Milyang (0527) 354-3009
	Hamyang Cultural Institute	967-4, Kyosan-ri, Hamyang-up, Hamyang-gun (0597) 63-2646
	Koseong Cultural Institute	(Premises of County Library) 88, Seooe-dong, Koseong-up, Koseong-gun (0556) 72-3805
	Haman Cultural Institute	208, Malsan-ri, Kaya-up, Haman-gun (0552) 83-2290
	Sanch'ong Cultural Institute	321-6, Chi-ri, Sanch'ong-up, Sanch'ong-gun (0596) 73-0977
	Hapch'on Cultural Institute	817-3, Hapch'on-dong, Hapch'on-up, Hapch'on-gun (0599) 31-2401
	Keoch'ang Cultural Institute	331-1, Jungang-ri, Keoch'ang-up, Keoch'ang-gun (0598) 42-6166
	Ch'angnyong Cultural Institute	28-27, Kyosang-dong, Ch'angnyong-up, Ch'angnyong-gun (0559) 33-3777
	Keoje Cultural Institute	294-1, Changseungp'o-dong, Changseungp'o (0558) 681-2603
	Uiryong Cultural Institute	877-24, Tongdong-ri, Uiryong-up, Uiryong-gun (0555) 73-2034

Current Status of
Cultural Institutes Nation-wide

Province	Name	Address
	Hadong Cultural Institute	450-5, Eupnai-dong, Hadong-gun (0595) 84-3929
	Sach'on Cultural Institute	(Premises of County Library) 45-4, P'yonghwa-ri, Sach'on-up, Sach'on-gun (0593) 52-4077
	Namhae Cultural Institute	345, Seobyon-dong, Namhae-up, Namhae-gun (0594) 64-6969
	Ch'angwon Cultural Institute	96-2, Shinwol-dong, Ch'angwon (0551) 84-8870
	Chinyang Cultural Institute	284, Sangdae-dong, Chinju (0591) 53-3171
	Ch'angwon-gun Cultural Institute	266-19, Chisan-ri, Chinbuk-myon, Ch'angwon-gun (0551) 43-9844
	Ch'ungmu Cultural Institute	188-3, Munhwa-dong, Ch'ungmu (0557) 646-3310
North Kyŏng-sang Province	**Kimch'on Cultural Institute**	1, Namsan-dong, Kimch'on (0547) 434-4336
	P'ohang Cultural Institute	55-3, Teoksu-dong, P'ohang (0562) 42-4711
	Kyongju Cultural Institute	198-4, Tongbu-dong, Kyongju (0561) 43-7182
	Yongch'on Cultural Institute	1-1, Ch'anggu-dong, Yongch'on (0563) 34-3030
	Andong Cultural Institute	446-2, Tongmun-dong, Andong (0571) 2-5825
	Yongju Cultural Institute	(Premises of Citizens' Hall) 470-62, Yongju 4-dong, Yongju (0572) 2-3300
	Kumi Cultural Institute	50, Songjeong-dong, Kumi (0546) 50-5575

Province	Name	Address
	Sangju Cultural Institute	(Premises of Sangju Cultural Center) 118-1, Namseong-dong, Sangju (0582) 535-2339
	Cheomch'on, Munkyong Cultural Institute	118, Chungang-dong, Cheomch'on (0581) 555-2571
	Kyongsan Cultural Institute	143-18, Seosang-dong, Kyoungsan (053) 82-0593
	Ponghwa Cultural Institute	288-4, P'ojeo-ri, Ponghwa-up, Ponghwa-gun (0573) 73-2350
	Kyongju-gun Cultural Institute	319-62, Angang-ri, Angang-up, Kyongju-gun (0561) 761-2341
	Keumneung Cultural Institute	565, Kyo-ri, Chire-myon, Keumneung-gun (0547) 435-0542
	Ch'ilkok Cultural Institute	273, Waek·van-ri, Waekwan-up, Ch'ilkok-gun (0545) 947-0450
	Yongdeok Cultural Institute	146, Teokgok-ri, Yongdeok-up, Yongdeok-gun (0564) 734-2456, 733-3883
	Koryŏng Cultural Institute	5, Chisan-ri, Koryong-up, Koryong-gun (0543) 954-2347
	Uljin Cultural Institute	77-2, Eupnae-ri, Uljin-up, Uljin-gun (0565) 83-2270
	Yongil Cultural Institute	39-13, Seongnae-dong, Honghae-up, Yongil-gun (0562) 61-0219,
	Yongyang Cultural Institute	292-6, Seobu-ri, Yongyang-up, Yongyang-gun (0574) 82-1378
	Yongp'ung Cultural Institute	463-1, Tongbu 4-dong, P'unggi-up, Yongp'ung-gun (0572) 636-6771
	Seongju Cultural Institute	393, Yesan-dong, Seongju-up, Seongju-gun (0544) 933-2443

Current Status of Cultural Institutes Nation-wide

Province	Name	Address
	Yech'on Cultural Institute	222, Nambon-dong, Yech'on-up, Yech'on-gun (0584) 654-3833
	Seonsan Cultural Institute	487-1, Tongbu-dong, Seonsan-up, Seonsan-gun (0546) 481-3113
	Ch'ongdo Cultural Institute	526, Peomkok 2-ri, Hwayang-up, Ch'ongdo-gun (0543) 71-2514
	Kunwi Cultural Institute	649, Tongbu-dong, Kunwi-up, Kunwi-gun (0578) 83-2003
	Euiseong Cultural Institute	509-3, Hujuk-dong, Euiseong-up, Euiseong-gun (0576) 34-5048
	Ch'ongsong Cultural Institute	290-3, Wolmak-dong, Ch'ongsong-up, Ch'ongsong-gun (0575) 873-2327
	Talseong Cultural Institute	353, Pudong, Hyonp'ung-myon, Talseong-up, Talseong-gun (053) 611-0010
	Ulneung Cultural Institute	273, To-dong, Ulneung-up, Ulneung-gun (0566) 791-0245
	Taegu Cultural Institute	7-4, Tongseongno 3-ga, Chung-gu, Taegu (053) 255-0964
South Cholla Province	**Kwangju Cultural Institute**	177-10, Sa-dong, Seo-gu, Kwangju (062) 68-4148
	Mokp'o Cultural Institute	(Former Municipal Yudal Library) 1-5, Taeeui-dong 2-ga, Mokp'o (0631) 44-4095
	Yosu Cultural Institute	303, Kwanmun-dong, Yosu (0662) 62-3377
	Sunch'on Cultural Institute	8-18, Changch'on-dong, Sunch'on (0661) 744-4502
	Naju-shi Cultural Institute	13, Keumkye-dong, Naju (0613) 82-5388, 32-5115

Province	Name	Address
	Kwangsan Cultural Institute	528-14, Soch'on-dong, Kwangsan-gu, Kwangju (062) 941-3377
	Tamyang Cultural Institute	72, Kaeksa-ri, Tamyang-up, Tamyang-gun (0684) 83-6066
	Hwasun Cultural Institute	San 62, Kwangdeok-ri, Hwasun-up, Hwasun-gun (0681) 374-0033
	Kangjin Cultural Institute	24-7, Namseong-ri, Kangjin-up, Kangjin-gun (0638) 33-7373
	Naju-gun Cultural Institute	(Premises of County Residents' Hall) 2-22, Namdae-dong, Naju (0613) 33-3839
	Yongkwang Cultural Institute	191-2, Munyong-ri, Yongkwang-up, Yongkwang-gun (0686) 51-3255
	Kurye Cultural Institute	291-8, Pongdong-ri, Kurye-up, Kurye-gun (0664) 782-8802
	Kokseong Cultural Institute	776-4, Eupnae-ri, 7-gu, Kokseong-up, Kokseong-gun (0688) 62-0890
	Hamp'yong Cultural Institute	(County Residents' Hall) 154-1, Hamp'yong-ri, Hamp'yong-up, Hamp'yong-gun (0615) 22-0505
	Chindo Cultural Institute	545, Kyo-dong, Chindo-up, Chindo-gun (0632) 42-1108
	Kwangyang Cultural Institute	312, Eupnae-dong, Kwangyang (0667) 2-0496
	Poseong Cultural Institute	902-13, Poseong-ri, Poseong-up, Poseong-gun (0694) 52-2629
	Changheung Cultural Institute	153-7, Kiyang-ri, Changheung-up, Changheung-gun (0665) 63-6362
	Changseong Cultural Institute	973-9, Yongch'on-ri, Changseong-up, Changseong-gun (0685) 92-1796

Current Status of
Cultural Institutes Nation-wide

Province	Name	Address
	Yongam Cultural Institute	157-4, Yok-ri, Yongam-up, Yongam-gun (0693) 73-2632
	Muan Cultural Institute	728, Seongdong-ri, Muan-up, Muan-gun (0636) 52-8648
	Haenam Cultural Institute	4, Seongnae-up, Haenam-up, Haenam-gun (0634) 33-5345
	Koheung Cultural Institute	122, Okha-ri, Koheung-up, Koheung-gun (0666) 35-5245
	Seungju Cultural Institute	55, P'yongjung-ri, Seungju-up, Seungju-gun (0661) 54-5851
	Wando Cultural Institute	791-1, Kunnae-ri, Wando-up, Wando-gun (0633) 52-4834
	Yoch'on-gun Cultural Institute	(Premises of Yoch'on County Office) 1094, Konghwa-dong, Yosu (0662) 64-1693
	Shinan Cultural Institute	(3 F., Shinan Welfare Center) 3-4, Manho-dong, Mokp'o (0631) 42-8131
	Yoch'on Cultural Institute	33, Hak-dong, Yoch'on (0662) 82-5388
	Tongkwangyang Cultural Institute	1313, Chungma-dong, Tongkwangyang (0667) 761-8585
North Cholla Province	**Cheonju Cultural Institute**	58-4, Kyongwon-dong 1-ga, Cheonju (0652) 88-7500
	Iri Cultural Institute	86, Namjung-dong 1-ga, Iri (0653) 855-2749
	Namwon Cultural Institute	226-2, Hajeong-dong, Namwon (0671) 33-1582
	Cheongeup Cultural Institute	685-9, Suseong-dong, Cheongju (0681) 32-8723

Province	Name	Address
	Kunsan Cultural Institute	14-1, Yonghwa-dong, Kunsan (0654) 42-0948
	Koch'ang Cultural Institute	236-5, Eupnae-ri, Koch'ang-up, Koch'ang-gun (0677) 64-2340
	Okgu Cultural Institute	731-15, Chikyong-ri, Taeya-myon, Okgu-gun (0654) 451-2138
	Imshil Cultural Institute	617, Ido-ri, Imshil-up, Imshil-gun (0673) 42-2211
	Kimje Cultural Institute	399-5, Seoam-dong, Kimje (0658) 547-4659
	Sunch'ang Cultural Institute	111-14, Sunhwa-dong, Sunch'ang-up, Sunch'ang-gun (0674) 53-2069
	Puan Cultural Institute	279, Seooe-ri, Puan-up, Puan-gun (0683) 64-5234
	Wanju Cultural Institute	545, Eupnae-ri, Kosan-myon, Wanju-gun (0652) 73-4335
	Muju Cultural Institute	231, Upnae-ri, Muju-up, Muju-gun (0657) 324-1300
	Iksan Cultural Institute	57-21, Namdang-ri, Hamyol-up, Iksan-gun (0653) 861-2022
	Chinan Cultural Institute	143, Kunha-ri, Chinan-up, Chinan-gun (0655) 33-1674
	Cheongeup-gun Cultural Institute	(Premises of Cheongeup County Office) 39-6, Yonji-dong, Cheongju (0681) 32-0222
	Changsu Cultural Institute	176-7, Changsu-ri, Changsu-up, Changsu-gun (0656) 351-5349

IMPORTANT INTANGIBLE CULTURAL ASSETS

Asset No.1
Chongmyocheryeak
Sŏng Kyŏng-rin
407-35, Hongun-dong, Seodaemun-gu,Seoul
Chosŏn Royal Ancestral Shrine Music

Asset No.1
Chongmyocheryeak
Kim Sŏng-jin
135-43,Wonseo-dong Chongno-gu,Seoul
Chosŏn Royal Ancestral Shrine Music

Asset No.1.
Chongmyocheryeak
Kim Chong-hŭi
Hwayang Villa A-201,
16-30, Kui-dong, Seongdong-gu,Seoul
Chosŏn Royal Ancestral Shrine Music

Asset No.1
Chongmyocheryeak
Lee Kang-dŏk
Yujin Apt. A-313,
48-84, Hongun-dong, Seodaemun-gu,Seoul
Chosŏn Dynastic Royal Ancestral
Shrine Music

Asset No.1
Chongmyo-cheryeak
Kim Ch'ŏn-hŭng
Yimkwang Apt. 3-603,
1015, Pangbae-dong, Seoch'o-gu,Seoul
Chosŏn Royal Ancestral Shrine Music

Asset No.1
Chongmyocheryeak
Lee Kang-dŏk
76-30,Wonseo-dong Chongno-gu,Seoul
Chosŏn Royal Ancestrsal Shrine Music

Asset No.2
Yangjupyŏlsandaenori
Sŏk Kŏ-ŏk
240,Yuyang-ri, Chunae-myon,Yangju-gun,
Kyonggi Province
Yangju Masque

Asset No.2
Yangjupyŏlsandaenori
Kim Sang-yong
239-18, Yuyang-ri,Chunae-myon,Yangju-gun,
Kyonggi Province
Yangju Masque

Asset No.2
Yangjupyŏlsandaenori
Roh Chae-yŏng
228, Yuyang-ri,Chunae-myon,Yangju-gun,
Kyonggi Province
Yangju Masque

Chongmyo cheryeak, *Chosŏn royal ancestral shrine music*

Asset No.3
Namsadangnori
Park Kye-sun
Chugong Apt. 28-306,
254, Shinhyon-dong, Seo-gu,Inch'on
Puppet Play and Other Folk Plays

Asset No.3
Namsadangnori
Nam Ki-hwan
Kyong-in Yollip 305,
524-24, Kajong-dong, Seo-gu,Inch,on
Puppet Play and Other Folk Plays

Yangjupyŏlsandaenori, *Mask dance*
drama from Yangju

Asset No.4
Kannil
Kim In
1979, Todu 1-dong, Cheju, Cheju Province,
Horsehair and Bamboo Hat-Making

Asset No.4
Kannil
Chŏng Ch'un-mo
242-46, Nonhyon-dong, Kangnam-gu,Seoul
Horsehair and Bamboo Hat-Making

Asset No.5
P'ansori
Chŏng Kwang-su
176-49, Puk Ahyon-dong,Seodaemun-gu,Seoul
Operatic Narrative Song

Asset No.5
P'ansori
Kim So-hŭi
24-1,Sokyok-dong, Chongno-gu,Seoul
Operatic Narrative Song

Asset No.5
P'ansori
O Chŏng-suk
Yang-u Apt. Ta-401,
252-1, Nonhyon-dong, Kangnam-gu,Seoul
Operatic Narrative Song

Asset No.5
P'ansori
Sŏng Ch'ang-sun
Hanshin 20-ch'a Apt. 339-1401,
60-67, Chamwon-dong,Seoch'o-gu,Seoul
Operatic Narrative Song

Asset No.5
P'ansori
Cho Sang-hyŏn
Shinshigaji Apt. 222-805,
Mok 6-dong,Yangch'on-gu,Seoul
Operatic Narrative Song

Asset No.5
P'ansori
Park Tong-jin
Pangbae Villa 305,
994, Pangbae 3-dong, Seoch'o-gu,Seoul
Operatic Narrative Song

Asset No.5
P'ansori
Han Sŭng-ho
520, Chongneung 2-dong, Seongbuk-gu,Seoul
Operatic Narrative Song

Asset No.5
P'ansori
Kang To-kŭn
547, Hyangkyo-dong,Namwon,
N. Cholla Province
Operatic Narrative Song

Asset No.5
P'ansori
Kim Sŏng-kwon
297-33, Kyerim 1-dong, Tong-gu, Kwangju
Operatic Narrative Song

Asset No.6
Tongyŏngogwangdae
Yu Tong-ju
230-1, Tongho-dong,Ch'ungmu,
S. Kyongsang Province
Tongyŏng Masque

Cho Sang-hyŏn, **P'ansori** *virtuoso*

Asset No.6
Tongyŏngogwangdae
Lee Ki-suk
270, Chongryang-dong, Ch'ungmu,
S. Kyongsang Province
Tongyŏng Masque

Asset No.6
Tongyŏngogwangdae
Kang Yŏng-ku
1084, Hwasam-ri, Yongnam-myon,
T'ongyong-gun, S. Kyongsang Province
Tongyŏng Masque

Asset No.6
Tongyŏngogwangdae
Kang Yŏn-ho
Kyongnam Apt. Na-403,
455, Misu 1-dong, Ch'ungmu, S. Kyongsang
Province
Tongyŏng Masque

Asset No.7
Kosŏngogwangdae
Hŏ Chong-bok
161, Pongam-ri, Tonghae-myon, Kosong-gun,
S. Kyongsang Province
Kosŏng Masque

Asset No.7
Kosŏngogwangdae
Lee Yun-sun
136, Seowoe-ri, Kosong-up, Kosong-gun,
S. Kyongsang Province
Kosŏng Masque

Asset No.7
Kosŏngogwangdae
Hŏ P'an-se
53, Tochon-ri, Maam-myon, Kosong-gun,
S. Kyongsang Province
Kosŏng Masque

Kosŏngogwangdae, *Mask dance drama from Kosŏng*

Asset No.7
Kosŏngogwangdae
Hŏ Hyŏn-do
75, Ryuhong-ri, Taega-myon, Kosong-gun,
S. Kyongsang Province
Kosŏng Masque

Asset No.8
Kanggangsullae
Kim Kil-im
919,Tongwoe-ri, Munnae-myon, Haenam-gun,
S. Cholla Province
Circle Dance

Asset No.8
Kanggangsullae
Park Yong-sun
733, Tunjon-ri, Kunnae-myon,Chindo-gun,
S. Cholla Province
Circle Dance

Asset No.9
Ŭnsanpyŏlshinje
Ch'a Chin-yong
111-38,Ŭnsan-ri, Ŭnsan-myon, Puyo-gun,
S.Ch'ungch'ong Province
Shamanistic Village Ritual of Ŭnsan

Asset No.9
Ŭnsanpyŏlshinje
Sŏk Tong-sŏk
135, Unsan-ri, Ŭnsan-myon, Puyo-gun,
S. Ch'ungch'ong Province
Shamanistic Village Ritual of Ŭnsan

Asset No.10
Najŏnch'ilgijang
Kim Pong-ryong
91-2, Nokbon-dong Unp'yong-gu, Seoul
Lacquer Ware inlaid with Mother-of-Pearl

Asset No.11-ga
Chinju Samch'ŏnp'o Nongak
Park Yŏm
150, Songp'o-dong, Samch'onp'o,
S. Kyongsang Province
Traditional Farmer's Band Music of
Chinju, Samch'ŏnp'o

Asset No.11-na
P'yŏngt'aek Nongak
Ch'oi Ŭn-ch'ang
283-1, P'yonggung-ri, P'aengsong-up,
P'yongt'aek-gun, Kyonggi Province
Traditional Farmer's Band Music of
P'yŏngt'aek

Asset No.11-na
P'yŏngt'aek Nongak
Lee Tol-ch'ŏn
98, Ssangyong-dong, Ch'onan,
S. Ch'ungch'ong Province
Traditional Farmer's Band Music of
P'yŏngt'aek

Asset No.11-da
Iri Nongak
Kim Hyŏng-sun
154, Namjung-dong 1-ga, Iri, N. Cholla Province
Traditional Farmer's Band Music of Iri

Najŏnch'ilgijang, *Lacquerware inlaid with mother-of-pearl*

Asset No.11-ra
Kangnŭng Nongak
Park Ki-ha
339, Hongje-dong, Kangneung,
Kangwon Province
Traditional Farmer's Band Music of
Kangnŭng

Asset No.11-ra
Kangnŭng Nongak
Kim Yong-hyŏn
32, Sach'onjin 2-ri, Sach'on-myon,
Myongju-gun, Kangwon Province
Traditional Farmer's Band Music of
Kangnŭng

Asset No.11-ma
Yimshilp'ilbong Nongak
Park Hyŏng-rae
P'ilbong-ri, Kangjin-myon, Yimshil-gun,
N. Cholla Province
Traditional Farmer's Band Music of
Yimshilp'ilbong

Asset No.11-ma
Yimshilp'ilbong Nongak
Yang Sun-yong
84, Kumda-ri, Pojol-myon, Namwon-gun,
N. Cholla Province
Traditional Farmer's Band Music of
Yimshilp'ilbong

Asset No.12
Chinjukŏmmu
Lee Yun-rye
1438-14, Sangbongdong-dong, Chinju,
S. Kyongsang Province
Chinju Sword Dance

Asset No.12
Chinjukŏmmu
Lee Um-jon
447-3, Okbongbuk-dong, Chinju,
S. Kyongsang Province
Chinju Sword Dance

Asset No.12
Chinjukŏmmu
Kim Su-ak
450-4, Ponsong-dong, Chinju,
S. Kyongsang Province
Chinju Sword Dance

Asset No.12
Chinjukŏmmu
Sŏng Kye-ok
469-5, P'anmun-dong, Chinju,
S.Kyongsang Province
Chinju Sword Dance

Asset No.13
Kangnŭngtanoje
Kim Chin-dŏk
616-16, Noam-dong, Kangneung,
Kangwon Province
Shamanistic Ritual and Festival
around May 5, Lunar Calender of
Kangnŭng

Asset No.13
Kangnŭngtanoje
Kwon Yŏng-ha,
254, Chibyon-dong, Kangneung,
Kangwon Province
Shamanistic Ritual and Festival
around May 5, Lunar Calender of
Kangnŭng

Asset No.14
Hansan-moshitchagi
Mun Chŏng-ok
159, Chibyon-ri, Hansan-myon, Seoch'on-gun,
S. Ch'ungch'ong Province
Hansan Ramie Weaving

Asset No.15
Pukch'ŏngsajanorŭm
Kim Su-sŏk
131-8, Yongnang-dong, Sokch'o,
Kangwon Province
Pukch'ŏng Lion Dance Drama

Kangnŭng tanoje, *Shamanistic ritual and festival held on the fifth day of the fifth lunar month*